Those Who Left The Dales

Those Who Left The Dales

The Upper Dales Family History Group

Edited by Glenys Marriott

This project was supported by Grassroots Grants, the Office of the Third Sector, the Community Development Foundation, The Yorkshire Dales Millennium Trust, and York and North Yorkshire Community Fund.

Published by Upper Dales Family History Group 2010

ISBN 978-0-9566547-0-0

Cover design by Clare Brayshaw

Front Cover – a postcard published around 1908 of passengers waiting at Aysgarth Railway Station in Wensleydale. Courtesy of Denny Gibson (Personal Collection)

Prepared and printed by:
York Publishing Services
64 Hallfield Road
Layerthorpe
York YO31 7ZQ
Tel: 01904 431213

www.yps-publishing.co.uk

Introduction – The 10th Anniversary Book – *"Those Who Left the Dales"*

Every family has a story to tell, and some are extraordinary. This is a collection of family stories gathered together by the descendants of those who made the great decision to move, sometimes a short distance, and sometimes right around the world. It is only in recent times that the vast wealth of information held by individual families has been recognised as a valuable source for understanding our economic and demographic history. Each move was the result of serious deliberation, and at a cost. The reasons were many, and whilst some went away to study at school or college, others left to be apprenticed, some to marry and some to take the king's shilling. The majority moved however for economic reasons. As traditional forms of employment such as lead mining went into decline people looked to transfer their skills to new areas of employment, or were bold enough to cross the seas and take their chances.

The result is that traditional dales names have spread around the world, and through hundreds of letters and cards, communication was maintained. In large families some sons and daughters would move, but they still maintained contact with siblings and parents in the dales. Some of these precious letters and cards are gathered together in this study. Each side of the family was enriched by contact with the other culture, whether it was Manchester or Manitoba, and many exiled dales folk were proud of their Yorkshire heritage. Migration was linked to age, and it was young people in their teens and twenties who were most likely to move, leaving behind an aging population. Between 1801 and 1821 the population reached a height of around 15,000 before dropping to around 8,500 in 1911. Those who were left in the dales concentrated on agriculture as the basis of their income, and as the population fell even the traditional crafts that serviced the local needs fell into decline. People emigrated to destinations all over the world, but predominantly to Lancashire and the West Riding of Yorkshire, New Zealand, Australia, Canada and America.

This important study draws together for the first time the invaluable research done by family historians across the world and illustrates just a few examples of the many who left the dales. It rapidly became apparent that the stories being supplied for our 10th Anniversary exhibition were too precious merely to be returned to their owners after the exhibition. We agreed to publish a summary of each story, and this book now forms the basis of a new archive of migration from the dales.

Our aspiration is for it to be seen as the basis for further research by a generation of new historians. Readers will note that no references have been included as they would have more than doubled the size of the book – individual authors will be delighted to discuss their papers and provide references so do please contact them direct.

Wherever necessary, appropriate permissions have been requested by the writer for the use of any photographs, although the majority belong to the authors or have been provided by other members of the group. Denny Gibson has been especially generous with her large collection of old postcards.

The chapters are not recorded in geographical or date order, nor are they grouped in family clusters. The reason for this is that each story includes more than one dales family and these appear and re-appear throughout the book. Marriage between families resulted in a complex labyrinth of relationships, some in the dales and others abroad or out of the county. We are therefore indebted to Marion Hearfield, one of our members, for her substantial index. Please refer to it regularly, as it is invaluable. Marion has tried very hard to make the index accurate and to include every person and every place named in the book. Please note that the Index numbers refer to chapter numbers, not page numbers. Women are indexed by their married names as well as their maiden names, when we can identify them. If a person also had a nickname or abbreviated name, that is indexed separately.

Dalesmen and women were involved in adventures across the world. Several were entrepreneurs and became extremely successful. They started major business empires such as Fenwicks in Newcastle and Christopher Pratts of Bradford, whilst others became saddle makers to Royalty. They took up glamorous lifestyles as horse trainers in Paris, or became band masters in the north east of England.

What is clear is that their descendants have inherited a passion for the dales, and feel that, wherever they live in the world, they are part of the environment which shaped their ancestors – at heart they are dalesmen and women.

This book is our tribute to those brave people who left the dales, and an acknowledgement of their achievements.

We are grateful to all the members of the group for supplying this unique insight into the life of dales folk.

Acknowledgements

We are grateful to Lord Crathorne, the President of the Cleveland Society, for agreeing to open the exhibition on 2nd October 2010 and to Rodney Tennant at Tennants Auction House in Leyburn for allowing us the use of his premises. Alison Tennant has been an enthusiastic supporter of our initiative and has worked hard to accommodate us.

A special thank you is due to Cllr. John Blackie, who immediately saw the importance of both the exhibition and the book, and was the first to give us financial support to 'get the show on the road.' We are also indebted to the members of the Yorkshire Dales Millennium Trust for their grant towards the running of the exhibition and the publication of the book.

Marion Moverley developed the theme of *"Those Who Left the Dales"* and devised the type of data to be included.

As always, Keith Sweetmore, the County Archivist, has been a great support and has supplied us with copies of original letters sent back to the dale from abroad. After the exhibition we are depositing with the North Yorkshire County Record Office copies of all the letters we have received, together with any originals.

Helen Bainbridge, the curator of the Swaledale Museum in Reeth, has always responded with enthusiasm to our many requests for help and we are grateful to her for her professional advice on staging the exhibition.

A special mention should be made of our advertisers; we are pleased to highlight the part played by long-established dales firms in supporting the economy of the area over many years.

Dr. Christine Hallas has given hours of support, behind the scenes, sharing her archives, photographs and maps, and her unparalleled knowledge of the reasons for the exit from the dales. She has been an enthusiastic supporter of our aim to form a dales migration archive. Her guidance has, as always, been worth following.

Duncan Beal and the team at York Publishing Services have given admirable support and have encouraged us throughout. We look forward to placing our next publication with them.

Two other supporters have offered special help privately – Blair Southerden and Jane Ritchie. They both know that we are grateful to them for their positive support for our project!

The history of the formation of the Upper Dales Family History Group

The Upper Dales Family History Group covers Swaledale, Arkengarthdale and Wensleydale, in North Yorkshire, and their tributary valleys. These are areas of outstanding scenery, with a range of wildlife habitats and a rich cultural heritage. We are located some 80 miles north east of Manchester; Leeds and Bradford lie to the south, while Kendal is to the west and Darlington and Northallerton to the east.

Like most groups, this one started after a chance discussion. Dr. Ann Hartley of Thoralby asked me if I had researched my family history. There was no local genealogy group although there were many experienced researchers. The North Yorkshire County Record Office was some 40 miles from the furthest Wensleydale villages which added to the challenges. After a year of planning, meeting key researchers, and assessing the viability of starting a new group, I invited people to a meeting in the Dales Countryside Museum in Hawes to consider the options. Over 60 people turned out and the proposal to start a new group had overwhelming support.

I approached the South Durham, Cleveland and North Yorkshire Family History Society – known locally as 'the Cleveland', and our new group was accepted as a branch operating under the Society's umbrella. The Friends of the Dales Countryside Museum also accepted us as an affiliated group, giving us access to their support and the museum's excellent facilities.

The group began in November 2000, holding monthly meetings with speakers in Hawes, Middleham or Fremington, to enable members to access the group across these scattered, fell-side communities. The early computerisation of many of our members led to us starting a computer club. This attracted many new members, and over the course of ten years the club has reduced from a monthly event to four per year, as more members have become accustomed to using computers in their research. Tony Keates and Pat Ryder still run this and have gained the appreciation of many dozens of members over the years. Tony was our original treasurer, eventually passing over to Don Farrar. David Trusson was asked to start an email group, and this has grown steadily over the ten years. Today it is a huge part of our activity, with over 500 members worldwide, all researching their ancestors from the Upper Dales. Kate Trusson, a talented quilting tutor, was also an early member of the committee, looking after the needs of Swaledale researchers.

Marion Moverley, a well known local and family historian and tutor, gave her support, and members were encouraged to attend Marion's lessons. She also ran transcribing workshops, encouraging high quality research in the group. Early in the life of the group she undertook to manage our programme of events and this has contributed much to the success of the group.

A founder member was Tracy Little, a local newspaper correspondent in Swaledale, who undertook to manage our publicity, and ten years later is still doing just that. José Hopper, a member of both the Metcalfe Society and the committee of the Friends of the Museum was also a founder member, and still represents the interests of Wensleydale researchers on the current committee. Evelyn Abraham, another founder member, contributed her support for ten full years, retiring in April this year.

Ann Hartley undertook to co-ordinate our research, resulting in further publications of the Bishopdale Booklets. These were published initially by Jean Kington, and passed over to the group to manage, on her retirement. Ann also led the group's contribution to burial transcribing for the National Burial Index. The Bishopdale Booklets are now produced by committee member Stella Birch.

Brenda Watering looked after our bookstall for many years, eventually handing over to Pat Ryder. We must also acknowledge the regular help given by Judy Farrar, who ensures not only that our register at meetings is kept up to date but that every visitor is greeted with charm, a smile and a name-label.

The current committee also includes our secretary Sybil Reed, who together with Marion and Tracy contributed to the final review of the contents of the book.

In the early days the group had pages on my original Bishopdale website, no longer in existence. Peter Underwood gave his immediate support to producing a new dedicated website, which is actively used today. It can be accessed at http://www.upperdalesfhg.org.uk/ He also took over the management of the email group. Peter and June have been strong supporters of the group, and although living at a distance, when they return to the dales they are always most welcome. Marion Hearfield and Ann Wilson support Peter in managing the email group and member Rennison Vayro has collated and developed an active list of website links numbering nearly 1000.

Our oldest, original member was the late Lucie Hinson, who celebrated her 90th birthday in 2001. Lucie contributed an amazing collection of magazines to the Dales Countryside Museum and kept us all on our toes. Lucie's son Colin Hinson is a trustee of GENUKI (http://www.genuki.org.uk/index.html) and he maintains the Yorkshire pages, which are a good starting point for anyone researching in this area.

In October 2001 the group held its first exhibition at the Dales Countryside Museum in Hawes. This was a grand affair, with 52 exhibitors displaying their research. Well over 600 visitors came and this resulted in new members for the group. We were delighted with the turn-out and the support from local residents. One such was Fremmie HUTCHINSON, a great dales character, who died shortly after the exhibition on 28th December 2001. He was thrilled to see his photographs on display. Another key person who attended was Marie HARTLEY, the well known author and researcher of dales events. We waited with baited breath as she stood before each exhibit, walked slowly through the exhibition, standing for long moments to read each display board. As she signed the visitors' book I asked her what she thought of the exhibits – forthright as ever, she responded "not bad at all for a start!" Those who knew her well would recognise this as true praise indeed. We are sorry that she is not still alive to see our 10th Anniversary exhibition.

In November 2002 we met to consider how we could support the Dales Countryside Museum with a new initiative – an open access room for the public to use the research facilities. A small group worked steadily to collate and record a range of research papers, adding to the already sizeable collection of the museum. Tony Keates and Pat Ryder from our committee still support this, together with other members of the group.

Between April 2003 and 2009 I stood down as chairman and left the group in the safe hands of firstly Tony Keates and then John Harland as chairmen. Throughout the next six years the group continued to prosper, at a time when some groups nationally and locally were folding through lack of support. With a varied range of speakers, study days and workshops the group tries hard to attract and keep new members and we hope that readers of this study will join us.

GLENYS MARRIOTT

Chairman
Upper Dales Family History Group
Email: glenys@bishopdale.demon.co.uk
August 2010

The area covered by these stories

Wensleydale and Swaledale: Administrative Areas

Not shown, but located to the south west of Bishopdale, are Wharfedale, and Langstrothdale, which also appear in the book.

We are grateful to Dr. Christine Hallas for providing this map, published originally in her book *"Rural Responses to Industrialisation – the North Pennines 1780-1914"* ISBN 3-906762-31-9

Programme of speakers at the 10th Anniversary Exhibition 2nd – 16th October 2010

Venue: Tennants Auction House, Leyburn.

Saturday 2nd October.

2 pm Exhibition opened by Lord Crathorne, Lord Lieutenant of North Yorkshire.

2.30 pm Presentation by Dr. Christine Hallas

Migration from 19th Wensleydale & Swaledale – Setting the Scene

Friday 8th October

11 am Presentation by Marion Moverley

London Connections highlighting dales folk who had business connections in London

2 pm Presentation by Blair Southerden and Jonathan Kirton

Kirton/Kearton emigration from Swaledale to St Vincent, Windward Islands 1764

Tuesday 12th October

11 am Presentation by Tony Keates

Using the internet for research

2 pm Presentation by Ron Spensley

Migration from Swaledale: the South Yorkshire Connection

Friday 15th October

11 am Presentation by David Pratt

The Christopher Pratt Story

2 pm Presentation by Dr. Duncan Bythell

Why move to Burnley? Mill-town life in late nineteenth-century Lancashire

Contents

List of Illustrations and adverts

1   The WILLIS family from Carperby to Wisconsin

Matthew WILLIS born 1799 at Carperby married Jane LONGMIRE, and emigrated to Wisconsin.

The WILLIS letters were bought by Christine AMSDEN, originally of Castle Bolton but now living in Canada, and recorded the lives of the two branches of the family – those who emigrated to Wisconsin and their relatives left in the dales. Christine deposited the originals of most of the letters with the North Yorkshire County Record Office in Northallerton in 2009. The additional letters she sent to me for the 10th Anniversary Exhibition and they too will join the others after the exhibition.

These letters give not only a clear view of life for those who left the dales, but also of those who remained. What was described regularly were the ordinary events of their lives – births, marriages, numerous deaths and those miscreant acts which gave rise to being memorable enough to record. On both sides of the Atlantic there were concerns about the cost of farming, poor weather and the advantages or otherwise of migrating. It is also fascinating to see how these letters link in to so many other stories told in this book. They fulfil one of the aims of the exhibition which was to attract and bring together these unique migrant records and exhibit them as a whole. They also tell the story of the women in the families, whose stories are often untold when history was written. Throughout the exhibition there were stories of women producing an average of ten children, often losing some at birth or to disease, and of their physically demanding lives with little offer of respite or recreation.

Members of the Upper Dales Group have been able from their own histories to piece together those mentioned in these letters and to show the strong links not only between families but between villages – a link strong enough to support any new emigrant when arriving in America. Even for those who did not emigrate but still left the dales, the links were strong and easily identifiable. For example, Thomas CARTER's father (chapter 9) Richard CARTER was a cousin of Matthew WILLIS. Richard's father John was the brother of Eleanor CARTER, mother of Matthew WILLIS. Likewise A.C.D. CURKEET wrote about the Matthew WILLIS homestead in *The Circuit Rider*. (See chapter 37)

Not every member of the family emigrated however. Matthew and Jane WILLIS left one daughter Elizabeth in the care of an aunt and uncle at Nappa, John WILLIS and his wife Alice SARGINSON. She was never again to see her parents. The letters tell the story of Matthew WILLIS and his wife Jane LONGMIRE and John HUMPHR(E)Y and his wife Eleanor who was Matthew's sister.

Matthew and Jane's children were:
John WILLIS born in 1837 at Preston, Lancashire
Elizabeth Longmire WILLIS born 26th February 1839 at Preston, Lancashire who remained in Nappa.
Thomas Carter WILLIS born June 1841 at Preston; his son was John Grainger WILLIS
Matthew WILLIS born about 1843 died on the voyage to America
James WILLIS born about 1845
Rose Ellen WILLIS born 1847 Wisconsin
Richard WILLIS born 1850 Wisconsin
Anthony Errington WILLIS born 6th April 1852 Wisconsin
Margaret Jane WILLIS born 1854 Wisconsin
Alice Ann WILLIS born 1856 Wisconsin
Robert WILLIS born 1859 Wisconsin

There are twelve letters written between 1849 and 1875, from Rama, Iowa Co. Wisconsin and Low Thoresby and Nappa, Wensleydale. A summary of the first letter is included here.

Letter 1. Low Thoresby April 1st 1849 letter from Jno HUMPHRY brother in law of Matthew WILLIS

Dear Brother & Sister Matthew Jane WILLIS, Once again I take up my pen to write to you in hopes this will find you all well for without health this world is but a desert and not worth living in, no matter where placed, whether in the Prairies of North America or the gardens of Old England, whether he is emcompaſs'd and bound up all winter by snow and frost or situated amongst the misty mountains of Wensleydale, but I hope before now you will be able to write without your Ink Freezing in your pen keeping and extra fire, I hope also that times will be better with you than when last you wrote to Nephew J. WILLIS......

Times are very bad here at present that is Farming, corn very low I sold 24 Busels of capital good Red Wheat sound as Braſs that weighs 9st 10lbs per (B...) for 6s per Bushel, last Thursday. Oats verry low about 2s to 3s per bushel, Fat Stock low Beef worth about 5s per stone good and Fat Mutton about 5d per st, Bacon is pretty well sold it has been about 6/6 per st but it is now only worth about 6s. Cheese is only badly sold from 50s to about 57s per cwt, wool is rather on the advance.... & holding cattle is very low indeed, can scarcely be turned into money. _ so you see if you have times bad in America we have them bad here. The prospect still worse, and Rents is as high as ever Rate, and then there is Highway Rates and Poor Rates, and then there is all Labour besides, that is where you have but one Ploughing we have perhaps two or three, and then we have to manure our Land and Lime it and after that is done and all other Labour, we can only grow corn every other year, and when that is done we can only get light crops say 20 to 35 Bus of Oats an Acre and from 15 to 25 of Wheat, and then we have joiners, Blacksmiths, Labourers and women to pay besides Housekeeping – you will perhaps say, well it might be better for you to come into America, myself think it would, but you send such Horifying accounts you terrify your sister Ellen that she dare not venture over the Sea into a country where the Frost is so excedingly severe as allmost to Freeze the Kettle to the Fire. And yet as long a journey by Sea and Land as it is and as cold a climate in winter and a Hot one in summer there are many cases of people coming to your place every year for instance this spring there have set of already from Swaledale and Arkindale from 100 to 200 persons and I supose there are a good many more preparing to go immediately, mow these persons have all either Friends or relations in your country and to your country they are going that is if providence permit, J DINSDALE from Askrigg his wife and cousin and her husband and I supose M DINSDALE almost wishes them all to come to him, both his mother and the remainder of his family, a quantity have also set of out of Coverdale and Netherdale

Now Dear Matthew you must not be offended if I ask you a few serious questions which I hope you will answer me candidly. Would any of these People's Relations have wished their friends to emigrate to a country where the advantages are no greater than the country they are leaving, and where the climate is still worse? Would they have wished them to incur expense and risk of life and Property for the sake of having them in the same predicament as themselves? even you seem to think England is preferable to America, then I wonder what can be the meaning of all this tide of emigration, one year after another, and each year more people emigrating than the former ones, is it because they are restleſs and unsettled and like change, if it is even for the worse, and another thing strikes me as strange, that tho' so many emigrate, yet few come back again and most of these few stay a few weeks or months and then return back here have been two or three over a while since but they have gone over again into their own western settlement, James DAVY of West Witton twice before you went croſsed (John DAVY was at West Witton in 1841) over the Atlantic and twice returned again, he is gone the third time last spring and is doing well.

Mr. Robt LODGE of Starbotton is made Bankrupt and will pay but little dividend. James ORTON has made an aſsignment and will pay but little, tis reported that C. ORTON our Brother will lose upward of £300 then to Crown All Wm Jno ANDERSON Esq. of Swinithwaite Hall has left the Country and all is going to be sold both Property and Furniture, ...and it is suposed that there will not be much to spare after all his Debts are paid, This you see Matthew we are only in a queer way in England, ...Ellen joins with me in kind love to Jane and our little Nephews and niece and hopes they will be all well when this arrives, and I must conclude and Rem your Afft Brother Jno HUMPHRY

GLENYS MARRIOTT glenys@bishopdale.demon.co.uk
CHRISTINE AMSDEN http://www.dalesgenealogy.com/letters/letters.html

2. The CROFT family of Middleham

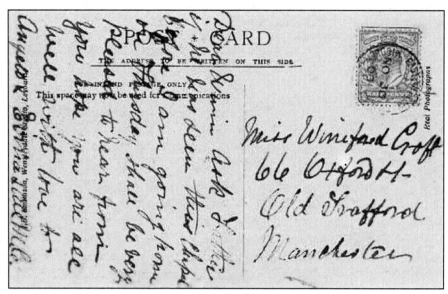

Old postcard to Miss Winifred CROFT

James Percy CROFT, born in Middleham 14th April 1861, son of Angelo James CROFT and his wife Mary née GILL, lived on Kirkgate with his family. Father Angelo was a *plumber and glazier*, following in a tradition where many CROFTS were plumbers, glaziers or painters in different parts of the dales, but all with their roots in nearby East Witton. Mary kept a *milliner's* shop on Kirkgate and in 1871 James was still there with the rest of the family. Then by the 1881 census he had moved to Leeds and was apprenticed to be an *organ builder*.

At 80 Woodsley Road, Leeds, just south of Woodhouse Moor Park, John WALKER was a *butter merchant;* he had a wife Jane and son, John Addison WALKER, a *music teacher*. The WALKERs had also moved from Middleham, where they had been *grocers*, to Leeds, and they took in young James Percy CROFT as a lodger. Angelo and Mary CROFT were Methodists, and this line of the CROFT family remained so. The WALKERs were also Methodists and young John Addison WALKER had been baptised at the Methodist Chapel in Middleham in 1855. So here we have a link between families, shared beliefs, shared dales background, and one taking in the other as a lodger. Did John WALKER, *butter factor*, sell butter from dales farms? He may well have done as local Leeds directories advised that a carrier travelled between Middleham and Leeds, stopping at Masham and Ripon, and would be at the Golden Cock on Kirkgate, Leeds, every Friday at 12.30 p.m.; and the local directory for Middleham informed the public that William SIDDAL set off from Middleham for Masham, Ripon and Leeds every Thursday, returning from Leeds at 12.30 pm Friday. So parcels, letters and messages could be sent quite easily from Middleham to Leeds.

There were several organ builders in Leeds, and it is not known who James Percy worked for, but once he had finished his apprenticeship he moved on to Manchester. He had left his heart behind however, and in 1888 on the 29th March, at Woodhouse Moor Wesleyan Chapel, James Percy CROFT *organ builder* of 11 Hamilton Street, Old Trafford, married Emily WHITEHEAD, *dressmaker*, of 56 Kings Road, Burley Fields, Leeds. Emily lived only a few streets away from Woodsley Road where James had been a lodger with the WALKERs. Now, the newly married couple were to make their home in Manchester.

They moved house in their early years together, first to 17 Clifford Street, Stretford, then to Dudley Street, Stretford, before settling down to live at 66 Oxford Street, Stretford with their four children. James Percy progressed as an *organ builder,* and Emily produced first of all Angelo James, named after his Middleham grandpa, in 1889, then Percy Emil in 1891, and then two girls. Evina Ruth born in 1895 was named after James's sister who had died and was buried at Coverham, and the last daughter was Winifred Maggie in 1896. Sadly two of the children did not survive into adulthood. Percy Emil died when he was 14, and Winifred died when she was 18. Angelo James married, but Evina never did, but what she did do was keep in touch with a wide network of relatives, visiting them in different parts of the Yorkshire dales, and sending postcards back to her family from her visits.

There must have been some novelty for the country cousins to have part of the family living in a big city, and my cousin can remember her mother sending a chicken or bits of pork from a newly killed pig, through the post from Teesdale to the CROFT relatives in Manchester, as late as the 1950s. Evidently she just wrapped them up and posted them.

The CROFT family had ancient roots in the Middleham and Coverdale area, and a search on the 1851 census of CROFTs who had "Middleham" as place of birth reveal that they were all living locally, none had strayed. That was to change however as by 1861 Hornby CROFT, son of Hornby CROFT the *painter,* had moved to Stockton on Tees where he was a *bricklayer,* and there he remained. He first lodged at the Spotted Cow in Stockton, and then lived on Neasham Street in 1871, moving to Paradise Place in 1881 where he remained until sometime after the 1901 census.

Duterau CROFT, another son of Angelo and Mary, brought up in Kirkgate, Middleham, went to Crowle in Lincolnshire where he trained as a *chemist and druggist.* Then he moved to Scunthorpe, before retiring to Blackwell near Darlington where he was very involved with Elm Ridge Methodist Chapel. He paid for a new organ there in 1836, and his niece from Manchester, Evina, came to the dedication. Duterau's brother, Thomas Lister CROFT came from Harrogate as well. Thomas had started to train as a *solicitor* at Middleham, then left and went to Pudsey. He set up his own solicitor's office in Wood Street, Wakefield, where he acted for different branches of his family in the Yorkshire Dales and Barnard Castle. Distance was not a problem as family links were what was important.

Honor Gill CROFT, the youngest daughter of Angelo and Mary of Middleham, also had an adventure. In the 1891 census she is at 8 Junction Parade, Brighton, with Christopher OTHER, born in Redmire, and his wife. Later Honor's cousin Rebecca became Mrs OTHER's *ladies' maid.* Honor came back however and lived in Middleham, then Thirsk.

The last CROFT who went far from home was William, son of Samuel, another *plumber.* William was nephew to Angelo, and he was a *plumber* also – but in Eastbourne! His wife Mary was from Bedale, and five children were born in Church Street, Leyburn, and then sometime between 1881 and 1887, when the last child was born, the whole family moved to 23 Gilbert Road, Eastbourne, Sussex, where another branch of the CROFT family set up as plumbers.

Some of the Middleham CROFTs made a shorter journey, to Darlington. These were related to the plumber CROFTs, but were a branch that were *boot and shoe makers.* Also Methodists, the children were baptised in Middleham, but Isabella lived on Bondgate, working in a grocery shop for her sister Margaret and brother in law Albert WALKER. James went to live at Green Bank Road, Darlington, and also worked in a shop.

One small family in the Yorkshire dales, and within a few years a network of cousins spread across the country. Some would keep in touch, some perhaps not. As the generations passed the links disappeared, until the censuses drew them together again.

MARION MOVERLEY 26 Lyons Rd, Richmond, Yorkshire, DL10 4 NS
moverley.lyons@virgin.net

3.   Henry and Elizabeth Cleminson HUNT

HUNT reunion Pennsylvania 1939

Henry and Elisabeth HUNT left the Yorkshire dales in 1830 with their son Timothy L. HUNT in the hope of a better life in a new country. On their arrival in America they purchased land near Johnstown, Cambria County, Pennsylvania and built a farm. Their eight children were born here, including Robert (my ancestor), William, James, Joseph, Ruth, Susanna, Elizabeth, and John. Of these only 2 did not live to adulthood, Joseph and Elizabeth. Henry died on 10th April 1849 and his wife Elizabeth put an advert in the Mountaineer Sentinel, Ebensburg, Pa, on Thursday January 17, 1850 stating *"Notice is hereby given to all persons interested, that Letters of Administration have been granted to the undersigned, by the Register of Cambria County, on the estate of Henry HUNT, late of Conemaugh Township, Cambria County, deceased. Those indebted to said are required to make immediate payments, and those having claims, to present them properly authenticated for settlement. Signed: Elizabeth HUNT, Adm."*

Elizabeth Cleminson HUNT died June 23 1895. Her obituary in the Tribune, Johnstown, Cambria Co., Pa. on June 24, 1895 read *"Mrs. Elizabeth HUNT died at the home of her son-in-law, Mr. Henry VARNER, one mile west of Fairview, yesterday forenoon at 6 o'clock, age eighty-six years and two months. Mrs. HUNT was one of the oldest and best known residents of Cambria County. She was born in Yorkshire, England and emigrated to this country with her husband, the late Henry HUNT, in 1830. The family located to Pottsville and after a residence of about a year at the place they removed to East Taylor Township, in which the deceased has lived ever since. After their removal to this county the husband found employment as a foreman on the construction of the Old Portage Tunnel, where he worked up to the time of its completion. He died in 1849. The deceased was the mother of eleven children, five of whom survive: Timothy L., of Roxbury; William, of Jackson Township; James, of Nebraska, John, of Altoona; and Susanna, wife of Henry VARNER, of Jackson Township. There are living about forty-five grandchildren and over fifty great-grandchildren. The deceased had been a devout member of the Methodist Church from girlhood and was well known for her charity and many deeds of kindness. The funeral will take place from her late home at 10 o'clock tomorrow forenoon, interment to be made in Wesley Chapel churchyard with services by Rev. J. L. SRUFFY of Conemaugh".*

The following day in the same paper notice of her funeral was given *"HUNT, In Jackson Township on Sunday evening, June 23, 1894 at 6 o'clock, Mrs. Elizabeth HUNT, aged 86 years and 2 months. Funeral at 10 o'clock tomorrow morning; interment in the churchyard at Wesley Chapel."*

Additional information about the family is recorded in a church article which stated that they were members of the Wesleyan Church in England, and first settled with the Methodist Episcopal Church in Johnstown. *"In due time preaching was established in Brother HUNT's house, then a church was built, and the second one now stands on the same site. Sister HUNT was converted at twelve years, and was married in her seventeenth year, her husband being already a member of the church. Hers was a beautiful, devoted and noble Christian life. She maintained the strict observance of the Sabbath, and it was a great grief to her to witness violations of the sacred day, especially on the part of professors of religion".* (Rev. J. L. STIFFY.)

I have a copy of a letter written in February 1849 to James PRATT back home in Yorkshire that includes the following:

"We are glad that you intend to come to America in the spring for we think you will do better in this country with your family than you are doing there. If you can raise the means to get to Philadelphia we can assist you from there to our home. .... W. SPENSLEY of Reeth recommended us to one Anthony BARNES who treated us like a father but we do not know whether he is living or not. The fare across the ocean is from £3 to £4.10 each person, children half price. We have not heard of Metcalf BELL this 8 or 10 years, as for Galana we do not know much about it, only it is a great lead mining place. We do not know the exact distance, but we suppose it is between 2 and three thousand miles from here........We would like to see you come this way. You could get work here, they are making a new Railroad from Harrisburg to Holidasburg. When you get there inquire for Jonathan BOWING. He is a pious local preacher & he will give you directions.....We farm our own we have 134 acres altogether. Between 30 & 40 acres are cleared. We have 2 horses, 6 cows, 9 head of young cattle, 50 sheep & 4 hogs.

Your affectionate & loving friends
Henry & Elizabeth HUNT"

James PRATT did not make the trip.

Robert HUNT my great great grandfather was born July 25th 1830 near Johnstown Pennsylvania and died December 24th 1886. His obituary was recorded in the Daily Tribune, Johnstown, Cambria Co., Pa; on Thursday, December 31st, 1886:

"HUNT, In West Taylor Township, on Friday, December 24th, 1886, Robert HUNT, aged 56 years and 5 months."

ANN WILSON momann1@aol.com

4. Bernard METCALFE to India

In January 1807 Bernard METCALFE was living in Natches, Georgia in America. He had begun proceedings to recover $675.55 from Messrs HAMMOND and BROWN, also of Natches. On 28th September 1808 they promised to pay him $885 and again on 21st January 1809 the sum of $208.04. On 26th May 1810 B & F METCALFE recovered the sum of $235.90 from George W. NICOLAS.

Cotton was being grown in India in the early part of the 19th century. However, to quote the Board of Directors *"The dirty and mixed state in which cotton is at present brought to Europe depreciates its price."* The East India Company (EIC) therefore decided to import specialist knowledge. On the 7th of May 1813 the EIC directors decided to increase the cultivation of cotton with the objective of improving its quality. Models of American machines for dressing cotton were obtained and studied. They also engaged the services of Bernard METCALFE. He was to be an assistant in the Commercial Department. Bernard METCALFE had, according to the directors, resided in Georgia for several years. He was a *merchant and dealer of cotton* and was considered a person of credit and respectability. His principal responsibility was to further cotton transactions but could be *"called upon to assist general business."* He was to make himself available to any location *"where his services can be most useful."* His pay was to be 110 pagodas per month to commence on the day he landed in India. The EIC paid for his passage to India, eating at the Commander's table of the ship called *Northumberland*; upon landing he was to be conveyed to Madras. He was advanced £100, which was to be recovered from his monthly pay.

On 3rd September 1813 Bernard METCALFE signed a contract promising to work for the EIC for a term of five years and gave a promise for his faithful performance of his engagement. The EIC also purchased two different machines from America. These were dismantled and six copies made; they were then distributed to the areas where cotton was grown. As Bernard METCALFE *"was well acquainted with the machines"* no great difficulty was expected. Bernard must have been working in India as nothing else is recorded until 1815 when he was to travel to central India, for which he was to be paid his regular allowance but was refused any extra beyond his regular amount. In January 1816 he was permitted to travel to China for the benefit of his health and he drew his salary four months in advance.

At the same time the building, which had been purchased, and some of the machines installed were to be sold. Clearly the machines had failed. They had failed to such an extent that when on the 10th January 1817 Bernard METCALFE asked for his allowances to travel to Bombay he was refused as *"no advantage can be anticipated employing him there."* Instead he was permitted to proceed to the Cape of Good Hope for his health, and also allowed to take an allowance of six months.

On his return on the 9th July 1817 he asked for his contract to be terminated and paid in full. An internal report dated 20th August 1817 states the failure of the project was due to the different spices grown in Georgia and India and not *"to the want of zeal or knowledge on the part of Bernard METCALFE."* As his services were no longer required his employment was ended with the EIC promising to pay their obligations under his contact in full. He asked to remain on full pay until his return to England but this was refused. Bernard METCALFE was buried 10th August. The balance of his estate, including some of his outstanding pay was paid to his mother Mrs Jane METCALFE of England.

The Metcalfe Society also has information on a Bernard METCALFE who was married to a Jane HOGG in Askrigg. He was the deputy registrar of Richmond. They had a son Bernard born 1771. Could he have been the same Bernard METCALFE?

In conclusion, in 1839 the E I C was still trying to improve the condition of cotton grown in India and Bernard METCALFE was still being referred to in internal reports in a very complimentary way.

This article was written from the records of the East India Company and records of the State Historical Society of Georgia USA.

GEORGE BUXTON g_buxton@talktalk.net

Tennants

AUCTIONEERS

The new purpose built Auction Centre

From the old to the new...

Upholding the same family tradition
for over 100 years

The Auction Centre
Leyburn, North Yorkshire DL8 5SG
01969 623780
www.tennants.co.uk

5.   HESELTINEs from Thoralby to Bradford: building the mills?

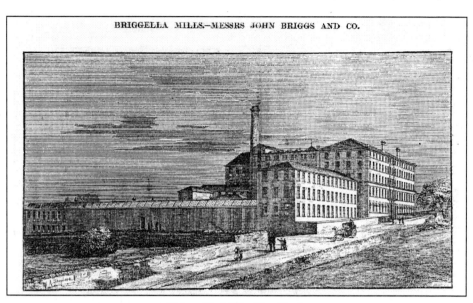

BRIGGELLA MILLS.—MESSRS JOHN BRIGGS AND CO.

Briggella Mills, Bradford

Our line of HESELTINEs is descended from Leonard HESELTINE from Thoralby (born 1698) who married Elizabeth METCALFE. The family was living at the Riddings in Thoralby and was mostly in farming. It is not clear who in our line first left the dales and why, so here is an overview of the information.

Leonard's great grandson, also called Leonard HESELTINE was born at Riddings, Thoralby on 6th September 1789 according to the Aysgarth register and christened in Aysgarth church on the same date. (More can be read about Riddings in Chapter 62.)

This Leonard first became a *stone waller*, which is not so strange, with the number of dry stone walls around the farms in the dales, and then later a *stonemason*. He was in Askrigg at least until 1849, but his wife, Alice GRAHAM, died in Bradford in 1850. Leonard was still in Bradford according to the 1851 census, with his two youngest daughters, and another widowed daughter with two children.

He is mentioned in Baines's Directory of 1823 as a *stonemason* in Askrigg. *Yorkshire Village* by Marie Hartley cites Leonard HESELTINE as *"an Askrigg man, received about £21 2s 5d for building the present village cross"* in 1830. He was also the stone mason responsible for building the Askrigg village pump, and encasing it in a handsome stone case in 1849. Both were still standing at the time of publication in 1953 and are still standing today.

In the *Trustees of the Market Tolls Book* for Askrigg there are several references to Leonard, including 2nd March 1831: *"To paid Leon. HESELTINE on a/c of new Cross £5 9th March, 1831 To paid ditto 2/11. By recd. From Leon HESELTINE for old stones 2/11 3rd June, 1831. To paid Leon. HESELTINE on account of bill £10 5th January, 1832. To paid Leon HESELTINE balance of bill £2/4/3 & stamp 1/2 £2/5/5 11th May, 1842. Paid Leonard HESELTINE for Mason's Work in repairing the Well in Pudding Lane £1/16 Oct 1849. Paid Leonard HESELTINE for Mason's Work at the Pump (as per bill) £2/11/-."*

Leonard's son Jeffrey married Mary CLARK in Askrigg, and baptised his first children in Askrigg. The first child he baptised in Bradford was in 1847. He was living in Bradford East according to the 1851 census. He was recorded first as a *stonemason*, and later a *paver* and a *road surveyor*. His eldest son moved from Bradford to Whitby. His youngest son, John, was a *cart driver*. This is the family line of one of the other members of the Upper Dales Family History Group (see also chapter 65).

Leonard's son John married Mary BRIGGS in Bradford in 1849, and lived in Bowling. He was a *stonemason* as was his son William. Whilst some of William's twelve children worked in the textile mills, others worked in shops.

The family stayed in Bradford until my husband, yet another John, left in the 1970's.

Three of William's sons fought together in the same regiment, the 1/6 Battalion of the West Yorkshire Regiment, in WWI. One of them, Harry Jeffrey, died in the Battle of Passchendaele, near Ypres. Before the war he worked in Briggella Mills (see photograph above). Leonard, my husband John's grandfather, also fought in this Regiment. He was a *painter* and *decorator*.

Leonard's daughter Jane Ann married William CLAYBROUGH in Bradford in 1845. Her husband died in 1850 after which she moved in with her widowed father.

Leonard's son Thomas married in Bradford in 1855, and lived in Bowling where he worked as a *stonemason*.

Since the textile mills were booming business in the 19th century, it seems likely that the pull to leave the dales was the possibility of work in building the mills and the houses for the mill workers.

ELIANE HESELTINE-MOK eliane.heseltine@gmail.com

6.   Ottewell ROBINSON – Fremington to London

Fremington – old postcard

Ottewell ROBINSON was baptised in 1776 in Grinton, the son of Thomas ROBINSON and Elizabeth his wife née TOMLIN. I do not know where he went to school nor where he did his legal studies but in 1794 he witnessed the marriage of Nathan HIRD and Mary METCALFE in Grinton so was presumably still living in Swaledale at that time.

On August the 4th 1814 he married Maria WALKER at Northill Bedfordshire. She was the daughter of William WALKER and niece of Christopher WALKER of Middleham. On her father's death in 1819 she inherited, in trust, his land in Yorkshire and Northamptonshire.

In 1815, at the baptism of their first son William Walker ROBINSON, their address was Argyll St and Ottewell's occupation was given as *Gentleman*. Further children followed, Elizabeth Mary (1816), Ottewell (1818), Maria (1820), Alfred (1822), Emily Ann (1824), Henry (1827), Charles (1828), Edward (1830) and Septimus Thomas in (1832). For all their baptisms his occupation was given as *Conveyancer* and only in the case of Septimus does he give a house number i.e. number 20. Edward was the only child not to survive into adulthood, dying at the age of two.

Ottewell's will was proved in October 1837 and although Maria, his wife, and her brother William, had been nominated as executors they both renounced and his son William proved his father's will. Maria was left everything to use towards the upbringing of their children. In the 1841 census the family, except for Charles, Henry and Alfred, were all together in Elysium Row, Kings Road, Fulham. William was a *solicitor* but Ottewell's occupation was not stated.

By 1851 Maria, Elizabeth Mary, William, Charles and Septimus were living in Park Terrace, Lambeth. Maria was a *land proprietor*, William a *Solicitors managing clerk* and Charles was a *Commission Merchant*. Maria remained in Park Terrace for the rest of her life. In 1861 she was living with Elizabeth, Charles and Septimus. Charles died in 1863 and was buried in Norwood cemetery on June the 24th.

Ottewell jr. became a clergyman, initially in Lincolnshire, then Yorkshire returning to London in 1854. He finally became Vicar at St Thomas's Southwark remaining there until he died in 1886. In 1860 he had married Mary Parkin BROCKLESBY, daughter of William BROCKLESBY, but they had no children and she predeceased him in 1881.

Maria had married William BELL in 1860 the son of a *brewer* in Fulham. Sadly William died in 1869 leaving Maria a wealthy but childless widow. She lived alone in Kensington until her death in the 1890s.

Alfred had followed his brother into the ordained ministry, ending as Vicar of Humbleton in East Yorkshire, where he served for almost 40 years until he died on Oct 28th 1902. He had married Ann Sophia SMITH, daughter of Charles SMITH, *a gold and silver lace maker and gentleman*, in 1850 at All Saints Church Fulham. They had a family of three boys and three girls.

Emily Ann married Paul MARGETSON in 1846, a *leather manufacturer* of Balham. Emily died in 1891 and Paul in 1897.

Septimus remained a *Colonial Clerk* all his working life living in Brixton and later Lambeth on the border with Kennington. He married Jessie CONSTANCE in 1861. They had three sons and one daughter and Jessie died in 1883. Septimus lived on with some of his family with him until 1914.

Henry, who had left home before 1841, was a *leather manufacturer* by 1859 when he married Susannah BETHAM. She was the daughter of John, a *shipping and commercial agent*, and Ann. The BETHAMs were living at 7 Park Terrace so were neighbours of the ROBINSONs. Henry and Susannah were married by his brother Ottewell on October 13th at St Mary's, Lambeth.

In 1861 Henry and Susannah were living in Brixton with their eldest son Henry Betham born in 1860. By 1871 they had moved into Angell Road and their youngest child Sidney Betham was just one month old. The family totalled six with three boys and three girls. In 1881 and 1891 Henry sr. and his family were back at 7 Park Terrace Brixton which they had perhaps inherited from Susannah's parents. When Henry sr. died in 1900 his address was given as Brackenbrough, Cedar Road, Beckenham. Susannah in the 1901 census was shown at 5 Cedar Road so presumably this was the same house.

By 1881 Henry jr. was at home with his parents, a *medical student* at London University. He was admitted to the UK medical register on July 28th 1883 and graduated with a BA in medicine and surgery. In 1891 he was living in St Thomas's Hospital as a *physician surgeon*. He moved up the ladder rapidly in his career, specialising in chest and thoracic surgery, publishing several articles and giving lectures. In 1893 he married Evelyn Louise MILLING in Tunbridge. Their only child Ronald Henry Ottewell Betham ROBINSON was born in 1896 at their home in Wimpole Street. In 1901 they are living at 1 Wimpole Street. Henry died in 1918 and Evelyn in 1949.

Ronald H O B ROBINSON known as "Joey" followed his father into the medical profession via Cambridge University and then at St Thomas's Hospital. He became President of the British Association of Urological Surgeons and, like his father, published many articles and gave lectures. He was also Honorary Secretary of the Royal College of Medicine, examiner in surgery at Cambridge and the University of Malaya as well as holding many roles within the Royal Colleges and other hospitals in London. He married Audrey WALKER and they had one child, a daughter. He died on the 6th February 1973 and a memorial service was held on the 8th March in St Sepulchre's Church, Holborn.

SHEILA HARRIS hsheila10@yahoo.com

7. WARRINERs who travelled from Redmire to Liverpool and beyond

The grave of Mary RAW and William WARRINER in Redmire churchyard

The head of the family was William WARRINER. Born in Redmire on 24th February 1784 he was the son of Matthew WARRINER and Eleanor ALDERSON. He married Mary RAW who was also born in Redmire in 1797, the daughter of Isaiah RAW and Mary JOPLIN. They had eleven children, all born in Redmire but eventually departed for Liverpool and in some cases farther away still.

The eldest child was Matthew who was born in 1816. He left home before the 1841 census and was in Liverpool working as a *joiner* and married to his first wife Jane RUSSELL from Cumberland. They had three children before she died in 1855. By then Matthew was a *licensed victualler* in the centre of Liverpool. His mother's cousin Henry JOPLIN from Reeth was already established in the trade in Liverpool and may have introduced him to the life. By 1854 he and his brother David bought a small brewery from the famous Liverpool brewer Robert CAIN. Mathew was a member of the Liverpool Licensed Victuallers and was the chairman for a number of years. His second wife Ann SCOTT from Whitehaven, with whom he had another daughter, took over the licence of his pub on his death. His obituary in 1865 in the Liverpool Mercury stated *"....the flag of the institution was hoisted half-mast high and the inmates of the cottages manifested their respect by drawing their blinds."*

The second child Isaiah, born in 1818, was named after his grandfather Isaiah RAW. Isaiah also left Redmire at an early age and began his new life in Liverpool as a *soda water maker*. He married the daughter of a *licensed victualler* called Hannah Mary ANDERS from Liverpool. Isaiah advertised and sold his soda water making kit in 1851 and was running several different pubs until his untimely death on 22nd September 1866 from *"cerebral effusion and albumineria"* aged only 47 years. He had eight children and the youngest Joseph Scott WARRINER was my great grandfather. He was only five weeks old when his father died.

The third son John was born in 1821 and after leaving home worked as a *servant* in Spennithorne Hall in Wensleydale. In 1852 he married a co-worker Ellen WILSON and they made their way to Liverpool where they also began new lives as *victuallers*. His eldest brother Matthew passed the licence for a pub in Gt. George Place over to him thus keeping the business in the family.

The first daughter was Mary born in 1823. In 1841 she was a *servant* at the home of the ESPINER family in Redmire and in 1851 she was a *nursemaid* at Spennithorne Hall. She married Joseph SANDERS from Eardisley in Herefordshire in Liverpool in 1858. In between I have no record of her movements but the CHAYTON family from Spennithorne Hall appear to have gone abroad and I presume she followed her siblings to Liverpool to find work. Her husband was a *cow keeper* in the Everton area of Liverpool. Her mother Mary was widowed on 14th November 1861 and by 1871 was living with Mary Jr. (Polly).

The next child William was born in 1825. He was a *coalminer* and then a *lead miner* in Redmire but by 1871 he had followed his siblings to Liverpool and also become a *licensed victualler*. He married Grace PARKINSON in Wensley in 1848 and they had 8 children all of whom were born in Redmire. They all appear to have moved to Liverpool. By 1881 he had become a *draper* and left his victualler days behind him. He died in 1885 aged 60 years.

David WARRINER was born in 1827. In 1851 he worked as a *waiter in a bar* owned by his cousin Henry JOPLIN. He married Isabella ARUNDALE, born in Buckden, in Liverpool in 1855, a year after he bought part of the Robert CAIN brewery with his brother Matthew. Later, Isabella's sister Ann married Henry JOPLIN. David was involved in several transfers of licence and business involving the sale of premises for the extension to Lime St Station in Liverpool before buying a farm of 14.5 acres in Huyton, on the outskirts of Liverpool. By 1892 he had emigrated to New Orleans with his family and set up offices for the Elder Dempster shipping line. David returned to England and died in 1899. He was buried in Anfield Cemetery, Liverpool.

Edward was born in 1830 and was in Liverpool in 1851 working as a *barman*. He married Catherine BUTTERTON in 1858 and they had six children. He remained in the pub trade for twenty years before deciding to become a *cow keeper* – an occupation he remained in until his death aged 57 years in 1887.

Joseph was born in 1832 and was a *lead miner* in Redmire before joining his family in Liverpool. He worked with Edward initially and then with David at the Masons Arms in Copperas Hill. He married Ellen DENNING from Ireland in 1874 and then decided to become a *dyer* and left the pub profession. He died in 1890 aged 58. They had no children.

Roger was born in 1835 and was an *apprentice tailor* in Gunnerside before leaving Redmire for Liverpool. He married Elizabeth BRACK from Liverpool in 1858 and they had ten children. Roger became a *merchant tailor* employing twenty two people in the heart of the tailoring community in London Road. He raised funds for the Wesleyan church and was a Freemason and at one time became Worshipful Master. Following the death of his first wife in 1876, he married Sarah BALM in 1877. He died in 1903 aged 68.

Robert was born in 1838 and I believe was in Redmire until his father died in 1861. He left for Liverpool where he was a *cow keeper* and married Ellen FOSTER from Kettlewell in Wharfedale in 1866. They had seven children some of whom went to the USA and others to Canada. He died in 1890.

The second daughter was Ellen born in 1843. Ellen stays at home until 1863 when she married John MASON. They had one child Mary E MASON in 1864. Ellen left Redmire with Mary and lived with her brother David, then with her brother William and then took over in Robert's home after his death. She then moved to live with Roger. By this time her daughter had returned to Redmire and was either living with or visiting her father. I have no idea if Ellen ever saw her husband or lived with him after her removal to Liverpool.

The mother of all these WARRINER children, Mary RAW lived her remaining days in Liverpool and died in 1880 aged 83, outliving many of her children. She had eleven children and 53 grandchildren. All seem to have helped each other and remained close and supportive thus bringing their Redmire upbringing to Liverpool and then further afield.

SHEILA MOSS 123 Hallow Road, Worcester WR2 6DF. sheilamoss123@btinternet.com

8. William THOMPSON 1830-1871 –
A Dalesman's Journey and Life in Australia

William's eldest son and first Australian generation – James THOMPSON 1867-1935

William THOMPSON was born on 10th October 1830 at Fremington in the parish of Grinton in North Yorkshire. He was baptised at St. Andrew's Church in Grinton ten days later, just five minutes walk through the fields from Fremington. William and his brothers spent their youth in Reeth and its surrounding area, but three of them left for Australia where they made their homes. This is their story.

In 1832 William's parents James William THOMPSON and Ruth URWIN were living in Reeth at the "Half Moon Inn". Later that year they moved to a corn mill at Witton le Wear, a small village north of Bishop Auckland, Co. Durham on the River Wear. In 1833 they returned to Reeth. William's father James started work at the Barras End Lead Mine. William started school in Reeth in 1834 under the tuition of William HARKER and afterwards under Quaker THOMPSON. By 1835 his father moved to Fremington sawing for the Old Gang Lead Mining Company. William then went to Wards Free School.

William attended school in Fremington from 1835 to 1842, and when aged about twelve, began his first job with the Copperthwaite Lead Mines working for Edward and Mr. HAMMOND sawing. As the eldest child in the family William may have been favourably placed attending school. His next younger brother James was living and working with his grandfather, James THOMPSON (1778-1849) at the Fremington Mill from at least eleven years of age. Between 1836 and 1847 three more brothers and two sisters were born.

William worked at sawing on his own for the next few years until aged 17 when he began working with his father. His grandfather James died in 1849 and left the rental from his estate to four other grandsons to be inherited by them in 1863 when the youngest of them turned 21 years of age. William's younger brother James was one of the four.

In 1850 a saw mill was *"put up in Arkindale"*. Consequently, the sawyers *"were all struck off"* except William and his father who was then given the management of the mill. The family *"shifted into Arkindale"*. William was living with his parents in 1851 with all his siblings except for Thomas who was with his uncle Robert at the Fremington Mill. The family was at the CB Yard. William and his brother James were wood sawyers; John was shown at *"home"*, whilst Robert was a *scholar*. James, their father, was still the *manager* of the sawmill. With lead mining and the associated wood sawing work decreasing, William moved to Shildon in Durham in 1856. His parents followed a few months later. Shildon was the northern end of the "Darlington to Stockton" Railway which opened in 1825, the first public railway.

William's father died 27th January 1857, and William emigrated to Australia in June of the same year. After a three-month journey from Liverpool on the *Donald McKay*, he arrived in Melbourne 30th Sept 1857. He ventured out to Melton, Ballarat and other country areas before settling back in Melbourne and working in a similar field as in Reeth at the Carron Road Yard for Messrs. Anderson, Sharp and Wright and continued until the 28th Dec 1866.

In the meantime his brother John arrived from England in 1859. He spent some time in Melbourne and then left for New Zealand. The last contact with William was a letter to him in 1867. His younger brother Robert also left England between February 1861 and September 1863. William noted him as going to the Crooked River gold diggings by steamer '*Tario*' in a journal entry dated 21st November 1863.

On the 29th December 1866 William married Amelia Elizabeth SIMPSON, the daughter of George Alexander SIMPSON (1822-1898) and Mahala HEWITT (1822-1861), a *printer* then *dairyman* in Port Melbourne. After leaving the Carron Yard in 1867, he commenced working at Sandridge Work Shops under Mr. Elsdon for the Melbourne and Hobson Bay United Railway Co., where he undertook probably the same work as at the Shildon railway works, cleaning and working on steam engines.

Amelia and William went to live at Sandridge in Melbourne, and the young couple had their first child James (my great, great grandfather) on 21st December 1867. William was an industrious man, making his own furniture and a violin that he played. For leisure, he attended the theatre with his good friends Mr. HEPPLE and Mr. APPLEGARTH. The family frequented the Church of England, and William quite often cited passages of gospel from Sundays' sermons. Annie WARD also visited the family frequently. He attended grand events of the time such as the departure of BOURKE and WILL's expedition and the visit of the Prince of Wales from England. William also received occasional news by letter from Yorkshire, such as the death of their mother Ruth on 11th December 1859. His letters were from his sister Margaret who remained in Reeth, eventually marrying John Wesley GOUNDRY in 1867.

William and Amelia's second child George was born 21st October 1869, followed by William on 29th September 1871. After renting several homes William and Amelia purchased their own home in Carpenter Street, Brighton in 1871. William had become increasingly ill however and on the 8th October 1871 died of *"Stomach disease"* only two days shy of his 41st birthday, and ten days after his third son William's birth.

Six years after his brother William's death, Robert married William's widow Amelia. He and Amelia did not have any children together, but continued raising his nephews. Sadly, Amelia passed away on 4th May 1883 only five years after they married and Robert two years after that on 6th August 1885. The three boys then went to live with their maternal grandfather George Alexander SIMPSON at his dairy in Port Melbourne.

Losing three parents in the space of fourteen years must surely have had an impact on them all, but their Yorkshire roots were not forgotten and have been proudly recounted to their descendants, along with the legacy of William's journal which he kept daily from his Liverpool departure until a few days before his death. The original is at the Victorian State Library in Melbourne for all to share in his journey from the Dales.

DEBRA ANDREASSEN familymatters@noraus.com

9. Thomas CARTER from Bainbridge to Middlesbrough

Miss Edith J. Carter being awarded the Freedom of the Borough of Middlesbrough 1934

Thomas Carter was born at Fieldgate farm, Bainbridge and christened on the 23rd January 1835 at St Oswald's church Askrigg. His father Richard was a *farmer* in a small way and until he was 25 years of age Thomas assisted his father in the work of the farm.

In 1861 he went to Middlesbrough determined to strike out an income for himself. He started a picture framing business and by his great natural ability, industry and enterprise soon established a prosperous connection. Ten years later he disposed of the business to Alderman Scupham and thereafter devoted his attention to building and speculative building operations.

In this business he was singularly successful, and it was not long before he had the distinction of being the largest individual ratepayer in the town. Being naturally of a retiring and altogether modest and unostentatious disposition, he was never eager for public life and although he was elected on the Town Council until 1876 he retired at the end of three years.

He remained outside the Council until 1890, when, yielding to a requisition from the Middlesbrough Temperance Society, he sought re-election, and was returned for the North West Ward. He retired again, but in 1894 he was returned this time for the Ayresome Ward, which he continuously represented until his elevation to the aldermanic bench.

He was a Guardian of the Poor for over a quarter of a century, and in this position he did much excellent work. It was work for which he was well suited, for he always took the closest personal interest in the welfare of the poor. As vice-chairman of the Board, chairman of the Finance Committee, and in other positions he rendered valuable service.

He was a staunch tee-totaller, and took a great interest in the work of the Middlesbrough Temperance Society, of which he was at one time President. He was an active Wesleyan and gave freely both of time and money in the interests of that denomination, and on several occasions he represented the Whitby and Darlington district, of which Middlesbrough formed a part, at the annual Wesleyan Conference. In politics he was a convinced Liberal, but he never took an active share in party polemics.

In 1887 the Corporation did him the honour of appointing him to the civic chair and his daughter Miss Edith J. Carter assisted him as Mayoress.

He was always an earnest supporter of the North Riding Infirmary, and of the House Committee of which he was chairman. The welfare of the institution he had ever at heart, and every effort that was put forward to enhance its usefulness and augment its funds had his practical sympathy and assistance. Gradually the House Committee increased in influence and in 1877 it was moved that three working men should be voted onto the committee *'as they would see for themselves the way in which the Institution was managed, and it was for their advantage to get the workmen to increase their subscription.'*

Thomas died on the 20th April 1904 at his home, Ayresome House, Newport Road, Middlesbrough. On receipt of the news of his death at the Municipal Buildings the Town Clerk Mr Alf SOCKETT gave directions for flags to be hoisted at half mast.

JAN GRADWELL jan.gradwell@btinternet.com

10. Anthony WILKINSON – a progressive man of Wyoming

Anthony Wilkinson

Anthony WILKINSON was born on 4th July 1838 at Howgill Thoralby. He was the son of Anthony and Alice (née SAYER) WILKINSON.

At the age of 19 he found work as *game watcher* at Rokeby Park and stayed there for two years. In 1863 he was appointed *game keeper* at Tolloch Castle, Rosshire where he stayed for a further four years.

He returned home to Yorkshire to assist his father in the work and management of the farm until 1873 when he left to take passage to America.

On arriving in America he first went to Dorchester Nebraska where he operated a meat market for about three years, sending wagons to surrounding areas and adjoining towns where he transacted an extensive and profitable business.

After three more years he moved on to Custer and took up a homestead and began in a small way raising cattle and sheep. He also owned a general meat market in Ansley, Nebraska. In this business he again met with success and desired to have a larger field for his stockgrowing operations.

He moved to Wyoming where in 1878 he bought a ranch near Archer and engaged in a successful business in raising sheep and cattle. He remained there until 1891 when he purchased a ranch property at Muddy Creek about a mile from Pine Bluffs. He extended his operation from year to year and became one of the biggest dealers and largest property owners in the state. He was also one of the largest landowners in the Western Country, having 8,300 acres at his home ranch, about 16,000 acres at Big Horse Creek and approximately 8,000 acres a short distance south of his home ranch making about 32,000 acres of land in Wyoming.

Extract from *"Progressive men of Wyoming"*

CHRISTINE HOWIE chowie@hotmail.co.uk

CAMPBELLS OF LEYBURN

still at the heart of the local community – naturally

 1920's

In a retail world dominated by major supermarkets Campbells of Leyburn is refreshingly different.

Still a family business after more than 140 years today's Campbells offers traditional values of quality products and real value in an ever expanding store.

 2010

Campbells of Leyburn now provides a wide range of everyday products, a selection of local produce, some superb fresh fruit and vegetables, probably the finest selection of wines and spirits in the area and our recently extended in-house butchery and deli offers the regions' finest meats and charcuterie.

You can now also buy wine online at:
www.campbellsofleyburn.co.uk

www.campbellsofleyburn.co.uk

4 Commercial Square, Leyburn, North Yorkshire DL8 5BP
Tel: 01969 622169 Email: enq@campbellsofleyburn.co.uk

Campbells — serving the Dales for more than 140 years – naturally

21

11.   Henry Octavius ATKINSON

A sketch of the forge at Gownleyfoot by Diane McLENNAN
www.dianemclellan.com

My ATKINSON story begins with a name, a place and an approximate date of birth: that, due to family circumstances, was almost all I knew about my grandfather.

The name was Henry Octavius ATKINSON and had it not been for his unusual middle name, I doubt I would have been able to find him in records. The place was Harrogate and the year of birth, 1877, was calculated from the fact that he was some twenty years or more older than my grandmother. They met and married in Canada during World War I; there were two daughters of the marriage but Henry had a secret, which resulted in two families being left without a father.

Researching Henry's family was a revelation. His father Octavius was a *blacksmith*, born in 1843 at Gollinglith Foot, known locally as Gownley Foot, near Masham. His father George, born in 1803 in the Masham district, was a *blacksmith*. He no doubt trained Octavius in the trade as well as another son Henry who later conducted his business in Healey and a third son Joseph who emigrated. Their mother was Rosamond CHERRY born in 1808 in Thornton Steward. George and Rosamond raised their family at Pastures End, Gownley Foot.

When Octavius married Esther RAYNERD of Colsterdale, in 1873, they moved to Tower Street, Harrogate, where Tave, as he was called by his birth family, set up his blacksmith shop. From these humble beginnings grew Octavius ATKINSON and Sons Ltd, a major employer at Starbeck, Harrogate. His primary business was in the design, fabrication and erection of steel buildings and general construction work. The company had agents in Canada, the Middle East, West Africa, Australia, New Zealand, India, Pakistan, USA and Central America. In the 1960s the company was taken over by Taylor Woodrow, but still traded under the name Octavius ATKINSON and Sons Ltd, with Octavius' grandson, William Octavius ATKINSON as President. However in the 1980s, the parent company moved operations to a brand new state of the art factory at Flaxby Moor Works, Hopperton. It is believed it was this move that contributed to the closure of the company, as expected export orders did not materialise and the company went into liquidation in the early 1990s.

Octavius' youngest son George Frederick born in 1882 was an *apprentice* at the Harrogate Water Undertaking in 1901 and also became a *civil engineer*. By the time, he married Dorothy ALLEN in Bilton, Harrogate in 1909 he was working for the Fylde Water Board, Blackpool, where he became Chief Engineer in 1924. (See chapter 64.)

John, one of Octavius' brothers, worked in London, first as a *butler* and later ran an inn there. Other brothers who left the dales include the youngest Robert who married Octavius' wife's sister Caroline and moved to Harrogate, where he worked with Octavius; George, who went to Leeds; Joseph and Bateman who emigrated to the US and William went to New Zealand.

I am indebted to Esther Pogue, the widow of a grandson of Joseph, for sharing his family tree with me and for the invaluable copies of letters to Joseph from other family members in England and New Zealand. Naturally, most of these letters tell us more about life in the dales than of those who emigrated, but there are also some between the brothers in America, which give an insight to life in their new land. I found those which referred to *"uncle and aunt"* in New York of particular interest, using them to research and identify these relatives.

We found two important clues, a letter from Aunt Mary, who was clearly *"uncle's"* wife; the second was a record in US Immigration records that a Bateman ATKINSON entered New York in 1836. This was prior to Ellis Island records and the record arose because under the rules of an Act in 1825, foreigners were allowed to occupy, use or own land or property. When an applicant made such a request, his date of entry was required. A search of US census records identified a Bateman and Mary ATKINSON, both born in England. When Uncle Bateman died, a nephew of Mary by birth, Henry G CRICKMORE, wrote to the brothers, Joseph and Bateman to inform them. A search of the cemetery records in Brooklyn revealed that H G CRICKMORE was buried in the same plot as Bateman and Mary ATKINSON.

I found two other descendants of Octavius who were brought up outside the ATKINSON family. They were half brothers, born a generation apart, who did not know the other existed. One lives now in Oxford; the other has lived in Sweden for more than fifty years.

This story is not my work alone. Many have contributed along the way, but mainly it is the result of painstaking research of our band of four, comprising along with myself, Liz HOLDSWORTH (whose ancestor Henry was a brother of Octavius), the late Sue WISHART (whose ancestor was another brother, George) and Esther Pogue (whose husband was a descendant of brother, Joseph). I am indebted to Tony CHEAL who has provided copies of deeds and local newspaper cuttings, which have helped enormously researching those who lived in Harrogate.

Two ex-employees of Octavius ATKINSON and Sons Ltd also responded to a message board plea for information about the company, providing interesting insights to the characters of their previous employers.

MARGARET HAWKINS snikwahrm@hotmail.com

Editor's note: Tony CHEAL is a local historian in Harrogate who maintains a vast index and record of people and places in Harrogate and the surrounding area. http://harrogatepeopleandplaces.info/

12. The LAMBERT family of High Blean – a Quaker family in Wensleydale

Anna LAMBERT

My ancestors came from the remote area of High Blean, far above Semerwater. Thomas LAMBERT was born in 1678, which event is recorded in the Aysgarth Parish Registers. It is one of the few occasions the LAMBERTs appeared in the conventional records of the Church, as at some point during his life, Thomas was drawn to the Light, and became a member of the Society of Friends – or the Quakers, as they are more popularly known. He married Margaret ROUTH in 1709, also a Quaker, and together they had five children. At some point the family moved to Kirkby Moorside, and then returned to live at High Blean. The children were recorded in the Wensleydale Monthly Meeting once they resumed life in Bainbridge. Thomas died in 1734, and was buried *"at Bainbridg burying place"*. His detailed Will also includes an inventory of £51 12/6d *of goods and chattels*. This comprised livestock, household goods such as *"A Cubbert and two chests"* and *"chairs and a longsettle"* along with *"cheeses, Beef meal and Wheat"*. The Will was witnessed by Richard ROBINSON and George METCALFE, but his widow Margaret had to enter into a £1000 bond with her brother Oswald ROUTH in which she committed herself to bring up her son Thomas LAMBERT (the younger) *"in the fear of God and in the discipline of the Church of England"*. She obviously did no such thing, as my 7 x great grandfather brought up all his children as Quakers.

Thomas LAMBERT (the younger) also lived at Blean, as a *farmer*, and it was his youngest son, David, from whom I am descended. His wife was Hannah WEBSTER, and they married on 9th May in 1781. Between 1792 and 1794 the family moved from High Blean to the other side of the valley to Browna Parrocks (Now called Browna Paddocks). Daughter Margery died aged twelve in 1797. Twins Francis and Mary survived infancy, which in itself is unusual, only to perish at the age of nine within two months of each other in 1799. Whatever tragedy struck the family, it also fell upon the LAMBERTs of Thorns House, killing three children and their mother in early 1800. All were buried at Bainbridge. David himself died in 1816, and also left a detailed Will. The sum total of his belongings did not, according to the Will, exceed £600 – but that is the equivalent of £35,400 in 2010 if using the retail price index as a "conversion". There were strings attached also to this will. His son David had to *"at his own expense properly fit up and furnish the stable and chamber... and proper convenience for fuel"* so that his mother could live there. David must have been a particular favourite, as he was the third born son, and although he was also required to provide legacies for his brothers out of the estate, it was David who got to keep the *"goods and chattels"*. This left my own ancestor – another Thomas LAMBERT (the *cow doctor*) with a legacy of £100, to be followed, after the death of mother Hannah, by a further one hundred and fifty pounds.

Thomas married at some point before 1817 as by this time he described himself as a *widower*. He presented himself to the Bishop of Chester's surrogate, and applied for a marriage licence. He described himself as a *butcher*, and took along with him Thomas DINSDALE, *farmer*, for support. Both described themselves as being from High Abbotside. His intended was Isabella METCALFE, and Thomas (along with Thomas Dinsdale) signed up for a £200 bond, to be paid over if any of the marriage rules were broken. As a Quaker, Thomas was not required to be *"sworn"*. Instead, he *"did affirm on the holy evangelists"* that he was a *widower*, and that his bride to be was over 21 and a *spinster*. They were married two days later, and remained man and wife for the next 45 years, when Isabella died.

It was a fruitful marriage, with eight living children as *"proofs of affection"*. Margaret was the eldest, and although she never married, had an "interesting" life. Born in Burtersett, she and younger sister Alice (born 1829) were both mysteriously baptised into the Church of England, in 1844. Alice was 14 and Margaret 21. They are both quite clearly described as the children of Thomas and Isabella LAMBERT, and their father, Thomas is described as a *Cow Leech*. The probable reason emerged in the 1851 census – they needed work. Margaret, sister Ann (born 1839) brother Oswald (born 1832) were all living in Leyburn at the home of Thomas EDMUNDSON, a *medical doctor*, aged 55, and described as *married*, although there was no wife in residence. The LAMBERTs were all *servants*. Also there was Thomas D. LAMBERT aged five and the son of Margaret. Young Thomas was later trained as a *Chemist and Druggist*, and operated a shop at 3, Market Place, Askrigg, which, given his start in life, indicates that someone took an interest in his education. Dr. EDMUNDSON died in 1866. Margaret went to live with her son for a while, but eventually moved to Aiskew, as *housekeeper* to Benjamin PURCHAS. She died in 1890.

Brother Francis LAMBERT went as a *farm servant* to Helwith (1851) and then to Paddington, London as a *servant* (1861). He had progressed to a *shop servant* by 1871, at 187 Edgware Road, Paddington.

Oswald, initially in service with Dr. EDMUNDSON, was the *coachman* for George ALDERSON at the Vicarage, Hornby in 1871. By 1881, he was living with his niece at Litherskew, Hardraw, and was a *domestic gardener*. He was still there in 1891, although now living alone, and described as *"retired"* – good going for a 59 year old man. By 1901, he had returned to West View, Burtersett, where he was *living on his own means*, with his nephew, Oswald METCALFE. He died in 1909, and his death was recorded by the Quakers in *'The Annual Monitor"* for 1910. His Will left £193 14/2d to his sisters, Ann ALLEN, Anna ROWNTREE (my 3 x great grandmother) and niece Mary Jane NUTTALL.

In July 1856 Anna, my ancestor, gave birth to a son, Thomas Lambert ROWNTREE. Alas, she was not married to the father. She later married Thomas ROWNTREE in 1857, at Hawes. It was to be one of the few occasions she set foot in a church. Later Anna and Thomas tried to get baby Thomas Lambert baptised at Hornby. In the margin of the register the vicar carefully wrote *"This child was born when the mother was a spinster – baptised after the marriage when the infant was 9 months old. Maiden name of mother Annie LAMBERT."* None of her other 12 children were baptised. Husband Thomas ROWNTREE was a *gardener* and in 1858 they were in Tunstall where Arabella Alice ROWNTREE was born. By 1859, they were in Staindrop, Co Durham and by 1863 they had moved to Middlesbrough, where Thomas had secured work as a *gardener* at Newlands. Anna's father Thomas LAMBERT went to live with them. His wife Isabella had died in 1862, and was buried in Friends Burying Ground, Bainbridge, although the Burial note is clearly marked *"not a member"*. Thomas LAMBERT died in 1867, aged 84. He also chose to be buried at Friends Burying Ground, Bainbridge, and whilst also described as *not in membership*, he was noted as being *"late of Burtersett, Cattle Doctor and Farrier"*. Anna LAMBERT and Thomas ROWNTREE were married for over 60 years. Anna died in 1919 and Thomas in 1922. He is buried at Patrick Brompton.

LIZ HAMILTON Bizzy@blueyonder.co.uk

13. Mary HARLAND's letter from Marrick to Quebec

This original letter was provided for the exhibition by Jon Cable in Highgate London. It is dated 1834 and was written on quite expensive paper with the countermark *'R Barnard 1833.'* The letter has since been deposited in the North Yorkshire County Archives in Northallerton.

The letter was sent *'by favour'* or outside the normal postal system from Mary HARLAND in Marrick to her sister Mrs. John Hannah CROFT c/o *Masson and Strang* in Quebec. Mary had addressed the letter incorrectly to *Messrs Masson Longstrang & Company* and this was corrected at some point in its journey.

Mary, the daughter of Charles LONSDALE, married John HARLAND, *gent*, at Grinton in 1819. She died at Marrick aged 50 and was buried in Grinton on 28th July 1847. She had two sisters named Hannah and Margaret and Grinton Parish Records show the marriage on 22nd April 1829 of John CROFT and Hannah LONSDALE witnessed by John HARLAND. Margaret LONSDALE's marriage on 18th September 1830 was to John WHITELL of Ravenstonedale and witnesses were John and Mary HARLAND, Jane CROFT, and Hannah CROFT. John, shown as a *mercer of Reeth* and Hannah, baptised Charles John on 9th April 1830 and Anne on 1st January 1832 but after that date there were no more entries.

Following the marriage of John HARLAND and Mary LONSDALE in 1819, there were the following baptisms at Grinton:

9th August 1819 Frances Wallington (buried on thirteenth August 1819.)
19th January 1823 Chas John Willington (born 14th January and buried 29th March 1823 at ten weeks.)
30th June 1826 Walter Willington. At the baptism John HARLAND was listed as a *Lieutenant in the King's Own*. Walter is the *Walter William* named in the letter. The transcription is as written.

'Marrick April 6th 1834

Dear Sister

I received your letter safe and was glad to hear that you had arrived as there was so many ships lost at that time it gave me great uneasiness we all so got Johns letter and was very sorry to hear that you had got hurt but I hope you are quite recoverd. This you will receive by Charles & John SPEAR they have come a foolish errant.

Poor Fanny is dead and was buried Easter Sunday and young Sally COATES is dead and Nelly JOPLIN & Ester ORTON and Nanny has got married & Francis LONSDALE is also dead and left 3000£ to his man servant

Mary ATKINSON has got married to John CLORE the butter carrier and that wretch Bess has come home to carry on her old business.

Old Nancy and Betty desires their love to you and they have lost little Jos in the meesels.
Jane COATES and Mrs COARSAN and Mrs THWAITES all begs to be remembrd to you

Mr Barker and Mary Elle desires to be rememberd to both of you. Mary is at home with her mother and we have got Eliza BRUNSKILL from Hoff.

My aunt Jane is going on in the same way and aunt Betty and family desires their love to you and James CALVERT daughter is dead.

Dolly WHALEY & Mr CHALDER Susan and all the rest of Marrick send their love to you and would be glad to see you again in Marrick.

Now I think I have sent you all the news that I can think of at present I should have rote to you before this but was waiting for their coming.

We had Johns mother down a few weeks ago and she says that they are determined not to send any money as they might be of their work and they would be obliged then to live on it — but know that with what money he has received and what he has sold the goods for that he has 70£. in the Savings Bank at preasant therefore he might have sent the 10£. We have not received a farthing of the book debts since you left and Thomas PEACOCK of Sturfit Hall says that he paid John at Lanquit and Lant ALLISON all so says that he paid him as well as several more of them as you must ask him. Mr HARLAND has been 6 weeks in London and he is now home or he would have sent the accounts with Charles but until some of the book debts is got in you are in debted to him.

I hope by this time you like your situation better and that John and the children is all well Walter often speaks of them and wishes he could ride on his pony to meet them but he says that if they do not come back again he hopes he will meet them in heaven.

Little Bessy is grown a fine child I never though that John would have left her but she is well provided for with the old people

Mr HARLAND send his kind respects to you both and if he has time he will rite at the same time if not he will rite by some of the vessels that is going from London as he will be there in a few weeks again.

Make my best respects to John and accept the same your self from your affectionate sister Mary HARLAND. I shall be glad to hear from you as soon as you receive this and let me know how all is going on and what you both think of Charles and John skeem as I think it a bad one.

(In child's writing Walter adds)

Walter love to cousin Charles and Ann unkle John and aunt Hannah (Mr & Mrs CROFT)"

Robertson Masson & Strang was a well known and large commercial trading company. In 1830 this firm consisted of three companies, W. & H. Robertson and Company in Glasgow, run by Hugh Robertson; Robertson Masson LaRocque, Strang and Company at Quebec, managed by John Strang. Hugh Robertson and Masson held more than 80 % of the capital of all three companies. In 1833 the total investment amounted to £80,200 and the value of the goods imported rose to about £100,000. In 1827 the sales in Great Britain of potash alone were worth £31,678. Masson had gone further than other Canadian businessmen in establishing contracts with the British market, but he was by no means the only one doing so. La Roque and Charles Langevin two of the people with whom he worked were part of this small but visible group.

Others mentioned in the letter were:

Sarah COATES of Reeth who died on 18th December 1833 aged 27 and was buried at Grinton. Eleanor JOPLIN widow of Cuthbert of Reeth who died 23rd February 1834 aged 56 buried at Grinton. Esther ORTON widow of John of Reeth who died 28th March 1834 aged 70 buried at Grinton. John CLOSE married Mary ATKINSON at Grinton witnesses John BRADBURY, Abb BRADBERRY, Mark ATKINSON on 20th March 1834.

I am grateful to John CABLE for contributing this original letter to the exhibition.

If any of the people mentioned in this letter are related to you please contact:

GLENYS MARRIOTT glenys@bishopdale.demon.co.uk

14. Emigration of George KEARTON and others from Swaledale to St Vincent, Windward Islands 1764

The present day entrance to the Kearton plantation on St Vincent. The building on the hillside is approximately where the sugar boiling plant was situated.

George KEARTON, baptised on 25th February 1722, was the fourth son of George KIRTON senior (sometimes Kearton) of Oxnop, near Muker. George senior was reputed to have been *"in his 125th year"* when he died in 1764. It was in the following year that George (Jr.) purchased a half share (moiety) of a plantation on the west coast of the island of St Vincent in the Windward Islands in the Caribbean. The other half share was owned by William LINDOW who owned other plantations on the island. George KEARTON sailed to St Vincent to manage the plantation which was growing sugar and coffee, valuable crops that were exported to England. The plantation lay on the west coast of the island at Kearton's Bay. The inventory of the estate identified it as Kearton's Estate at Barrowally (sic); the town is now named Barrouallie. An indenture held at the National Archives, dated 23rd January 1770 between William LINDOW and George KEARTON, described the plantation of 123 acres lying within the parish of St. Patrick.

The total value of the buildings amounted to £3,319 0s 0d. In addition the property included a number of slaves. They were identified by name and value starting with Cato – *a driver* (£130), Mingo – *a boiler* (£130), Jeremy – *a doctor* (£80) Hector – *a distiller* (£70) and Jingo – *a cooper* (£120). Four boys were valued between £60 and £70 each and a male child at £12. Thirty one males were identified in total together and valued at £2,357. Twenty five female slaves are identified of whom two are children valued only at £5 the pair. Only Mareyan had an occupation, washer, and their values ranged from £20 to £80. The total value of the female slaves was £1,240. The livestock included mules, horses, asses, bulls, cows, sheep, and cows all together valued at £682 15s 0d.

George KEARTON wrote his will on 5th July 1773 in which he left his 123 acre share in the plantation to his nephew John KEARTON, the son of George's eldest brother, Anthony. John was living with, but not married to Ann DOYLE and they had two sons named Anthony and George (2). Anthony was the elder son and it was reported that he travelled by way of the newly independent United States. George (2) was born in Muker in England in 1775 but by 1777 the parents and two boys had travelled to St Vincent. These years coincided with the occupation of the island by the French. John KEARTON became a member of the St. Vincent Assembly which continued to administer and run the island and also of a Peace Commission which had probably been set up to encourage and hasten a settlement between the French and the English. This was achieved in 1783 under the Treaty of Versailles. In 1787 John was commissioned as a *captain* in the St. Vincent North Regiment of Militia and it is highly probable that he and the regiment were heavily engaged in the war with the Carib Indians on the island. George KEARTON (Jr.) died in April 1783 and was buried at St George's Cathedral, Kingstown on 23rd April of that year. He was aged about 61.

John KEARTON and Ann DOYLE had a further three children on St. Vincent. Named Jennet Spooner KEARTON (after her grandmother Jennet SPOONER, daughter of the Rev. John SPOONER of Greenside at Ravenstonedale, Westmorland), William Lindow KEARTON and Thomas KEARTON. Baptisms were recorded at St. George's Cathedral on 20th October 1782, 12th May 1785 and 18th June 1788 respectively.

George (2) was undoubtedly employed on the Kearton estate. Between 1800 and 1804 the baptisms of four "coloured" girls were recorded at St. George's. They were named Frances, Maria, Elizabeth and Fanny and the father was named as George KEARTON Esq. of England. The last three baptisms make clear that the child was freed at birth. On 6th June 1810 he married Mary Gerald COLCROFT at St. George's. Mary was aged 18 years having been born on St. Vincent in 1791. One child, Mary Elizabeth KEARTON was baptised on 11th February 1811.

John KEARTON's death is unrecorded but occurred between 1810 and 1813. In his will he left his moiety of the Kearton estate to Ann and subsequently to his sons *"in fee"* – that is as a legal estate of inheritance. This was not permitted in law as children born out of wedlock were not permitted to inherit property. So began a long legal challenge made by George Henry KEARTON/KIRTON, *an attorney* and first cousin of John. The challenges are recorded in detail in Jonathan KIRTON's paper on this family and in his book *A Kirton Family History*.

At some point between 1810 and 1825 George (2) bought out his brother Thomas's interest in the plantation for an annuity of £500 per year. His mother had died some years earlier (before 1820) and her will dated 1818 left her property in trust. To her two sisters Eleanor DOYLE and Elizabeth BUCKLEY (widow) she left five hundred pounds each; in the case of Elizabeth this was to be paid in cash, in the case of Eleanor, she was released and discharged from a debt incurred when Ann had purchased a lot of land in Barrouallie. To her granddaughters Frances MORGAN, Elizabeth PAUL and Beury IALZELL she left one hundred pounds each. Her sons George and Thomas received five hundred pounds each. Ann's will directed that certain named slaves and their children should be released and set free. The residue of her property was left to her granddaughter Mary KEARTON. Ann's will was not registered until 1836. It is unclear whether this delayed in any way the payments of the legacies contained in it, but certainly the effect was to put control of the plantation firmly in the hands of George (2).

The Gentleman's Magazine of 1827 recorded the death of George (2) KEARTON Esq. of Kearton Hall, St. Vincent in Stanhope Street, London whilst on a visit back to England. He died on 22nd January 1827 and was interred at the Walcot Burial Grounds at Bath, Somerset. His wife Mary and daughter Elizabeth were living in Bath. By 1851, Mary Gerald KEARTON *a widow and annuitant* was living in the High Street, Barnstaple in North Devon. She died aged 78 at Bedford and her death was reported in The Times on 30th January 1869. Her daughter married James CROSBY the Police Magistrate of St. Vincent. She predeceased her mother, dying in Georgetown, Demerara (British Guiana) on 13th April 1858.

Acknowledgements: This summary is based on a paper which appears on www.svgancestry.com by Jonathan G KIRTON of Montreal, Canada. In this paper he acknowledged the assistance he received from the late Lt. Com. George Cecil David KEARTON, Royal Navy and Royal Canadian Navy retired (1921 – 2001) and his sister Mary Diana DYKE. Copies of George Henry KEARTON's papers were made available to Basil E KEARTON of Te Kuiti, New Zealand whose book *Yorkshire and Yonder, Families of Keartons* was published in 1995. Photograph of Kearton's Plantation copyright of Nicholas Graham SYKES, the son of Edward Kearton SYKES.

BLAIR SOUTHERDEN blairsou@globalnet.co.uk and
JONATHAN KIRTON jonathankirton@sympatico.ca

15. "More like a Century" – The World War I diary of John (Jack) PRESTON of Askrigg.

John (Jack) PRESTON was born in 1883 in Askrigg in Wensleydale, the second son of James PRESTON 1859-1934 and Margaret Ann CHAPMAN 1861-1946 both of Askrigg. They lived in West End House and farmed the land just north of St Oswald's Church.

In 1910 Jack married Elizabeth (Lizzie) Preston BANKES in Liverpool. Lizzie was the daughter of William Lightfoot BANKES (1833-1900) of Liverpool and Margaret PRESTON (1851-1909) of Askrigg. Jack and Lizzie were first cousins and their common grand-parents were John THOMPSON Woodward PRESTON and Elizabeth GRAHAM of Askrigg. In October 1910 Lizzie gave birth in Liverpool, to Constance (Connie) Margaret PRESTON but Lizzie died within a few weeks of the birth.

When WWI started in 1914 Jack was living and working at West End House Farm, along with his daughter Connie, his parents, sister Isabel CHAPMAN, brothers James Graham and Frank Baden. The oldest brother, Charles William, had married and moved to Lancashire.

Jack was enlisted in the Army and left Askrigg in April 1915. He did not return until April 1919. He spent about five months in Gallipoli, Turkey under constant shelling and then was evacuated to Alexandria, Egypt where he spent the rest of the war. He was a member of the RASC (Royal Army Supply Corp.) S4/090172 and made the rank of *Sergeant*.

His younger brother Jim was killed in France in 1917 when he was only twenty years old. Jack kept an extensive personal diary and wrote many letters home which are included in the exhibition. The last sentence in the final diary described how *"these four years felt more like a century."*

Jack was the founder and secretary of "The Gallipoli Association" for survivors of the campaign. He did not re-marry and lived in West End House until his death in 1948.

JOHN BAYNES WHITTON, Jack's grand-son. Arizona, USA jbwaz@cox.net

George & Dragon Inn

Hotel and Fine Dining

Aysgarth, North Yorkshire

Telephone: 01969 663358 Fax: 01969 663773
E-mail: info@georgeanddragonaysgarth.co.uk

Real Ale, Real Welcome!

In the heart of the stunning Yorkshire Dales National Park, on the edge of a pretty village, near the spectacular Aysgarth falls, the George & Dragon Inn has greeted travellers for nearly 300 years.

This 17th century Coaching Inn is perfectly located for exploring Wensleydale and touring the beautiful Yorkshire Dales.

John and Collette will give you a warm welcome serving real local ales from the Black Sheep Brewery and Yorkshire Dales Brewing Company and fine wines from every corner of the globe. Relax in front of a real log fire in the winter months, or amongst the flowers on the patio with summer views of Pen Hill.

16. The CURRY family of East Witton

Harry RAPER (1786-1868) on 30th June 1856 on his 70th birthday.

My mother's maiden surname was CURRY and using several sources I traced her family back to East Witton and in doing so I found a large family of cousins spread all over the world. I could not have traced these people without the help of the dales email group which enabled me to contact a Jane CURRY in New Zealand. She sent pages from the diary of Harry RAPER *master carpenter* of East Witton with information about the marriage of his daughter Ann RAPER, the birth of his grandchildren and his daughter's death. The information I have about the family in Ireland came to me from a David UPSHON in South Africa who has researched the CURRY family for many years.

On 11th February 1832 Joseph CURRY *schoolteacher* in East Witton married Ann RAPER at East Witton church; this couple were my great, great, great grandparents. Joseph and Ann CURRY had three sons born in East Witton, Henry CURRY my ancestor, born 26th October 1832, Matthew CURRY born 9th April 1834 and John Thomas CURRY born in 1836 who died 8th September 1836. Ann CURRY née RAPER died 21st February 1838 and was buried in East Witton graveyard with her son.

Joseph had left the dales by 1841, then remarried and he and his new wife had a further twelve children. His eldest son Henry CURRY remained with his grandfather Harry RAPER while the younger son Matthew CURRY moved with him to Otley.

Matthew CURRY born on 9th February 1834 in East Witton lived with his father and stepmother in Dewsbury in 1841. By 1851 he was apprenticed to a Benjamin DAWSON *joiner* of Dewsbury. On 24th January 1857 he married Mary Ann WALTON at The Parish Church, Northallerton. Records showed he had children in Stockton on Tees and Newcastle upon Tyne in the three years before he moved to Ireland. He settled in Abbeyleix, Queens County, Ireland where he and his wife raised 20 children. Matthew's descendants have been traced to New Zealand, Australia, Canada and Ireland.

Henry CURRY my great great grandfather grew up in East Witton and served as a *joiner's apprentice* to his grandfather Harry RAPER. He married Isabella SHIELDS on 5th June 1858 at the Parish Church, Houghton le Spring in Co. Durham. Isabella was born in East Witton and lived next door to Henry in 1841 but I do not know when she moved to Houghton le Spring. By 1861 the family were found in Great Bedwyn, Wiltshire. The Earls of Ailesbury who owned the Jervaulx Estate in the dales also owned an estate in Great Bedwyn. In 1871 his wife Isabella CURRY was a widow living in East Witton with five children. Records showed Henry Raper CURRY was buried on 20th April 1866 at Great Bedwyn. He was *Agent* to the Marquis of Ailesbury and left a widow and five children. He died of *phthisis (tuberculosis.)* Isabella CURRY returned to East Witton and lived with her parents and then in 1891 with her brother Joseph SHIELDS *landlord* at the Blue Lion. She was *schoolmistress* at East Witton school for many years and died 23rd April 1918 and was buried at East Witton church.

Five children of Henry RAPER CURRY were raised in East Witton:

Annie Elizabeth CURRY born 19th March 1859 in East Witton married James ELKINS on 15th April 1884 at All Saints Church, Knightsbridge and lived in London from that time with her husband and two children.
Thomas William CURRY born circa 1862 in Great Bedwyn, Wiltshire worked as a *draper's assistant* in Ripon in 1881. I have been unable to trace him from that time.
Isabella Edith Elizabeth CURRY born circa 1863 in Great Bedwyn married John William TROTT on 15th October 1898 in St Catherine's Chapel, Feltham, Middlesex and settled in Scarborough with her husband. Records indicated there were no children.
Margaret Ann CURRY born circa 1866 in Great Bedwyn died 1872 in East Witton.

The fifth child Henry Thomas CURRY, born on 15th September 1860 in Great Bedwyn, was my great grandfather. From 1871 onwards he lived in the dales and married Elizabeth ATKINSON on 13th January 1889 at the Wesleyan Chapel in Bedale. Elizabeth was the daughter of Henry ATKINSON (1836-1908) *master blacksmith* of Masham. In 1891 Henry Thomas CURRY was recorded as a *brewer's traveller* living on College Lane, Masham very close to the current Theakston brewery. He died on 23rd February 1898 in Masham when the cause of death was *phthisis (tuberculosis) of 12 months and exhaustion*. He had five children all of whom were born in Masham but left the dales:

1. Hilda Edith CURRY born in 1889 was unmarried in 1911 and worked as a servant in Knaresborough for a family called Barstow. She argued with her mother about the man she wished to marry and disappeared. I have never found any trace of her since 1911.

2. Elsie Annie CURRY born in 1891, worked as a nurse in London in 1918 when she met a wounded Australian soldier Hans Andreas KNUDSEN. They married on 29th March 1919 at St Stephens, Coleman St, London and after visiting his parents in Denmark emigrated to Australia. She died on 23rd November 1923 West Maitland, New South Wales, from a perforated appendix.

3. Margaret Dorothy CURRY born in 1895 married Ernest GLADWYN on 17th July 1918 at Holy Trinity Church, Wibsey, Bradford and lived in the city where she had two children.

4. Robert Vivian CURRY born in 1897 married Letticia Olive SPENCE on 19th November 1925 at the Wesleyan Methodist Chapel, Wycar, Bedale. They owned a garage and cafe at Leeming Bar north of Masham on the old A1. Robert was unwell so he and Olive moved to Southbourne at some stage where Olive opened a private hotel. They had one daughter Elsie.

5. The fifth child William Henry CURRY born on 31st May 1893 was my maternal grandfather. He married Bertha LICKLEY on 28th Aug 1917 at Eastbrook Hall, Bradford. On 10th May 1921 his wife Bertha died in childbirth along with their second child, their first child being my mother Margery Elizabeth CURRY (1919-2002). After WWI he lived in Bradford, trained as an *accountant* and worked privately after qualification. He acquired a brush making firm (making brushes and combs for the mills) and my uncle took over the running of the company after his death. The family shares were sold eventually to a partner in the company in order to provide a pension for my grandmother. He married Annie SAVAGE in 1922 in Selby and they had three children, two of whom are still living. He died on 12th March 1951 at Scalebar Park in Ilkley.

LIZ HOLDSWORTH yzzil.yrruc@btinternet.com

17. Richard PEACOCK (1820-1889) – Locomotive Engineer extraordinary

Richard PEACOCK

Richard PEACOCK was born at Healaugh, Swaledale on 9th April 1820. His parents were Ralph PEACOCK and Dolly ROBINSON. He was their seventh son. His father was a *lead miner* in one of Swaledale's many lead mines. Ralph was a man of many talents, but lacked the education and opportunities to develop them fully. Nevertheless, he rose to the position of *overseer* of several lead mines.

Ralph was a mechanical genius and this interest led him to visit Darlington in 1825, to view the new *"marvel of the world"*, the Stockton and Darlington Railway. His son, Richard, accompanied him, and, although only five years old at the time, he remembered this visit clearly. It was to be a seminal influence in his future career. Ralph too was impressed and when, in 1830, the Leeds and Selby Railway Company won Parliamentary approval to build its railway, he sought work in its construction. He was appointed *assistant superintendent* in the construction of the Leeds tunnel, and later of Leeds station. This was to be Yorkshire's first main railway line, and is still in use to-day. This appointment, however, obliged Ralph and his family to leave their beloved Swaledale and move to live in Leeds.

Young Richard fared well at school in Leeds and, in 1830, at the age of ten, he transferred to Leeds Grammar School. He left there at the age of 14 to take up an apprenticeship with the Leeds locomotive builders of FENTON MURRAY and JACKSON. He was remarkably talented in his chosen career and advanced rapidly, so much so that at the age of 18, he was taken on as *Locomotive Superintendent*, by the Leeds and Selby Railway, which had opened in 1834. In those early days of railways and steam locomotives, such things were possible.

In 1838 (at the age of 18) Richard married Hannah CROWTHER, a Leeds lass, who was to bear him two sons, Ralph, only a month after their wedding, and Joseph in 1839. Sadly Hannah died in 1854. Some 18 months later Richard married Frances LITTLEWOOD and their union was blessed with two daughters and a son, but alas Frances too died young in 1870.

In 1840 the Leeds and Selby Railway was merged with the York and North Midland Railway, which was owned by George HUDSON, the "Railway King", who was destined to fall from grace some years later.

Richard was a casualty of this merger so he moved on to the Great Western Railway, where he worked under the famous Isambard Kingdom BRUNEL and his chief engineer, Daniel GOOCH. Then a year later, in 1841, Richard gained a position as *Locomotive Superintendent* of the Sheffield, Ashton-under-Lyne, and Manchester Railway, which was under construction at that time. He chose and developed a site at Gorton, Manchester, for the company's works, where locomotives were built and maintained by the company and its successors for many years.

For 14 years Richard PEACOCK held this position during which time he befriended a Manchester locomotive engineer, Charles BEYER, who was employed at SHARP Brothers, another Manchester locomotive builder. They discussed setting up their own company to manufacture steam locomotives and in 1854, the world-famous firm of BEYER PEACOCK and Company was born. A site for their works was available almost adjacent to the works of his old company, and so it was purchased and developed, perhaps much to the chagrin of his old employers.

The new company was remarkably successful, exporting its products all over the world, and Richard PEACOCK loved nothing better than to deliver them himself. Such tasks took him to many distant countries. In 1870 he was at St. Petersburg, Russia, delivering engines for the Grand Russian Railway.

He was an affable man who was much liked by his workforce. He also took an interest in local Gorton affairs and was elected as the first Chairman of the Gorton Board of Guardians. He held this position until 1866, when the pressure of business obliged him to resign. He was a founding member of the Institute of Mechanical Engineers and, in 1849, he became a member of the Institute of Civil Engineers. He was President of the Openshaw and Bradford Mechanics Institute from its inception and President of the Manchester Steam Users' Association from 1866; he was also a Justice of the Peace. In 1885 he was elected as the first Member of Parliament for the newly created Parliamentary Division of Gorton. All these offices he held until his death. He was a Liberal and, during his period in Parliament, he fought for Home Rule, reform of the House of Lords and disestablishment and disendowment of the Church of England and the establishment of Local Government.

Another enterprise, with which he was closely involved, was the planning of the Manchester Ship Canal. In this he collaborated closely with the main protagonist, his great friend and neighbour, Daniel ADAMSON. The latter was born in Shildon, Durham in 1820 and married a Swaledale lass, Mary PICKARD, at Aysgarth in 1845. Like Richard, Daniel also came to Manchester where he made a sizeable fortune in the manufacture of Lancashire boilers. Although both men saw the Bill for the Ship Canal succeed in its passage through Parliament, and the start of construction, neither of them lived to see Queen Victoria open it in 1894.

Richard PEACOCK was in many ways a great benefactor to the people of Gorton. He was a devout Christian, of the Unitarian persuasion, and built both a fine stone church at Gorton, and a school nearby, entirely at his own expense. Both still exist to-day although the school has been converted into dwelling accommodation. He died on March 3rd 1889 at his stately home, Gorton Hall, and was buried in a vault in the graveyard of the church he built at Gorton. A remarkably fine memorial was erected over the vault, and his workforce erected a large bronze plaque in his memory. It can still be seen to-day, set in the front wall of his church.

RICHARD McGARRY rick_mcg@tiscali.co.uk

18. John, Joseph and Edward RYDER of Braidley, Coverdale

Braidley, Coverdale

John, Joseph and Edward RYDER were born at Braidley, in Coverdale, three of the five sons of Edward and Margaret RYDER (née YEOMAN).

John was baptised in 1817 at Coverham, had very little schooling and at 12 years of age was sent to work for his grandmother for his board and clothes. At seventeen he found other employment at eight pounds a year, and later secured a position as a *coachman* for a lady with whom he remained until 1842 and then set off for Liverpool and onward to New York.

He does appear in the UK 1841 census at home with his parents at Braidley together with brothers Jacob, Henry and Edward but without their brother Joseph.

In 1846 Nicholas YEOMAN of Horsehouse sent a letter to his son Richard in Ohio. He sent it with a message from Margaret RYDER to her son, also called John. Nicholas mentioned that John's departure appeared to be as a result of an argument with his parents.

To go to America would seem a bit drastic, but lack of employment probably was the driving force. Richard, John and Joseph lived near one another whilst growing up in the dales, and remained neighbours in America.

John's voyage lasted five weeks and then he travelled west by canal to Oberlin, Ohio, where he worked as a *stonemason* for a short time. He moved on to Huron County and bought 50 acres of land and farmed there for ten years, later moving to Hull's Prairie on 120 acres to which he later added 40 acres.

He married Betsey WILLINGTON in 1850 who also emigrated from England, and in the Federal Census for 1850 brother Joseph was living with them. John and Betsey went on to have 13 children and reared them to adulthood.

John died in 1895 in Wood County Ohio. His life was recorded in Beers, *"History of Wood County"* which stated he was considered to be *"a pioneer agriculturists of Middleton township, Ohio. A man of broad views and High Christian character."*

Joseph was baptised in 1822, and he next appeared living with his brother John, and John's wife Betsey in Ohio, as recorded in the 1850 USA Federal Census. It is not known whether they had travelled out together, or Joseph had joined them later.

In 1857 Joseph married Sarah WHEATON, (née CLARKE) a widow with seven children, who had emigrated with her husband John in 1840 from Wisbech in Cambridgeshire. John Wheaton died in 1856.

Joseph and Sarah had two daughters named Jenny and Lilian. Joseph enlisted as a *Private* on the 6th June 1861 in Company G, 24th Infantry Regiment, Ohio and received a disability discharge two years later on 16th Oct. 1863.

Joseph died in 1877, and was buried in Riverside Cemetery, Ridgefield Township, Huron County, Ohio next to Sarah.

Edward was baptised on 11th September 1831 and was recorded living with his parents in the 1841 UK census. He married Hannah ALLEN of Hawes in 1863 at Hawes, though both were resident at Gayle. Their first two children were born at Gayle and the following four children at Aigburth, Liverpool.

They moved from Gayle to Aigburth sometime between 1867 and 1870 and he became a *cow keeper* at 16 Aigburth Vale. By 1891 he had retired to Sefton Grove where he was recorded as a *"retired cow keeper."*

Edward died in 1899, intestate, and Hannah died ten months later. Between them they had acquired a substantial amount of property to the gross value of £3,115, which in 1899 would be the equivalent of £268,000.00 using the UK Retail Price Index for 2010.

I am indebted to Sherri Ryder DZIENIS (USA) a direct descendant, and the late Roger DAVIES for information about John and for help in tracing Joseph to Barb WHEATON. In addition I am grateful to Joan BLAIR (née RYDER) for information about Edward.

This family belong to my husband Raymond RYDER who checked these facts.

PAT M. RYDER Telephone 01969 622333 patricia5ryder@btinternet.com

19. Thomas Lindley CROFT from the dales to Cleckheaton

Thomas Lindley CROFT, aged 14, front row, fourth from right, seated.
Outside the Officers' Mess at Catterick Garrison when working for contractors.

"I'll tell you what to do" – this was a favourite saying of my grandfather Thomas Lindley CROFT. He was born on 3rd May 1900, into a third generation of *plumbers and glaziers* and had several uncles and cousins pursuing the same trades. His family originated in East Witton and then moved to Middleham before settling in Richmond. He was the son of James CROFT and Jane Elizabeth HAYWARD. The HAYWARD family ran a well-known boot and business in Richmond. Thomas had a sister Elsie who was three years older than him. They all lived with James' widowed father Henry Lindley CROFT at 6 Great Channel (now known as Frenchgate). The plumbing business was almost opposite in Ryders Wynd. James died from meningitis in 1905 at the early age of 34. Five years later James' father Henry died aged 86.

Tom was a choir boy at St. Mary's Church, Richmond. At 14 he was employed by contractors who were building Catterick Camp.

In 1916, when Britain was embroiled in World War I, Thomas aged 16 decided to leave beautiful Swaledale for thriving, industrial Cleckheaton in the West Riding of Yorkshire. He worked as an office boy at ELLISON, CORDINGLEY Ltd., a company of heating, chemical and general engineers. This included the repair of steam wagons which were in common use then. I have a letter from a man in charge of the office in which he told Tom's mother of an altercation where *'Tommy had offered to fight Mr. CORDINGLEY, which is very amusing because Mr. CORDINGLEY is of a remarkable big stature and the two together would remind you of the old adage of dignity and impudence.'* This resulted in Tom sending his mother a letter of explanation. Fortunately Mr. CORDINGLEY saw the humour in the situation, noted a spark of Swaledale spirit, and decided to keep him on!

In 1918, aged 18, Tom married Lucy May BOOTH aged 19. Their son George Lindley CROFT, my father, was born the year after in 1919. Although they were married young, they were together for 66 years until May's death in 1984.

Tom worked his way up to become *Director* and then *Managing Director* of the company. It changed its name to Cleckheaton Engineering and Motor Co. Ltd, having developed a garage showroom for selling and servicing cars. Tom was well – known as a character, famous for his forthright views and his trilby hat, worn permanently outdoors and often indoors too. I can remember him sitting on a high stool at a Dickensian style long desk, wearing the trilby at a jaunty angle on the back of his head! He also favoured three-piece suits, complete with watch and chain on the waistcoat. Part of his job involved visiting auction sales of government and war surplus and other unwanted equipment, buying Lancashire boilers or thousands of bolts and nuts for re-sale.

He was a keen motorist, owning a car in the mid 1930s. He also loved caravanning. His first touring caravan, bought around 1955, was based at Lake Windermere. We all used it including his daughter Audrey and her family. It was also towed from Northern Scotland to Wales and Cornwall pulled by his redoubtable Standard Vanguard. He loved boating and bought a cabin cruiser in which we plied the waters of Lake Windermere for many years. He was still driving until his early 80s.

Tom retired at the age of 70. His son George took over the position of *Managing Director*, having worked with his father since leaving school. Between them they worked 108 years for the company.

He relished the joys and challenges of life and was always proud of his Swaledale roots. He died in 1987 at the ripe old age of 86 – the same age as his grandfather.

MARGARET E. GREEN croftgreen@hotmail.com

20. The RUSSELL Family from Castle Bolton to Fullerton Nebraska in 1881

John and Hannah RUSSELL, Nebraska

It was in 2002 whilst searching for my RUSSELL family that I came across the RUSSELL name in Fullerton, Nebraska in America. Somehow I just felt that they were connected to my own RUSSELL ancestors. Looking for further information I found a book about Fullerton, which contained names of people and their history, who had emigrated there during the 1880s. In this book there was a John RUSSELL together with his wife Hannah and their six sons who had travelled to America in 1881.

John RUSSELL was born in Castle Bolton, Wensleydale, in 1821 and his wife Hannah was born in Redmire in 1831. The first of their sons William was born in Redmire, followed by John and Mary Ann, both born at Castle Bolton. The last four sons George, James, Walter and Edwin were all born at Wensley. My RUSSELL ancestors were born in Castle Bolton – from my seventh great grandfather James RUSSELL, who was born in the middle of the seventeenth century, until my third great grandfather George RUSSELL, born in 1789. This convinced me that my first reaction of being connected was correct but I still wanted this to be confirmed.

I set about finding a possible address or telephone number for any RUSSELL that I could find in the telephone list of Fullerton. The first Russell listed was Arthur Laird RUSSELL and he was the grandson of John RUSSELL. I duly sent him a letter, working my way down the list, until three months later I heard from a Wilma RUSSELL, that her mother-in-law Grace RUSSELL (née MILBY) was the widow of Arthur, and she had passed on my letters to Wilma as she knew that she was interested in Family History. From what Wilma had written, she was convinced also that we were related. After further letters and much research between us, we found the connection.

My fourth great grandparents were James RUSILL (1755 – 1790) and Elizabeth HORN (1760 – 1798) who were married in 1780 and had six children all born in Castle Bolton. Their second child, a son William was born in 1782 and his brother George RUSSELL the sixth child of James and Elizabeth was born in 1789. George married Margaret BELL in 1812 and they were my third great grandparents. William, his brother, married Ann STOREY in 1808, and they had eight children. Their sixth child was John RUSSELL who was also born in Castle Bolton in 1821, thus making me the first cousin four times removed of John RUSSELL. This maybe a little distant, but we are related just the same!

Wilma is the widow of Richard Laird RUSSELL who was the great grandson of John and Hannah and she has always taken a great interest in both her own Kindhart ancestry as well as the RUSSELL history. She has a number of files on the 6 sons and their descendents, and was also able to relate the story of why John and Hannah went to America, the story of their travels there, where they settled and the work they did. A lot of the present day Russell families still live in and around Fullerton and most can tell the story of John and Hannah's move to America.

From my own research I had found that John had started his working life in lead mining like many of the men who lived in the dales. His mother died in 1832 and his father in 1833, so John being the eldest still at home was left to look after his sister Elizabeth (Betty).

At the time of John's marriage to Hannah in 1857 he was still living in Castle Bolton and had become a *mining agent*. They lived in Castle Bolton until 1863 when George their fourth child was born. John was now a *farmer* and the family was living in Wensley.

Although John had travelled to America before at the time of the Gold Rush, wanting a better life for his wife and sons, he decided once more to make the journey to America.

With the knowledge of the length and difficulty of the journey and the safety of his wife and children, it must have been a very difficult decision for John to decide to make the journey again.

I am so grateful to be allowed to tell the story of John and Hannah and their life with their family in Fullerton.

Mrs DODD BARNARD (née Russell) Mill Lodge, 2 Pocklington Way, Heckington, Sleaford, Lincolnshire, NG34 9UJ. Telephone 01529 460208. barnardjodo@tiscali.co.uk

21. Cow keepers from the Dales to Liverpool

Haygarth of 31 Harper Road Liverpool

The nineteenth century was a period of depression in the Yorkshire Dales, Westmorland and Cumbria. Many families were unable to make a satisfactory living for themselves or their families. This was due partly to the closing of the lead mines, an agricultural slow-down, the Enclosure of the Commons and, in Dent, the system of partible inheritance.

It is not known which families were the first to make the decision to travel to Liverpool and to open a dairy to provide milk for the mushrooming industrial population there. However they met with some success and it was not long before they persuaded family, friends and neighbours to join them.

By the mid nineteenth century Liverpool had grown in size, with busy docks and a flourishing seaport together with an influx of Irish immigrants escaping the famine. Not only did the resident population require milk, supplies were needed also for the many ships that were using the port and also the seamen's families living in the small cottages clustered around the dockside.

Local farmers could not keep pace with the demand for fresh milk. More and more families moved in from the Yorkshire Dales and cow-keeping became a viable and often profitable occupation.

Cow-houses were built at the corner of almost every street in the centre of Liverpool and the outlying districts. The complex consisted of a terrace house (and often the one next door) built of brick, with a dairy for butter-making, a shippon, cellars to keep the milk cool, a hayloft over the horse's stable, a space for the trap or cart, a muck midden and a cobbled yard. It was surrounded by high walls with large wooden gates for the cart to pass through.

The larger cow-houses had their own field or big garden at the back enabling the cows to be left to graze during the day. Most of the smaller dairies had little or no land, however, and the cattle were kept in confined spaces for lengthy periods, some never going out except into the yard. The work of a *cow-keeper* was very arduous every day of the year.

Mrs Cindy JONES has passed on her memories of the dairy where she was brought up as a child:

"There were 20 cows in the shippon which my father and the cowman·Joe milked each day. The bottling was done by hand after being passed through a cooler and then a cardboard top was put on. Before that the milk was served from a

churn and ladled into the jugs brought to the dairy or delivered by horse and float. Bottle washing was done outside in big metal sinks using revolving brushes and then the bottles were loaded into crates and put into a giant steriliser. Milk measures were a gill, half pint, pint and quart. My mother kept a book in the dairy of people who paid at the end of the week (hopefully) and I remember the names in it were often 'descriptions' rather than surnames i.e. 'ivy leafed jugwoman', 'kissable lips', 'dirty dog woman' etc…hardly politically correct now but nobody got upset then."

Later, strict regulations were brought into force and a milk-testing scheme was introduced. Hay had to be bought from the local farmers or in one of the markets. In addition the cattle were fed on a mixture of pea meal, brewery grains, molasses from the sugar refining plants and linseed oil mixed with warm water. The cows were also fed pieces of turnip, cabbage leaves and cow-nut. Barbara PHYTHIAN's father, Mr ALLEN, led his cows to graze in Princes Park. In later years cows were allowed to graze on Everton Football ground as the grass had not been treated with fertiliser!

In some cases, cows would be brought down from the dales. With the coming of the railway cows could be moved more easily and certainly Lime Street Station was famous for its cattle traffic. Some sons and daughters intermarried with locals in spite of being considered foreigners because people couldn't understand the dialect! Yet there was a strong dales feeling. There was also considerable intermarriage within the dales community itself: the FAWCETTs and the ASKEWs; the GOTHs and the HAYGARTHs; the WILSONs and the LAMBERTs among others.

When it was time to retire many older people would leave their sons and daughters to manage the dairies and would return home to the dales. The work was hard and demanding and many men did not live to see old age and their wives took over the running of the dairy. When James SUNTER from Hawes died in 1909 his son Thomas took over.

One of the highlights of the year was the Annual Show run by the Royal Lancashire Agricultural Society. Others were the Great Liverpool Show and the Liverpool Cow keepers Association Show which eventually merged with the Liverpool and District Livestock Show. Several dalesmen were consistently successful in winning prizes for the best cow.

The heyday of cow-keeping was in the period from the latter end of the nineteenth century to just before the 1914-1918 war. The First World War changed everything. The women were left to run the businesses entirely on their own whilst their men folk were away fighting; cow-keeping was not a reserved occupation. The younger children were expected to do their share of the work. Between the two wars there were great improvements in refrigeration and transport. Very high standards were necessary for the milk supplied to schools. There was a growing threat from the formation of larger dairies which could arrange to have milk from long distances delivered by railway early in the morning. All this contributed to the decline of cow-keeping as an occupation.

When Liverpool was heavily bombed during World War II, whole streets were destroyed including many cow-houses together with their stock. The aunt of Cindy JONES kept a cow, Dolly, who won several cups. Dolly's stable was wrecked after a bomb landed in the street adjacent but Dolly survived, saved by the ceiling beams which had fallen down leaving her a space to cower in. The number of large dairies was increasing and milk production was being regulated by the Government; the distribution of milk was zoned until 1948. The new Co-operative Societies were able to give *"divi"* or dividend on milk purchases – a great incentive. Pasteurisation was now compulsory. By 1949 only 129 cow-keepers remained and few of them were delivering their own milk. Instead they sold their milk to the large dairies. The bringing in of the five day week was another blow – many dairies had one or two employees in addition to the family. The last cow-keepers were Mr CAPSTICK in Marlborough Road who finally gave up in 1975 and a Mr WINN who kept his licence but no cows.

JOYCE SCOBIE joyce@scobies.org.uk The Sedbergh and District History Society

22. Wesleyan emigration to the Natal, South Africa

Bedale Hirings, circa 1908 old postcard.

John WESLEY had many followers in North Yorkshire but by the mid 1800s there was some dissent within their ranks. Some of the more radical members had broken away and formed the Primitive Methodist movement. It may have been because of this unrest that a large number of Wesleyans decided to emigrate to the Natal area of South Africa in the 1840s/50s. There were several schemes to assist emigrants, the most well known being one organised by an Irish man called BRYNE. He bought up huge areas of land and then charged emigrants £10 which provided free passage and 20 acres of land on arrival. BRYNE did eventually go bankrupt. Another was the Rylands scheme which was more orientated towards Wesleyans. It was run in a similar way by RYLANDS a wealthy Wesleyan *business man* with the intent of helping would be settlers.

At Osgodby Hall, near Thirsk, an enterprising young farmer called Henry BOAST, a native of North Dalton in the East Riding, who was a local Wesleyan *preacher*, studied all the schemes available at the time. BOAST decided to organise a private syndicate, predominantly of Wesleyans, to go in a similar way. Two of the party, Wm. LUND from Sheriff Hutton and James TUTIN from Brompton, near Northallerton, went out several months ahead of the party and deposited £2,000 with the Colonial Land & Emigration Commissioners, for land to be divided amongst the emigrants according to how much each could afford to buy. This sum was also to cover the cost of chartering a ship from Hull. It was the latter which turned this syndicate's emigration into a total nightmare

Most of BOAST's 'followers' were farmers and tradesmen from the Bedale, Thirsk and Easingwold areas and in 1850 almost 200 of them prepared to leave their native patch for South Africa.

Amongst this group was a Bedale man, William SMITH who for many years had been a *grocer* next door to what was then called The Royal Oak, at the north end of Bedale. This inn had been kept by his father also called William SMITH. The younger William had been born in Burneston in 1790 and married his first wife, Elizabeth KAY, from Thirsk, in 1828. They had five children before Elizabeth died in 1837, aged 35. William's second wife was a widow, Isabella (Cranswick) WHITRIDGE who had a son, Matthew, born in Kent. Her parents had moved from the East Riding of Yorkshire to Aiskew and her father, Matthew, had been a noted Wesleyan preacher in the district for many years. There is a memorial plaque, dedicated to him, in Bedale Methodist Church. William's family increased by a further three children after he married Isabella. In 1850 William was almost 60 but he and Isabella took seven of William's eight children, plus step son Matthew WHITRIDGE with them to the Natal. The only member of the family not to go was his daughter Hannah SMITH, who was 18 at the time. In the 1851 Census she was 'living in' with a farming family James and Helen GOTHORP of Langwith House, Well near Bedale, working as *governess* to their six young children.

The SMITH family enlisted to join Henry BOAST's party, along with others from the Bedale area. Henry BOAST chartered a ship called *The Pallais* and the group were set to sail in April 1850 from Hull. The ship was inspected by port officials who deemed her un-seaworthy and too small for the number to be carried. A major blow! BOAST had to quickly find another more suitable ship and get all the provisions needed, etc. on board. In the meantime the group had to take lodgings in Hull. BOAST sought compensation from the ship's owner and the matter was taken to court.

The Hull Packet reported daily on the plight of the group and the court proceedings. The owner denied responsibility for the state of *The Pallais* as BOAST had seen it and signed a contract to the effect he was satisfied with it. As a *farmer* and not a naval man he no doubt did not realise *The Pallais* was not suitable. BOAST eventually chartered *The Haidee* to sail in June but some of the party had abandoned the plan and returned to their native places. The party was in dire straights and all the Wesleyan Chapels in Hull and district organised collections of money to help them. BOAST was reported to be under much stress when he fell ill with typhoid late in May and died a week later. The BOASTs had three small children and his widow also became ill and was reported as *"unlikely to survive"*. She did recover and fortunately her ageing father, Joseph SMITH, hurriedly joined the party and sailed with his daughter and took charge in place of his deceased son-in-law.

The Haidee was at last ready for embarkation at the end of June but they had not lost sight of land when she sprang a leak and had to return to port! On the 10th July they set sail once more but two of their party, young men named LECKONBY and PRESTON, had contracted small pox. The journey took over four months and on reaching Durban they found *The Haidee* was too large to enter the port. They had to anchor three miles out and disembark via the use of 'surf-boards' which caused them much difficulty. They had intended arriving by July/August, which would have been the right time to plough their newly acquired land and plant crops. As it was almost Christmas, they were held up yet again and had to live in tents and a rented warehouse before they could move on to their allotted land and start cultivation and build homesteads. Isabella SMITH baked a Christmas cake in a clay oven which was cut out of a clay hillside.

The story is also recounted in a book written by a descendant of WILLIAM SMITH, Mrs. P. WADSWORTH of The Natal, South Africa. This book contains very interesting extracts from a diary, kept during the voyage on *The Haidee*, by Amy PLUMMER. This young woman emigrated with her sister Jane and brother George. They had been brought up in the York area but may well have been related to the PLUMMER family of Bedale. The diary, which is now in a South African archive, gives a wonderful insight of life on board *The Haidee*, as she made her way to Durban with a "cargo" of devout, hard working Yorkshire folk. They were united by their religious beliefs, all from similar backgrounds, some related to each other and many who became related, through marriage, after arrival in their new country. A Passenger List, for this voyage of *The Haidee*, has been obtained but unfortunately it does not give their places of abode in Yorkshire. A copy of Mrs. Wadsworth's book has been deposited with the Bedale Museum.

Henry BOAST was from a well established East Riding farming family. Born and brought up in North Dalton, he moved to Osgodby in 1843, possibly the year of his marriage. He was the nephew of Mark BOAST, a very well known anti-corn law pamphleteer. Also with the group was a relative, Doctor Charles BOAST, who had been recruited to travel with them as their medical officer.

DENNY GIBSON dennygibson@hotmail.co.uk

23. ESPINER of Castle Bolton cum Redmire. "They Left the Dales" but who were they?

The wedding of Harriet Rebecca ESPINER to John Charles BUBLITZ
She was the daughter of Paul William ESPINER, the farmer who emigrated.

The Surname ESPINER could have a Norman/French Origin or be derived from SPENCER or Le DESPENCER. The first sighting of this family in Wensleydale was the marriage of James ESPINER to Elizabeth TWIDDAL.

Bishops Transcripts record that *"James ESPINER and Elizabeth TWIDDAL were married November ye 18th 1705."* No earlier record shows where James was born although other early International Genealogy Index listings in the North of England include:

> *Frances ESPINER married Richard HOLLINGWORTH in 1641 at Sutton in Ashfield Notts*

> *Thomas ESPINER and Ann ESPENCER married at Wragby, Yorkshire (Pontefract area 1730-40's)*

James and Elizabeth had three sons born at Redmire but two births have not yet been found. They are George and James who married and had children, and *William son of James ESPINER was baptzd October the 4th 1708 (BT).*

The family was listed in the parish until 1841 when James a *farmer* and Elizabeth were at North Gate Redmire.

(BT) 1793 April 6th Eleanor dr of Dorothy ESPINER Buried

Jane ESPINER married 20th Nov 1809 at Castle Bolton to Simon HARKER.

William ESPINER (born 1735, son of James and Ann) must have left by 1762 when he married Margaret ION at Bedale. His family at Bedale were recorded as ESPIN.

George ESPINER (born 1777, son of James and Margaret) also married in Bedale in 1818 to Mary and they appeared in the 1841 census there:

> *1841 Shepherds Yard, Bedale, Yorkshire. George ESPIN abt 1786 Yorkshire, Ostler; Mary ESPIN abt 1786 Yorkshire.*

ESPINERs at West Witton.

John ESPINER who was born in 1845 at Redmire became a *landowner* in West Witton, whilst a son James Bearpark ESPINER was a *land agent* still there in the 1911 census, as was his son John James aged nine months living with his SMORTHWAITE grand parents.

ESPINERS at Bedale.

Ann ESPINER (born in 1764 the daughter of William and Margaret) married George PURVESS on 19th February 1792 at Bedale and their descendants also 'left the dale' to move to other parts of England. William ESPINER was baptised at Bedale on 1st January 1798, the son of Elizabeth. This may have been the same Elizabeth born at Castle Bolton in 1764 who married George BUTTERWICK and died at Scruton. This family also left the dale and descendants have been located in the USA. William was a *stonemason* and a headstone was erected in Bedale Churchyard for him which also included a son, and William's wife Dorothy. He died in 1871 and Dorothy died after him in 1889.

It is from the following branch that we can follow four families who left the dales. The eldest son George remained in Bedale but two sons emigrated to New Zealand. Paul William became a *farmer* at Waimate Plains, Taranaki, whilst George Henry became a *school teacher* at Bunnythorpe, a village in the Manawatu - Wanganui region of New Zealand's North Island.

Both have interesting descendants in New Zealand, Australia, the USA and back in England. A son of Paul, Percy Gerald was killed in WWI, with the New Zealand Rifle Brigade at Havrincourt, France on 12th September 1918. He was buried at the Grevillers (New Zealand) Memorial, Pas de Calais, France.

Another son of George was John ESPINER who moved to Loftus and established a mineral water manufacturing company.

Francis moved to Bradford and his son William was with the railways moving first to Wressle, then North Ferriby. His grand-daughter Kathleen Mary married the author's brother John ANDREW. Francis had a grandson Arthur Charles killed in WWI a *Private* in the East Yorkshire Regiment 13th Battalion. He was killed on 14th August 1916 and was recorded on the Loos Memorial Panels 40 and 41.

The New Zealand family of George Henry included Henry John ESPINER a retired *consultant general surgeon* living in Bristol UK. His sons are Mark ESPINER, a *journalist*, and Tom ESPINER, a *computer specialist*.

Eric Arnold ESPINER became a *professor* and graduated in medicine from the University of Otago in 1957. He co-founded the internationally renowned Christchurch Cardio-endocrine Research Group (CCERG). His son Colin ESPINER became the political editor of *The Press* and in 2008 won the Qantas Media Award as New Zealand's best political commentator.

Guyon ESPINER TVNZ's political editor has covered politics from the press gallery in Parliament since 1998. For three years Guyon was a *political journalist* and columnist for the *Sunday Star Times* newspaper, at the Parliamentary Press Gallery in Wellington.

Stephen ESPINER became a *teacher* BA (Cant) PhD (Lincoln).

The family of Paul William in New Zealand include his great grandson David John ESPINER a *chartered accountant* in his own firm at Whangarei and Adam James ESPINER a *web designer* in Australia.

MARK ANDREW faxmark@blueyonder.co.uk

24. Ellen ROBINSON of Askrigg, 1830-1902

Ellen ROBINSON, my great grandmother, was born a daleswoman but was carried off by a transient *soldier*. He became a *civilian surveyor* and she travelled around England with him before finally settling as a widow in Whitley, Northumberland.

Ellen came from a well-established dales family. She was christened at Hawes on 21st February 1830 but later records say she lived in Askrigg with her parents James and Margaret ROBINSON. She had several siblings, Eden, Mary, Joseph, William and possibly others.

Her father was christened on 18th May 1794 at Askrigg and married Margaret KETTLEWELL on 15th April 1816 at Askrigg, when he was almost 22 years old. He was a *grocer* and was probably the son of William ROBINSON, also a *grocer* in Askrigg, according to the *Yorkshire Poll Book* of 1807. In various census listings, James was also *a chemist, druggist, postmaster and registrar of births, deaths and marriages*.

Ellen's mother, Margaret, died in 1853. James remarried twice more, in 1856 to Elizabeth MORTON, at Askrigg Chapel and subsequently to Christian THWAITE in 1863. He died in 1879, aged 85.

In 1851, at 21 years old, Ellen was still living in her parents' house in Askrigg and was described as *"assisting in the house"*.

On 18th January 1855 Ellen, now 24, married John Havey BROWNRIGG, 27, a *private* in the Royal Sappers and Miners, at Askrigg Chapel by licence. Witnesses were Eden ROBINSON, William ROBINSON, George Alderson ROBINSON and Elizabeth TIPLADY. George Alderson ROBINSON appeared to have been her cousin, son of James's brother, and a wealthy owner of several properties in the area.

Who was John H. BROWNRIGG? He was born in London on 25th May 1827, the oldest son of George BROWNRIGG, a *butcher* in South Audley Street, London. J.H. BROWNRIGG's middle name was spelt in several different ways in different documents – Havey, Heavey, Harvy and Hardy. HEAVEY was his mother's maiden name, so that seems likely to be the correct version. Presumably he was able to support Ellen comfortably, as in addition to his army pay he had money left to him by his maternal grandfather. He was mentioned in his father's will but only because he was to receive nothing! The will said he was *"otherwise provided for by the will of the late Timothy Heavey."*

I have not discovered how he came to be in Askrigg, or how he met Ellen, but would welcome further information. The marriage certificate gave Askrigg as his place of residence but it is possible that he was just there temporarily. It may be relevant that in the 1851 census he was a *Sapper & Miner on survey*, lodging with an *agricultural labourer* in Riplingham, Yorkshire. There were no other soldiers lodging in that village, so it seems that he was sent out alone on survey work. His military records have not yet been found. He and Ellen were married by licence, not the more usual banns. Ellen must have stayed in the dales because their first child, George, was born in the September quarter that year in Askrigg and christened on 27th January 1856.

When John left the army, he practised the profession of *surveyor*, presumably having learned the skills in the Sappers and Miners. The couple then spent many years moving around the country. Their daughter Margaret was born in 1858 at Brough, Westmorland. In 1861 the census shows them living at Broadlease Farm, Buscot, Berkshire. Their second son John was born in 1868 in Hexham, Northumberland. No other census shows them together at the same address, so perhaps he had many short-term jobs and she did not always go with him. I have found no definite record of his whereabouts after 1861.

In 1871 Ellen was temporarily back in the dales and was in Reeth with her children Margaret, aged twelve, and John two. Her father, James ROBINSON, aged 77, was head of household at nearby Hill House and Ellen's son, George, a 15 year old *student*, was living with him. James was by then a retired *druggist and grocer* in charge of two acres. There was also a *groom, a housekeeper* and their children. This was clearly a well-to-do establishment. Hill House was owned by and normally occupied by his nephew, George Alderson ROBINSON. It is now the Burgoyne Hotel.

Ellen's husband was not present at her address in the census of 1871. He could possibly be the Mr. BROWNRIGG, a boarder at the New Inn, Park Street, New Windsor, Berkshire. That person was married, aged 42, born at St George, Hanover Square, a surveyor of hills, woods and forests. All this matches JHB, except that his age would be 43 or 44.

Clearly, he reappeared on the scene, as their third son, James Robinson BROWNRIGG, was born in 1872 at Darlington, County Durham. Ellen would be about 42 at the time of this birth. James was my paternal grandfather.

In 1881, Ellen was living at 8 Powlett Street, Darlington, with sons James Robinson aged eight and John aged twelve. The family must have moved there in the year before his birth. Ellen was not recorded as a widow but I have not found her husband in this census. The oldest son, George, now 25, was in the army, having enlisted under the name of George ROBINSON. (See chapter 69.)

In 1891 Ellen was a widow, living at 16 Stephenson Street, Darlington, with daughter Margaret, aged 32, who was *manager* of the Co-operative Society. This entry was extremely difficult to find as it was indexed under the surname Brmuringg!

By 1901, she and Margaret had moved to Northumberland and were living at 26 Trewit Road, Whitley. Whitley is now called Whitley Bay because of confusion with Whitby in Yorkshire. Margaret was a *manageress mantle fitter*. Ellen's youngest son, James Robinson, had become a *constable* in the Northumberland police force and was recently married, so perhaps this was why she moved there.

Ellen died at home in Whitley on 4th February 1902, aged 71, with Margaret in attendance. The cause of death was *aortic incompetence and general anasarca*. I have so far been unable to discover when her husband died.

All three of Ellen's sons joined the Ninth Lancers. The two younger sons, John and James Robinson, both served in the Boer War. John, a *corporal*, was killed at the age of 31 on 10th July 1900 at Bloemfontein. I believe he was unmarried. James Robinson was wounded in the arm in March 1900 and later returned home to Northumberland, where he was a *police constable* in several towns. He also had three sons, one of whom was my father, and a daughter.

Ellen's choice of names continued to the next generation, as these three sons were called George, John and James Leslie. Ellen died before my father was born, so he never knew his grandmother from the Yorkshire Dales.

Ellen's descendants live in Australia, County Durham, and possibly Halifax.

ALLAN BROWNRIGG great grandson ambrownrigg@optusnet.com.au

25. Taverns across the sea: SAYER(s) Publicans from Aysgarth to Ohio

The SAYERS Family of Niles, Ohio 1902. Front: Francis (Frank) Holmes SAYERS, Elizabeth (Lizzie) SAYERS, Francis SAYERS, Rose SAYERS. Back: Jane (Jennie) SAYERS, Nicholas (Nick) SAYERS, Elizabeth, (Lizzie) SAYERS, William Yates (W.Y.) SAYERS, Mary SAYERS

Manifest of the passengers taken on board the Ship Atmosphere. Francis SAUYER Age: 19 Gender: Male Place of Origin: England Port of Departure: Liverpool, England Port of Arrival: New York Arrival Date: 18 May 1857

When Francis SAYER disembarked at New York's immigrant reception centre in 1857, he put behind him the most arduous leg of a journey that had carried him from the Yorkshire Dales.

"4 June 1758 I James SAYER of Thornton Rust bequeath my mine shares in Mosdale unto my nephews." Maybe it was to escape *"going down the pits"* of County Durham that prompted Francis' trans-Atlantic odyssey.

"Baines 1823 Directory: SAYER Francis, victualler and butcher, Miners' Arms, Aysgarth." It was Francis the elder who had taken the first of the SAYER journeys away from the Dales. Keeper of the Miners' Arms in Aysgarth (now the Palmer Flatt), he inherited a place in the dales' lead mining enterprises. From at least 1810 until 1827 records demonstrate Francis' involvement in church, community and business affairs.

"1822/23 1s 1d To F. SAYER as per bill – ale celebrating churchwardens' attendance of Bishop."

"April 1824 To F. SAYER for ale when rendering up leads at Sunday time 16s 6d." Did a decline in the lead mining industry initiate a decline in business? Marrying a first cousin, elevating his status as a businessman, and "padding his resume" are subtle clues, but Churchwardens Records of 1827 to 1832 seem to build a case for obstreperousness in Francis' character. Evidence of the family's financial straits also appears in the *"Aysgarth Parish Marriage Records: 1798 March 28 SAYER, Francis & Elizabeth SAYER. Entry of Death GRO London 17th August 1855 E. Hetton, Durham Francis SAYERS Master Butcher."*

"1829/04/20 Coals for Francis SAYER no further allowance unless he gets his son and daughter to church."

1830/02/08 Ordered F SAYER, 4 days at 10p per to work from 8 to 5 o'clock; if this don't sort you out, ticket for the workhouse for yourself and your wife Francis WINNINGTON, Chairman."

Thus to the coal fields of Kelloe, near Durham where their son William, *"pitman"* in the 1841 census, became his parents' breadwinner. He wed in 1834. First a daughter, Elizabeth, then Francis the eventual immigrant, Jane, and Richard expanded the family. Richard and mother Hannah however died of complications. Growing up in a reduced economic state young Francis experienced the rigors of life in the pits. The accidental death of Elizabeth's husband in 1854 and the passing of his gaffer in 1856 added motivation for one who had experienced both the possibilities of ambition and the poverty of the lack of opportunity.

"United States Census 11th June 1860 Mifflin Township, Allegheny County, Pennsylvania. Francis SAWYERS Age 22 Male Coal Miner Born: England." Francis fetched up in the coalfield just south of the city, boarding with English-born miner William Chapman YATES. He applied his knowledge of mining to a career and his gift of grandfather-guided gab to charming Chapman's 16-year-old daughter Lizzie. *Probate Court, Cambridge, Ohio July 8, 1861: I hereby give my consent for my daughter Lizzie M. YATES who is a minor to join in marriage with Francis SAYERS who is full age William (his X mark) YATES."* He and Lizzie returned to Pennsylvania with their Ohio-born son William Y. and added daughters Hannah and Mary before investing in a small grocery shop in an Ohio mining village in 1870.

Francis took United States citizenship in 1868 and a move to the town of Niles in 1873. *"State of Ohio Certificate of Naturalization. Francis SAYERS... renounced allegiance to... Victoria, Queen of Great Britain... and is duly admitted to citizenship of the United States of America 21st day of September AD 1868."*

"Directory of the Mahoning Valley 1877: SAYERS, Francis, Union House, Main near Mill (Niles)." Ownership of the Union Hotel and Tavern meant Francis had returned the family name to prominence. Lizzie, Jennie and Nicholas joined the three older siblings and tavern profits fostered real estate investments, a barbering career for young "W.Y." and a two-story home in an upscale neighbourhood.

"Trumbull County General Index to Deeds. July 14, 1891 SAYERS, Francis, from John & Anna M Stringer Range 3, Lot #95 in Niles Village $1805. Niles Official City Directory 1893-94: SAYERS Francis (Elizabeth), residence: 37 N Chestnut."

In 1880 the centuries old SAYER(S) naming tradition was renewed with the birth of Francis H. The stage was set for "W.Y.," "Nick," and "Frank" to climb to positions of influence in Niles. In the '90's W.Y. went from barbering to a partnership in Nick's business. A staunch "Lincoln Republican" like his brother, Nick was elected to a council seat, while Frank purchased the tonsorial business.

"Niles Business Directory: 1899, SAYERS & Seaburn 14 E Church Bicycles, Furnaces, Roofing & Spouting. Ordinances of the City of Niles – By order of Council: Nick SAYERS, Chairman Fire and Police Committee." Their sons' ambition and success enabled Francis and Elizabeth to sell the tavern. Francis the *"greatly beloved pioneer citizen"* and Elizabeth the *"woman of beautiful virtues" "passed to the great beyond,"* in 1914 and 1920, respectively.

"Niles Daily News March 6, 1909: County Recorder SAYERS, ravenously hungry while recover(ing) from a fever, asked his doctor to "measure that piece of toast (so it) won't be any smaller than it has to be." W.Y. duly assumed the role of family patriarch acquiring the title "Daddy" SAYERS. A century later the SAYERS are all gone, but an address among the stately homes of SAYERS Avenue still carries a certain cachet.

None of the SAYERS followed the publican footsteps of their forebears, but another chance for alcohol purveyance came with Prohibition in 1919. Who was better equipped to illegally defy the provisions of the legislation? There was the political punch of W.Y., Nick's expertise in piping and ductwork, and the gathering spot and potential distribution point of Frank's barber shops. Renovations of houses in the 1970s revealed clues: a trove of bottles under one porch and a vat and piping in an attic.

The SAYERS presence in Niles has disappeared, but at least one descendent felt the impact of Francis and Lizzie's "Little English Culture." A sojourn working in "t'aud coontreh" triggered familiarity and old documents established a research path leading "home." To paraphrase scholar and humorist Canon Sydney Smith (1771-1845): *"Never ask a man if (his ancestors) came from Yorkshire; if (they did), he will surely tell you, if (they did) not, why humiliate him?"*

DAVE MOORE, Webster, New York k1ark@rochester.rr.com

26.   The RAW family from Low Row to Haworth

Some members of the RAW family migrated to the West Riding before the significant dales exodus of the 1870s and 1880s. The 1841 censuses for Swaledale show 32 separate RAW households. Almost all were in Melbecks Township, and 23 of the heads of the families were lead miners. By 1881 there were as many RAW family members in Haworth as there were in Melbecks. This story concentrates on the children of Anthony and Ann RAW of pre-1841 Low Row, one of whose grandchildren bought the Haworth house now owned by my friend Pat Emery. Pat was actually researching the Revd. John WADE of Haworth but her online search took her to one of my Swaledale essays. We wondered if it were possible that the George RAW who bought her Haworth house at an auction at the Black Bull had come from Swaledale? Well yes, it was. George was born in Haworth in 1846 but his father, named Thomas, was born at Low Row in 1816.

Anthony and Ann RAW baptised all their children at the Low Row Independent chapel. The baptisms were Elizabeth on 20th April 1806, George on 21st February 1808, Anthony on 8th July 1810, John on 13th December 1812, Thomas on 21st January 1816 and Mary on 7th February 1819. In the 1841 census we found that Ann and all the sons plus Mary had moved to Stanbury, a mile from Haworth; and that all except Ann worked in the wool trade. There were two Swaledale burials for an Anthony RAW, one in 1822 and the other in 1834, so maybe these events were connected.

We satisfied ourselves that it was the right Thomas and set off searching for more. The parish of Haworth included the nearby hamlets of Stanbury and Oxenhope which, in those days, had a joint population greater than Haworth. The 1841 census shows Ann as a *widow* with unmarried sons George (30) and John (25), both *wool combers*, and daughter Mary (20) a *power loom stuff weaver*. Anthony (25) was settled at New Mill, Henfield Side, with his local wife Esther (20) and both were also *wool combers*; Thomas (20), another *wool comber*, was living in Stanbury with his local wife Sally (20), also a *stuff weaver*, and baby daughter Mary-ann.

The occupation of *woolcomber* was described in *Babbage's* 1851 report to the Board of Health together with the awful and unsanitary conditions of Haworth: *"Many of the inhabitants of Haworth pursue the occupation of combing wool for the factories. This business is carried on in their houses. In order to obtain the proper temperature for this operation, iron stoves are fixed in the rooms ……, which are kept alight day and night, and the windows are seldom, if ever, opened, excepting in the height of summer. In some cases …. this business was carried on in bedrooms, which consequently became very close and unhealthy from the high temperature maintained by the stoves, and the want of ventilation."*

The tines used in wool combing were fearsomely long and strong enough to pull through each other, combing the washed fleece chunks into silky strands. Thomas and his brothers stood all day at wall-fixed combs, dragging a second comb through the tangles then starting all over again. BABBAGE described attic rooms in Haworth itself in which he found four beds occupied by eight quarrymen, and six wool combers who worked and slept there. The long rooms were six feet wide and seven feet high, and hot. The sick relief rate in Haworth was 30% higher than in the nearby hamlets.

By 1851 mother Ann had died but John, George and Mary were still living together in Stanbury and still working at their same jobs. Also in the house was a one month old called Anthony described as John's nephew. The Keighley registrar recorded the death of an Anthony in 1852 so he may have been one of the 41% of Haworth children who died before the age of six (*Babbage*). In 1851 Anthony and his wife Esther were shown as *wool combers*. By 1861 they were doing the same job at Haworth Hill Top but by 1871, when Anthony was 60, he was a *farmer* of 16 acres back at Stanbury and Esther had stopped working. They had no children who survived. Anthony's death was registered in 1875 aged 64.

By 1861 George had married Hannah HEY and was living at Oldfield Gate with his wife and her father a *retired weaver*. George was a *night watch*. By 1871 the couple was at Town End at the top of Haworth. Now we are getting close to Pat's house, which is called Town End Cottage. In 1871 George was a *machine wool comber* and Hannah still a *worsted weaver*. I think George died in 1873 and by 1881 Hannah was living alone, at

North Street, Town End. There were no surviving children from George and Hannah's marriage. Brother and sister John and Mary were still unmarried at this time. In 1861 John was a visitor aged 45, at the home of Stanbury friends now living in Little Marsden, Lancashire. He and the couple all said they were *power loom weavers*, so maybe he was boarding there. By 1871 Mary was recorded in Haworth, married to Lancashire-born *farmer* Thompson SMITH, with her brother John, now a *wool comber* again, boarding with the couple. There were no surviving children for either John or Mary.

Thomas, the youngest son was recorded in the 1851 census with his family in one of the seven houses on Belle Isle, Haworth, just off Mill Hill. *"Thomas (34 b Smarber, Yorkshire), overlooker; wife Sarah (30 born Oldfield) 'domestic', daughters Mary Ann (12) spinner, and Elizabeth (9) scholar, both born Stanbury, and sons George (5) and baby John Anthony (9m) both born at Lees."* Apart from Thomas's birthplace, all of these are within a mile of Haworth parsonage, where the Revd. Patrick Bronte was campaigning so hard for a decent water supply. Belle Isle itself still exists, close by the huge mill at the bottom of the hill near the railway station. Thomas had obviously made an impression as a reliable and hardworking man, and had been promoted.

In 1861 the family was still at Belle Isle and Thomas was an *overlooker of power looms*. Thomas and Sarah had six children. The oldest, Mary Ann (21) was a pupil teacher and George was still at school which was unusual. The younger children were John Anthony aged ten, James aged eight, Merrilean aged five and Merinah aged two. As part of the improvements suggested by BABBAGE, in 1856 the Local Board of Health published a list of eight houses that would be compulsorily supplied with water. The RAW family at Belle Isle occupied one of them. However, by 1871 Thomas and his wife Sally had moved the family out to a farm at Hollings, on top of the moors and away from the squalid conditions of the town. Thomas was now working as a *farmer*. Sons John Anthony and James were both *overlookers*, Merillian and Merina were both *spinners* though Merina, aged 12, still went to school part-time. Their youngest child, Frank Thomas, had been registered in Shipley in 1864. Thomas died in 1877, aged just 59, and Merina died in 1878, aged 19. Their early deaths could well have been the result of unhealthy working conditions, or decades of bad water.

In 1881 Sally, Merillian and Frank Thomas (17, *tin plate worker*) were still at Hollings, living next to James. By now James had taken up *farming* full time at Hollings, and had a wife and three little daughters. Ten years later Sally, Merillian and Frank had moved to a smaller house at Shaw Top, Oxenhope but in 1901 Sally aged 78 and Frank, still unmarried and aged 37 were at Station Road Oxenhope, living next door to Merillian. She was still a weaver but now married to *plasterer* Amos SMITH and no doubt the happy mother of James Bertram W aged eight.

Thomas's son John Anthony did well. By 1881 he was a *coal merchant* living at Belle Isle. In 1891 he had moved the family to 50 Main Street in Haworth and was a *hosiery manufacturer*, whilst his eldest son George Herbert was an *assistant designer* in one of the local worsted mills. In 1901 John was the *manager of a yarn warehouse* and had moved again, this time to Hainworth Wood Road on the hill down towards Keighley. George Herbert (24) was now a *plumber and gas fitter*, Fred W. (22) a *piano tuner and repairer*, Charles Thomas (19) *a joiner and builder*. What a productive family.

Thomas's eldest son George had married Martha HARTLEY, only daughter of a *cabinet maker*. In 1881 George and his new wife were living with her mother in Well Lane, where the HARTLEYs had lived for decades, in the centre of the upper town. He was a *yarn merchant*, employing one man; his wife was a *milliner and dressmaker*. George and Mary had one son, Frank Buckley, and they lived within 100 yards of Well Lane for the next thirty years. By 1901 they had moved to a much bigger house in Changegate, and shortly after that they bought the cottage that 100 years later belonged to my friend Pat. Had his uncle George from Low Row lived there earlier? We are not sure, yet.

MARION HEARFIELD, Stroud, Gloucestershire, and PAT EMERY, Haworth, Yorkshire
marion@hearfieldresearch.com website: http://www.johnhearfield.com/Marion.htm

27. Two Rev Thomas LODGEs and their successors from Langstrothdale

Beggarmans, the birthplace of the two Rev Thomas LODGEs

This research started with a name on the LODGE Family Tree of a Thomas Rev born 1767 at Beggarmans to a Thomas LODGE and Elizabeth WALLACE. Being new to family history I thought this was an unusual name especially as one of his grandsons was also called Thomas Rev. My husband's aunt by marriage Mrs Muriel RAW of Kettlewell explained that Thomas was actually a Reverend in the Anglian Church and was a *Perpetual Curate* at Middlesmoor in Upper Nidderdale.

Thomas LODGE was the fourth child of Thomas LODGE and Elizabeth WALLACE who were married at St Michael and All Angels Church, Hubberholme on 5th July 1761. Their children were Robert born in 1762, Anne born in 1763, John in 1765 and Thomas in 1767. All were baptised and buried at Hubberholme. Thomas went to the Threshfield Free Grammar School near Linton-in-Craven. He then entered St. John's College Cambridge at Michaelmas Term 1786. He was awarded his B.A. in 1790 and M.A. in 1794, and was ordained a *deacon* (Winchester) March 6th 1790. He subsequently became a *priest* (York) on July 15th 1792. His first Parish was at Botley near Southampton where he was *Curate* from 1790-92. He then returned to Yorkshire to become the *Perpetual Curate* at St. Chad's Church, Middlesmoor in 1792 until he died on 22nd May 1827. On the 5th May 1794 Thomas was married at Pateley Bridge to Ann KIRBY and their children Thomas and John Kirby and only daughter Elizabeth were all baptised at St. Chad's Church at Middlesmoor. Thomas died in June 1809 and was buried in Hubberholme, as was his daughter Elizabeth in October 1821, Rev Thomas who died in May 1827 and his wife Ann who died in 1837.

John Kirby LODGE married Elizabeth FOSTER, daughter of John FOSTER and Elizabeth WALLACE of Outershaw, at Hubberholme on 10th October 1822. Their first child was Thomas born in 1823 at Outershaw and later baptised in Hubberholme Church. The family then moved to West Burton to farm. By April 1824 John Kirby had died and was buried in Hubberholme. Following his death Elizabeth his widow gave birth to a daughter also called Elizabeth Ann who was baptised at St Andrew's Church Aysgarth by Rev. J.S. LODGE. By 1837 Elizabeth Ann was also interred at Hubberholme having died at Outershaw where she and Thomas had been living with family. Their mother Elizabeth LODGE married again to Dr William BALDERSTON, *Surgeon*, a widower from Sedbusk at Hubberholme in 1829.

The second Thomas Rev was the son of John Kirby LODGE and Elizabeth FOSTER. He entered Trinity, Cambridge in the Michaelmas Term of 1844 gaining a B.A. in 1848 and a M.A. 1851. He was ordained a *Deacon* (Ripon) in 1848, Priest in 1848 and became a *Curate* at Hawes from 1848-1855. While curate at Hawes he was married in 1848 at St Stephen's Church, Kirby Stephen to Jane LODGE. She was the only daughter of James Burton LODGE of Askrigg and Ruth GRIME of Swaledale. They lived at Simonstone and four of their five children were born there and baptised at St Margaret's Church Hawes. He was Curate at St Margaret's from 1848 until he left in 1855 to be a *Perpetual Curate* of St Luke's Church at Skerton in Lancaster. Their fifth child was born and baptised there. They stayed until 1868 which left a gap of three years until he was appointed in 1871-1872 as *Curate* of St Mary's Church Warthill near York.

On 31st December 1872 Rev Thomas died and was brought back from Warthill to Hubberholme to be buried on the 3rd January 1873. His wife Jane then came back to Askrigg to live at LODGE's house with their children. In 1878 their eldest daughter Agnes Elizabeth married Rev. Christopher WHALEY at Askrigg. They had one daughter called Ruth Agnes Mary born in 1881. Christopher became *Vicar* of St Oswald's Church Askrigg.

Jane LODGE died at Askrigg on March 15th 1887 and she was buried with Thomas at Hubberholme on the 18th March. Their second daughter Annie Kirby married William BALDERSTON, a step grandson of her grandmother Elizabeth BALDERSTON (née LODGE) in 1894 at Chapel-le-frith, Derbyshire. They had no children.

John James Grime married Sarah Ann PRESTON in 1893 in Blackburn and they had only one child Bernard Grime LODGE. John GRIME's wife Sarah Ann died in Dentdale in 1897 and was buried at St. Oswald's Church Askrigg. Bernard died on the battlefields of Flanders in the First World War. His name is commemorated on the Tyne Cot Memorial in Belgium. John James GRIME died on 2nd April 1945 at Askrigg in his 90th year and was buried in Hubberholme.

Jane Ruth LODGE, the only daughter of Rev Thomas and Jane not to marry, died 4th March 1923 and was also buried at Hubberholme.

Thomas Robert, the last child born to Thomas and Jane, was married in 1902 at Hampstead in London to Winifred Marion SKEFFINGTON (born in 1877). She was the daughter of Martin S. SKEFFINGTON and Mary WEARNE of Kensington. They had two children, Thomas Cecil born in Pudsey in 1905 and Iris Winifred J. born in 1906, possibly at Askrigg. Thomas Robert died in 1936 in Settle and was also buried at Hubberholme, the last of this line of LODGEs to rest in the church yard of their ancestors.

Iris Winifred J., their only daughter, was married in 1927 in Ulverston to John LAMB and they had two sons and a daughter. Thomas Skeffington received his schooling at Giggleswick and Westminster Schools He became a Labour Party supporter. At the outbreak of the second World War he joined the Royal Navy. In 1945 he became the Member of Parliament for Bedford until 1951. He died at Brighton on 23rd March 1994, the last of this line of LODGEs to own Beggarmans.

The two Rev Thomas LODGEs and their descendants left their place of birth in the Dales, moved across dales and counties but came back to live or to marry at Hubberholme Church. Nearly all were buried there or within a thirty mile radius of Langstrothdale in Upper Wharfedale.

Those who did not return were Bernard Grime LODGE who died on the battlefields of Flanders in 1917 and Thomas Skeffington LODGE who lies somewhere on the South Coast.

MAUREEN HESELTINE maureen.heseltine@btinternet.com

28. LONGSTROTH Family and their journey across the plains of America

Stephen LONGSTROTH and Ann GILL

Stephen LONGSTROTH was born in 1789 in Langcliffe and he married Ann GILL in 1815, at St Oswald's, Arncliffe. Their first eight children were all born there. He left the dales around 1833 and moved his family to Clitheroe, Lancashire where another four children were born. The family had been christened into the established church in 1838 but Thomas became ordained into the Mormon faith. Later that year he became authorised to preach the gospel and in 1839 he was ordained as a priest.

Stephen was a very devout man, and whilst still in England, the family had much to endure as their chosen religion was frowned on by the established church. He lived in relative poverty with his family in Clitheroe; by the 1841 census six of his children had died. On 5th Feb 1842 Stephen set sail with his remaining family to America, where like many other Mormons he anticipated being able to *"lie with the saints in Zion"* and practise his religion without persecution. He left Liverpool with nothing and six weeks later arrived in New Orleans. Over the next twelve years he wrote a series of letters to his family in the dales telling of his journey across America. The earliest letter in 1844 was from Rockport when Stephen described his hopes of making a good living, moving to Illinois and building a house for his family. He explained that Rockport would not be a good place to settle because of the lack of employment due to all the work being done by slaves.

Stephen next wrote from Nauvoo of his journey to his new home. His letter in 1845 from Nauvoo described the difficulties *the Saints were experiencing and of the "hoast of henermies"* and of how they *"threatened to drive us out."* The 1848 letter from St Louis related how he fought the mob. They were trying to drive the Mormons from the city and how his family had to flee Nauvoo. They became part of the Brigham Young's pioneer group who trekked to the Great Salt Lake Valley.

The 1850 letter from the Great Salt Lake tells of the great trek across the plains. Stephen spoke of his new home and how the Great Salt Lake City was prospering and how *"thousands of men going to the gould mines pass through... and how a great many have dyed."*

In his final letter in 1854 from Great Salt Lake City he told of the cost of provisions and how he was starting to *"feel a little of the infirmities of hould age"*. He talked about his older children and was circumspect in what he said about his daughter's marriages. He did not tell his family back home that both Sarah and Nanny were married to Willard RICHARDS and there was no mention of plural marriages or polygamy. In all his letters Stephen talked about his religion and how his family back in Settle should consider their positions as regards their faith. His last letter described how he wished he could spend some time back in the dales. Stephen (1861) and Ann (1878) were both buried in the City Cemetery Salt Lake City.

Sarah, Nanny and Alice LONGSTROTH – sisters from the Yorkshire Dales

Stephen and Ann LONGSTROTH's three daughters, Sarah, Nanny and Alice were all born in Arncliffe. Their lives in America consisted of complicated social structures and plural marriages. Polygamy, at that time, was part of the Mormon faith and as their father was part of the church hierarchy they would have understood the doctrine regarding plural marriages. Evidence from family testimonies and Mormon historic documents showed Willard RICHARDS was married to all three sisters. Willard's granddaughter Minerva E. Richards KNOWLTON wrote the following: *"When Joseph SMITH told Grandpa to take another wife, he had no one in mind and Joseph said 'what about some of the women you met in England' and Grandpa immediately thought of the LONGSTROTH family, so Grandpa asked the parents of Sarah aged 16 and Nanny aged 14. The girl's parents thought Nanny was too young so Willard said 'Let me marry her and she can come back and stay with you and when you feel she is ready you can send her to me.' With the consent of the girls this was agreed. The girls were married to Grandpa in January 1843, Nanny went back to her parents and they were both sealed to him in 1846 in the Nauvoo Temple, and it was only after this time that the marriages were consummated."* These two marriages are in the Nauvoo Temple records but the marriage to the third sister Alice is less clear. In the document *Identifying the Earliest Mormon Polygamist, 1841 – 44*, there is a reference taken from Willard's diary which says *"At 10 pm I took Alice LONGSTROTH by the hand of our own free will and avow mutually acknowledge each other husband and wife, in a covenant not to be broken in time or eternity, to all intents and purpose as though the seal of the covenant had been placed."*

RICHARDS and his new wife Alice, sister to Sarah and Nanny, had mutually consented to a plural union between themselves without the aide of an outside officiator. He married his first wife Jenetta in 1838 and had over ten wives, with six of these wives bearing him fourteen children. Sarah had four children and Nanny three. In the 1850 Utah census Willard was living with Sarah and their children, whilst Nanny was living next door with three children and his children from his marriage to Jenetta were living at the other side with his mother, next door to Stephen and Ann LONGSTROTH. Willard RICHARDS died in 1854.

Alice LONGSTROTH (1824-1909) officially married twice, first to Moses WHITAKER c. 1846. He died in 1851 and then on the 11th December 1853 Alice was sealed to George Darling WATT, (the 'first' Mormon convert from England) as his third wife. He was later to take more wives and sire over 20 children. Alice had no children either by Moses WHITAKER or George D. WATT and she died in 1809.

Sarah LONGSTROTH (1826- 1858). Very little is known about Sarah other than her marriage to Willard RICHARDS and that she had four children, William Brigham, Joseph Smith, Pauline and Sarah Ellen.

Nanny LONGSTROTH (1828 – 1911) arrived in America at the age of eleven.

Nanny LONGSTROTH (1828 – 1911) arrived in America at the age of eleven. When the family moved to St Louis she worked for a wealthy family. She was seventeen when she was sealed to Willard RICHARDS and had three children, Alice Ann 1849, Stephen 1850 and Mary Asenath 1853. After she was widowed, Nanny and three of Willard's other wives married Willard's nephew Franklin Dewey RICHARDS. He was believed to have at least ten wives. Two years later the family moved to Framlinton, where they ran Richard's Rock Mill. Nanny was the last of the Longstroth children who were born in the dales to die on 7th January 1911 in Salt Lake City and she is still regarded as one of the foremost pioneering woman of the church.

JANET WESTWELL nwjw@live.co.uk

29. The PLEWES Family from Hauxwell to Province of Ontario in Canada

Terra Cotta, Ontario, built in the early 1860 at Plewes Mill.

All the Ontario Plewes' family members in my study are directly descended from Franciscus PLEWES and Alice HADSWELL who lived and died in the Bagby, Hauxwell area of North Yorkshire during the middle of the 17th century.

John PLEWES was born in Specton, near Flamborough Head in the East Riding of Yorkshire, in 1796, the son of John PLEWES of Hauxwell, in the North Riding of Yorkshire and Elizabeth VICKERMAN who was born in Foster on the Wolds, near Driffield. John married Ann STABLER in Sigglethorn near Hornsea, East Riding of Yorkshire on July 5th, 1821. She was born in Overton, Yorkshire. They came to Canada in 1850, settling in Acton, Ontario along with their children. William PLEWES, brother of John, also left Yorkshire for Ontario, Canada and may have come with John and Ann.

John operated a Grist Mill on Black Creek in Acton, Ontario on what is now the site of a modern mill at the outflow of Fairy Lake. John died on August 16th, 1851 in Acton after spending only one year in Canada.

The town of Acton, along with Georgetown and the villages of Stewartown, Glen Williams, Terra Cotta, and Norval make up the present town of Halton Hills, and are located about 50 km west of the former city of York, now known as Toronto. Terra Cotta, Glen Williams and Norval are located on the main Credit River that flows south into Lake Ontario at Port Credit, now part of the city of Mississauga.

The town of Georgetown was first settled at the confluence of Black Creek and Silver Creek. A mill was built there by George KENNEDY from Ireland, hence the name Georgetown. The main Credit River also flows through the north of Georgetown before meeting up with Silver Creek in the village of Norval. The site of the George Kennedy Mill had previously been known as Hungry Hollow, due to its impoverished inhabitants.

In 1859, John and Elizabeth's son Simon PLEWES, who was born 1831 at Catwick, near Beverley, in the East Riding of Yorkshire, purchased the water rights, land and buildings that were Henry TUCKER's grist mill and saw mill. The $5,000 purchase took place at an auction in Georgetown, Ontario.

On January 12, 1863, Simon married Janet SMITH at Halton, Ontario. Janet was born in 1838 in Canada. They had six children and settled in the village of Terra Cotta on the Credit River. The village was known as Plewes Mills, the town name changed to Salmonville in 1866 and then Terra Cotta in 1891, and is named after the red clay located in that area of the Credit River Valley.

The impressive Plewes house still exists in the current Terra Cotta. The ten room home can be seen today and is currently still in use as a home. Unfortunately there is not much left of Simon PLEWES' grist mill. Simon drowned in the mill race on his property on Black Creek in Acton in 1876 and is buried in Acton Cemetery. However his widow Elizabeth was able to purchase several lots at the village of Terra Cotta after his death.

Why did William, John and Ann PLEWES leave Yorkshire in 1850? It seems they had substantial financial resources, at least enough to enable them to operate a grist mill upon their arrival to Ontario. Their descendants became quite successful as they built and operated mills on many of the rivers of southern Ontario. The most likely reason for their immigration was that much of the North Riding of Yorkshire was in an economic depression in 1850, particularly in the Dales where lead was mined and processed.

William PLEWES was also born in Specton in 1804, and was the brother of John and uncle of Simon. He moved to Kimberley on the Beaver River in 1877. William purchased the burned-out mill from a Scotsman named John GILRAY in 1865. The mill was rebuilt in 1877 and is now a wine store in the village of Kimberley. The limestone cliffs in the beautiful Beaver Valley must have reminded William of parts of Yorkshire.

David PLEWES, son of John PLEWES and Ann STABLER was born at Catwick 1828 and moved to Acton with his parents. He worked as a miller and ended his career as a well known *grain merchant* of the Board of Trade Building in Toronto. He was at one time the owner of large flour mills in Brantford, which is located on the Grand River. The Grand River headwaters are located north of Luther Marsh and the river flows south to Lake Erie. David, a well known Methodist, laid the corner stone of Acton Methodist church on September 17, 1875. On July 1st, 1901, David preached at the silver anniversary sermons at Acton Methodist church. *(Acton Free Press, August 17, 1905.)*

In 1879, James Stabler PLEWES was born on September 25th, 1845 at Acton, Ontario. He was the grandson of John PLEWES and Ann STABLER, and was listed as being one of the first settlers in Ryde Township, located in the present day Muskoka Lakes area, north of Lake Simcoe. James owned a sawmill at Barkway, not far from the present town of Gravenhurst. Timber, mostly white pine, was harvested in this area. His son Adolph PLEWES was born on August 16th, 1879 in Simcoe, so it is likely that James' wife Esther VARLEY lived at Simcoe North, to the south of Ryde Township, along with their children. *(History of Ryde Township, 1979, Robert J Boyer.)*

In 1879, John PLEWES was born at Dundas, Ontario on March 23, 1850 and he was another grandson of John and Ann PLEWES. He had settled in Bracebridge in the Muskoka District with his wife Sarah Elizabeth NEY. Their four children were all born at Gravenhurst: Sarah Catharine PLEWES, born October 12th, 1879; John MacCauly PLEWES, born Feb 15th, 1881; Jessie Mabel PLEWES, born June 14th, 1883; Robert Simon Frederick PLEWES, born June 12th, 1887.

With special thanks to the Esquesing Historical Society for use of their archives.
www.esquesinghistoricalsociety.ca.

GERALD HUNT ghunt4@hotmail.com

30. The HORN family journey to New Zealand on the Ship *Queen of Beauty*

(Departed Gravesend, 4th May, 1863 and arrived Auckland 9th August, 1863)

G. W. HORN (Jeremiah's son) standing bottom right hand corner and his son Charles HORN as a boy (my grandfather) kneeling top right hand corner at the lead mine c.1900 New Zealand

This is the story of the following families who planned to leave the Dales to sail to New Zealand:

Jeremiah HORN (born at Preston-under-Scar in 1816) his wife Margaret RUSSELL (Castle Bolton) with their children Frederick and George HORN.

Daniel HORN (Jeremiah's brother) Mary Ann HOODLESS (wife) and son James HORN (from a previous marriage); Mary Ann's father Barnard HOODLESS who was 60 yrs old also accompanied his daughter.

The families decided to emigrate to New Zealand after finding life tough making a living at the Mallerstang Colliery in Westmorland. Also, they did not have the capital to invest in the Burtersett Quarry at Hawes. Jeremiah was listed as *quarry manager*. An undated card was printed from Burtersett stating that the men were determined to try to improve their lot. Daniel and Jeremiah said that on the back of the card it outlined that the man who took on the quarries made his fortune. Unlucky for Jeremiah and Daniel, but lucky for us!

The *Queen of Beauty* was a ship of 1235 tons and she carried 257 passengers. If our forbears knew the facts before leaving the UK then they were exceedingly brave people. Disease, mutinous crews, major storms, shipwrecks, fires, collisions with ice bergs or other vessels, un-seaworthy craft and drunken captains meant that many thousands of would-be settlers never reached their chosen country. The American Civil War was in progress during the journey of this ship and about five weeks after leaving the UK, about 50 miles off the coast of Brazil, she was intercepted and challenged by the famous Confederate Cruiser *Alabama* a celebrated raider of the civil war. She fired three shots at *The Queen of Beauty*.

The captain decided he had better heave to and allow the raiders to come on board. They proved to be a rough lot armed with revolvers and cutlasses so no doubt caused fear among the passengers. However the boarding party found the captain's papers to be in order, so after partaking of some of the ship's liquor supplies they departed leaving all hands very relieved. The fact that The *Queen of Beauty* was an American designed and built ship may have caused the Confederates to assume she was a Northerner.

The *Queen of Beauty* dropped anchor in Auckland, New Zealand on 10th August, 1863. The first item of news conveyed to the passengers was that war had broken out with the Maori people and fighting was going on within twenty miles of the town. Small boats came alongside and thus ended the long journey of three months. Farewells were spoken with real regret with everyone joining in a universal wish for fortune and prosperity in their new homes.

The families moved north to Whangarei and because of their mining experience took up land and put down two shafts hoping to find gold but struck a coal seam instead. This was the first coal found in this area at that time but not exciting. Jeremiah and Daniel must have had some good reputation as the newspaper said … *"though not prophets like their biblical namesakes of old, they were exceedingly wise and well read men who could talk and debate on many scientific and social reform subjects, in all of which they were keenly interested…"*

The family mined in various areas and Jeremiah HORN's son George William HORN was a *lead miner* at the Try Fluke mine at Kuaotuna. My grandfather Charles HORN was a boy in the early 1900's and he also helped in the mines with his father George William HORN.

In 1914 G. W. HORN and his sons bought 240 acres of land at Te Aroha and developed this land which was covered in brush and bush into what is today's most profitable pastoral dairy land in the world. The family used the first milking machine invented and became a very well established family dairy farm. Charles HORN's sons Alex and Chas HORN took over the farm during the 1960's and 1970's. They employed share-milkers on the property and Charles HORN (my grandfather) branched out into the bee industry and was the oldest beekeeper in the southern hemisphere when he died. This family dairy farm is now owned by Charles HORN's grandson Steven CLEMENTS who is also my brother.

My uncle Alex HORN (1921-1993) was a *fighter pilot* during World War II over the pacific and has written a book called *Wings over the Pacific* produced by Randon Century.

My mother Jessie CLEMENTS (HORN 1926) is the last surviving Horn in New Zealand from the Charles HORN (1885-1973) and Ellen FERGUSON (1887- 1970) family.

I am the grandson of Charles Frederick HORN (1885-1973). I have been living in New York for four years and am originally from New Zealand.

ASHLEY CLEMENTS clementsnz@gmail.com

31. The MILNERs of Swaledale to America

The Milner's Arms, Idle, Bradford

The MILNER family was a large Swaledale clan based for centuries around Muker and Thwaite. They were spoken of as one of the *"Twelve Tribes"* of Swaledale and the name echoes down through the Muker parish records along with those of their cousins the ALDERSONs, FAWCETTs, METCALFEs, HARKERs and others. However, unlike these, the MILNER name no longer appears locally as the family disappeared abruptly and permanently from the dale in the middle of the 19th Century.

Like many dales folk the MILNERs probably had Viking ancestry as *"Mylnari"* was the Old Norse name for a corn miller. While the Danes settled the flat lands in the Vale of York, the Norwegian Vikings preferred the hill country of the Pennines. They settled in the areas around Muker, Keld and Thwaites.

In the year 1500 Ralph MILNER of Muker and Richard MILNER of Calverts Houses were hunting deer without licence on church lands, and Wills written in Latin on vellum show MILNERs living at Calverts Houses in the time of Henry VIII. In the 1539 *Swaledale Muster Roll* the MILNERs supplied nine *archers* *"Able persons for the war, hosede and harnessed"* plus one *billman*. After the reformation the MILNERs owned Oxnop Hall. A 1666 murder inquiry took depositions from 18 MILNERs from a total of 105 for the dale, and records from the 1600s and 1700s have MILNERs living at Calverts Houses, Ivelet, Muker, Thwaite, Kisdon, Skeugh Head, Scar House, Usha Gap, Rash, Oxnop and Gunnerside.

Along with the KEARTONs and CHERRYs, the MILNERs were for generations *gamekeepers* to the Lords Wharton, but like many Swaledale people they were mostly *farmers* and *lead miners*. Around 1800, James MILNER was a *yeoman farmer* of Thwaite, but he also had lead mining interests and was involved in the Beldi Hill disputes. The Beldi Hill disputes broke out in 1769 between rival factions claiming ownership of the valuable lead mining rights in the area. The legal arguments spilled over into an open turf war with riots, acts of sabotage and violent confrontation between the mining gangs. A lead mine known to this day as *"Jammy MILNER's Levels"* is a few hundred yards west of Crackpot Hall.

Certain Christian names and nicknames reoccur in generations of MILNERs – Elizabeth (Betty), Mary (Mally), Margaret (Peggy), Agnes (Annas) and Rachel for the girls and James (Jammy), Edmund, William, Ralph, John and Edward for boys. Exceptions were the wonderfully named Tristram MILNER and Marmaduke MILNER, both of Calverts Houses. Marmaduke's descendants moved to Leeds around 1600 and became Aldermen and Mayors of the city. They made a fortune in trade with the Netherlands and bought Nun Appleton Hall from the Fairfax family. The First Baronet Sir William MILNER was MP for York.

Members of the MILNER family were among America's founding fathers. Richard *"Milmer"* arrived at Jamestown with the first supply convoy to the Virginia Colony in 1608 – 12 years before the Pilgrim Fathers landed. Robert MILNER (24) arrived on the *Francis Bonaventure* in 1620, settling at West and Sherlow Hundred. The year 1635 saw 18 year old Samuel MILNER sail on the *Philip* for Virginia and Michael MILNER settled in New England. An entire family comprising Joseph, Daniel, Anne, Sarah and Ralph MILNER arrived at Philadelphia in 1683. When the Swaledale lead industry collapsed in the 1800s, families began to drift away to the new mill towns and coalfields, and to Australia and America. Nineteenth Century mining booms in these countries led to mass emigration and many MILNERs settled in Lafayette, Wisconsin.

This extract from the passenger list of people emigrating to Lafayette County, Wisconsin shows an example of how many miners left the country:

SS Saxony Master; *Josiah Knowles. Liverpool – New Orleans. Dep. 19 Feb 1849; Arr. 30 Apr 1849.*
MILNER, *William 50 Male, Miner*
MILNER, *Thomas 27 Male, Miner*
MILNER, *James 23 Male, Miner*

Young Thomas MILNER never lived to see his promised land. After landing in Louisiana he developed a fever and died on the boat heading up the Mississippi. He was buried on the riverbank near St. Louis. His brother James married in Wisconsin, had a son, Lon MILNER, and founded an American branch of the family. However, the MILNER name was frequently corrupted by emigration officials to *Miller.* These *New Americans* would have found themselves among many familiar Swaledale friends and relations. For example, Ruth MILNER born 1779, the daughter of John MILNER and Margaret HARKER, who married Francis REDFEARN at Muker and emigrated to the mining boom towns of Lafayette County. Towns with evocative names such as Leadmine, Galena and New Diggings soon exceeded the population of the nearby city of Chicago.

A member of the Teesdale branch was young Mally MILNER, a beautiful but lowly servant girl who married into the aristocracy and became Mary, Countess of Strathmore. Her son John Milner BOWES was incredibly wealthy; a *landowner, ship-owner and coal baron.* He helped finance George STEPHENSON's railways and his racing stables bred four Derby winners and won the first Triple Crown. Guests at his shooting lodges included kings and emperors. He built the Bowes Museum at Barnard Castle to house his huge art collection, but he left no heirs so all this vast wealth passed into the hands of the Royal Family. In what must have been a huge and dramatic upheaval, the MILNER family disappeared altogether from their historic Swaledale homelands within a space of only 10 years. In 1861 there were still upwards of 30 MILNERs and their in-laws living around the village of Keld alone, but by 1871 they had gone. All apart from young Ellen MILNER, who was from Teesdale, and had come to work as a domestic servant at Satron.

The bulk of the MILNER family moved with their HARKER in-laws from Thwaite to Witton-le-Wear in County Durham. The HARKERs were *carters,* which must have come in useful during the move. In Weardale they were *farmers,* with some younger sons getting jobs in the booming coal mine and railway industries. Witton Park Farm became the MILNER home for 100 years. There were connections – the local landowners were the CHAYTORs of Witton Castle and William CHAYTOR was magistrate for Richmond and Swaledale. The CHAYTORs were also close family friends of the BOWES LYONs. The move occurred shortly after the death of the Countess of Strathmore. Had Mary MILNER remembered some of her relatives in a private legacy, helping to fund their relocation?

However one of the most interesting stories involves John MILNER who was born in England in 1585. He sailed for the Virginia Colony and in 1639 at the age of 54 he married 21 year old Elizabeth ROLFE. Elizabeth was one of the very first children born to settlers in the North American Colonies. She was the daughter of Captain John ROLFE and Jane PIERCE of Jamestown. Jane was Captain ROLFE's third wife. His second wife was a Native American girl, the daughter of a chief. In other words she was an Indian Princess – and her name was Pocahontas.

JOHN MILNER STUBBS jmstubbs@talktalk.net

32. Hannah (Alton) BUXTON

Hannah BUXTON
Hannah born 26th January 1791, daughter of Thomas and Hannah (Spensley) ALTON. Married George BUXTON 14th July 1812. Emigrated to the USA 1849. Died Benton, Wisconsin April 1873.

Hannah was born 26th January 1791 the daughter of Thomas and Hannah (Spensley) ALTON and married George BUXTON 14th July 1812; they had a family of six children. They were Richard, William, my great grandfather, Hannah who married John PEDLEY, Thomas who died in 1826 aged 8 years, and George who moved to Trimdon Grange about 1850. John emigrated to Wisconsin with his mother and he wrote a number of letters to his relatives. George their father died on 5th October 1825. Family members were regular worshipers at Gunnerside Methodist Chapel. When George died he was an *Exhorter*. Hannah, her youngest son John and daughter Hannah, her husband John PEDLEY and their family of Ruth, Hannah, Mary Ann and Jane emigrated to Benton, Wisconsin in America. They sailed on the ship *Saxony*. Due to the bad conditions one of the children Jane died on the voyage. Hannah died in Benton and is buried in Providence Cemetery Wisconsin.

After George's death Hannah become an *ore washer* cleaning up the lead as it was brought out of the ground. Parish relief was available, but the recipient had to be desperate. Hannah was a member of the Gunnerside Methodist Church where George BUXTON was buried. In 1848 young men returned from Wisconsin to tell people the advantage's of moving there. John and Hannah decided to go, in the belief that anything was better than their lives there. I often think of the heartbreak when some members of a family wanted to go and others did not. They all knew they would be unlikely to meet again.

Richard BUXTON, born 10th April 1813, was the eldest son and married Isabella CLOSE in 1839. They went to live in Bradford, in the West Riding of Yorkshire. The conditions were, if anything, worse than Swaledale. Bradford factory owners refused accommodation to families with young children. When Isabella and a child died in 1846 Richard returned to Swaledale with his son George.

Dixon COTTINGHAM had married Isabella METCALFE and their children were Mathew, John, Dixon and Joseph. When their father died Isabella was left in the same situation as Hannah. In 1848 Richard and Isabella (Metcalfe) COTTINGHAM married in Gunnerside, where they continued to live and work in Gunnerside. Richard worked at Whitaside lead mine and he also operated a small-holding to provide fresh food. Isabella also had a daughter called Hannah born 1850. They continued to live in Gunnerside until 1853 when they also emigrated to Benton. They went first to live at Big Patch, moving to Benton before 1860. A son William was born in December 1854.

With the commencement of hostilities in the Civil War in America, George, son of Richard and Isabella (Close) BUXTON joined Company I of the 3rd Wisconsin Infantry Regiment. He was posted to Harpers Ferry, where he was injured in a skirmish and died 10 days later. Hannah, daughter of Richard and Isabella (Cottingham) BUXTON married Christopher LOONEY from the Isle of Man. He was killed when a mine tunnel collapsed on him after only six months of marriage. Hannah married Joseph GELLING and they had Richard, William, Frances, Ernest and Raymond. Joseph GELLING committed suicide in 1910.

Several of Hannah's COTTINGHAM step-brothers lived in Dubuque, Iowa where they started an insurance company, still in operation today. William BUXTON (1854/1910) aged 15, was in attendance at Christopher LOONEY's accident. He then went to Dubuque, Iowa where he helped John HARKER, born at Satron in Swaledale, who owned a grocer's shop. When John HARKER decided to go to Mitchell, South Dakota he sold the shop to William who subsequently married Mary Louise GELSTON. By 1880 he moved to Minneapolis where he bought and sold farms, houses and factory buildings. William and Mary had sons Homer, Lynn, Benjamin, Roy and Jay. In 1900 he moved to Rialto, California where John HARKER also lived, working with citrus fruit. Naturally William also became involved in growing citrus fruit. He became president of the local bank and Water Company and organised the marketing and selling of the fruit. He owned the hotel and built one of the largest houses in Railto. At the time of his death he was one of the most respected and trusted business men in the town.

His son Homer died when young whilst Lynn owned several agencies for motor cars including Packard. Benjamin raced cars and became quite well known in Southern California and owned a garage in Railto. Roy was drowned in Lytle Creek. After the death of his wife in 1921, Jay worked his way round the Pacific for several years. On his return he became interested in gliders and became Southern California president of the Soaring Society. He designed and built gliders and held many world records for duration, and height. Jay's daughter Lucretia, who was a model, accompanied her father on many trips. None of his sons joined him in the citrus fruit companies.

John BUXTON, who emigrated to Benton with his mother in 1849, wrote several letters to my great grandfather and afterwards my grandfather. It took him several years to reply to one of them. Both he and Richard gave updates on members of the family. John returned to the dale for a visit, but arrived just after the death of my great grandfather in 1884. He had missed seeing his brother by only a few weeks. In his Will he did not mention Ann (Buxton) WINTER as she had asked too often about his wealth! Ann was my grand-father's sister.

A second letter was written by Richard just before he died to his brother, my great grandfather. I believe he was feeling very sad and lonely and reminisced about members of his family who had died; he still held the keys to Benton church. In closing his letter he writes *"As I sit here often a tear will trinkle down my cheek"*. This moves me as of his five children one lived in Dubuque 40 or 50 miles away and another son some 1500 miles away.

In conclusion, I feel huge respect for members of my family in the trials and tribulations they faced.

GEORGE BUXTON 20 Smisby Road Ashby de la Zouch Leicestershire LE65 2JL
g_buxton@talktalk.net

33. The CHANDLERS of Laverton (*or what a difference a day makes!*)

Thomas CHANDLER died 20ᵗʰ September 1885 aged 48

John CHANDLER of Laverton appeared to have been a prosperous business man, farming eleven acres as well as trading as a *butter factor* and running a weekly carrier service from Kirkby Malzeard via Ripon to Leeds and back. The 14ᵗʰ November 1851 started out as a normal day for John's wife Mary and their children until John suddenly dropped dead, aged just 38. The inscription on his gravestone in Kirkby Malzeard churchyard reads:

Sudden death came from above
And would not be denied
To separate the hands of love
That was so closely tied
His widow'd wife and children dear
Are left a while to sojourn here
But hope to meet on that blest shore
Where sin and death divide no more

A *fit* is given as the cause of death on his death certificate. The informant on the certificate was William RICHMOND who had been present when John died, presumably whilst at work. It must have been an enormous shock to the family, especially Mary with her seven children, the youngest not yet a year old. John's untimely death would have had a profound effect on the family finances and the futures of his children. By the time of the 1861 census almost 10 years later, the family had dispersed far and wide.

The oldest child, Thomas went to school until at least the age of 14, an indication of the family's comfortable financial situation. When his father died suddenly Thomas was about 15. The 1850s were a time of great change for him. Thomas moved to Leeds to work on the railway, where he met Matilda THOMPSON and in late 1859 they had a son, Thomas Chandler THOMPSON. In the spring of the following year, Thomas and Matilda married and in March 1861 they had another son John Henry, who was just 13 days old when the 1861 census was taken. At this time, Thomas was 24 and was working as a railway guard, living at 15 Lisbon Street in Leeds, with his family and mother in law.

By 1866 Thomas had become a *station master* and the family had moved to Hampsthwaite station near Clint (Harrogate). Here two more boys were born, Christopher H. in 1866 and George Alfred in 1868. The family was recorded as still living there in the 1871 census. When Thomas died in September 1885, the death was registered in the Ripon area and he was buried in Kirkby Malzeard cemetery. Matilda and the family continued to live in Leeds, however, according to the censuses that followed.

Elizabeth, the only girl in the family, was still a scholar in 1851 at the age of 13, showing that the family had an admirably forward thinking attitude towards the value of education for girls as well as boys, at a time long before school was compulsory for either sex. By the time of the 1861 census, Elizabeth was working in Tadcaster as a *house servant*, aged 22. It is likely that she married sometime in the next decade, possibly to a William LEEMING.

William was also a scholar at the time of his father's death. By 1861, aged 20, he was working as a grocer's assistant, living in at Brownhill, Batley. In 1865 he married Honore GILL in Pateley Bridge and by 1871 they were living in Victoria Street, Alverthorpe near Wakefield, where William was an *assistant grocer*. In 1875 he was widowed but remarried Harriet IDDISON in 1877. By 1881 they are living in Denmark Street, Belle Vue, Sandal Magna near Wakefield, with their three daughters, aged between five months and three years. William had risen to the position of a *grocer* managing a Co-operative Society store. In 1891 the family were at the Co-operative stores in Normanton with seven children. William lived to be 70 and died in 1911 in the Wakefield area.

John moved from Laverton to work at a corn mill at Sawley, and then in 1863, aged 20, he married Mary GILL in Pateley Bridge. By about 1869 they had moved via Leeds and Birstal, to the grocer's shop in Sharer Hill, Heckmondwike and had three children. John was working as a *commissioning agent* for beer and groceries. Tragically, like his father before him, John died aged only 32 in 1875, leaving Mary with their four young children and another on the way. In 1881 the family was still together in Heckmondwike, where Mary was working as a housekeeper to support both the younger children as well as 17 year old Emily who was an invalid. Amazingly, even in these circumstances, Maria was still at school at the age of twelve.

Christopher Charles married Elizabeth GILL in Ripon in 1868 which made no less than three CHANDLER brothers marrying three GILL girls! In 1871 they too had left the dales and were living in Pitt Lane, Liversedge, but Christopher was out of work. Ten years later they were at 46 Willow Lane, Burley near Leeds and Christopher was a *general labourer*.

Joseph, who was just two when his father died, had a very different upbringing to that enjoyed by his privileged older siblings. By the age of twelve he was living at Aldfield, working as a *plough boy*. Later he followed his brothers into the grocery trade in Birstal, near Dewsbury. In 1868 Joseph married a local girl, Sarah Elizabeth Pyrah WILSON, who was only 16 years old. Their son George Pyrah CHANDLER was born very shortly afterwards. Once again tragedy struck and on 3rd April 1869 Joseph died of '*low continued fever*', aged 20, leaving Sarah widowed at only seventeen. In 1871 she and little George were living back with her father and step mother in Batley. George also died young, at 18 in 1886. It was not until four years after her son's death that Sarah, having been *a widow* for 21 years, finally remarried to Isaac SQUIRES in 1890.

Robert Henry first appeared on the census taken on 30th March 1851, aged three months and was less than a year old when his father died. He was the one member of the family who did not leave the dale. Instead he went just as far as Kirkby Malzeard to take up an apprenticeship to a wheelwright. He then moved around the immediate area to Grewelthorpe, Carlsmoor and Dallowgill where he worked as a *wheelwright, joiner and farmer*, until his retirement to Glasshouses. He died aged 72 and is buried in Kirkby Malzeard cemetery. In many ways this is a sad little tale but it is also a tribute to the strong women who held their families together when fate dealt them a cruel blow.

CAROL METCALFE carolmetcalfe2008@yahoo.co.uk

34. John HEWGILL of Carperby and George Musgrave BINKS

The following was reported in the Penrith Herald on Saturday, February 28, 1874 headed *"American Emigration."*

"Some time ago we had the following extract from a New York paper: -

The Russian emigrants have been sadly disappointed, and, in some instances, most shamefully treated in Dakota. They purchased land in the neighbourhood of Yankton, and they found but shallow mould with gravel beneath, which broke their ploughs. Water was scarce and bad, and many died of diseases occasioned by its use. A farm was sold to a Russian who speaks no English, a portion of the money was paid, and when the unfortunate man sometime after showed his title to the property, his papers turned out to be only his first citizenship papers. Having the seal, the Russian was deluded into the belief that he had a genuine deed in his possession. But few of the emigrants will remain in Dakota, which is not the Eden they expected to find it, but rather the Eden of Martin Chuzzlewith's experience.'

Referring to the above extract, we have received the following letter from the Rev. G. M. BINKS, Congregational minister, at present residing at Castle Bolton, Bedale:................

"Dear Sir,

Sometime ago, being at the house of Mr. W. HEWGILL, of Carperby, in this county, I saw in your paper an extract from an American paper, in reference to a number of Russian emigrants who had gone to Dakota Territory, U.S. America, and had been imposed upon, the country being little better than a wilderness, the water unfit for use, etc.

In the interests of truth and justice, I forwarded your "Herald" to the Government officers of Dakota.

They have now forwarded me a copy of a paper published at Yankton, which I send you, containing a denial of the slander. May I ask you to give the same a place in your paper.

I am well known to both Mr. William and Mr. John HEWGILL of Carperby, Wensleydale, being my native place. For some years I have been engaged as a Congregational minister of the gospel in Dakota Territory. I therefore know the country well, and a finer country I never saw – a fine climate and a rich soil, surpassed by no country as a home for a working man.

I have no pecuniary interest in sending this letter, but write simply in the interest of truth,

Respectfully yours, G. M. BINKS."

The following is the statement referred to by Mr. BINKS, and is signed by a number of leading German-Russians and other well-known citizens:-

"The undersigned German-Russians who have recently settled in Dakota have read the above extract, and in reply state that it has not the slightest foundation, being false in every particular. The citizens of Dakota have been uniformly kind to us, courteous and neighbourly, and have spared no pains to make our sojourn pleasant and agreeable. The soil in this portion of Dakota is deep, rich, and very productive, and the climate salubrious and very healthy. We find good wholesome water, generally in from ten to thirty feet, and in but two or three instances have we been obliged to go deeper.

To our knowledge, there is not one word of truth in the statement that any attempt has been to swindle or deceive our people in the purchase of lands. We intend to remain in this territory because we like the soil, climate and people, and where we can obtain free farms from the general government."

George Musgrave BINKS was born in Castle Bolton on 16th April 1836 and baptised on 26th June 1836, the son of Thomas B. and Ann FAWCETT who married 22nd September 1817. His biography is recorded in the *"History of Minnehaha County, South Dakota"* by Dana R. Bailey. Apparently he attended school for just forty-two days. When seven years old he became apprentice to a butcher and remained there two years before going to work in a lead mine. He went on to become *superintendent and manager* of the Keld mining works. In 1867 he emigrated to the United States and lived in Bureau County, Illinois where he was employed in the coal mines for two years. By 1869 he went to Iowa and became a *Methodist preacher*. He moved again in 1871 to Vermillion, Dakota; and again in 1873 when he returned to England where he urged emigration to Dakota. He returned in 1874 to Sioux Falls where he took up a homestead and a tree-claim in Split Rock township, with four hundred acres of land besides some city property. The biography says that BINKS was a unique character, and well known all over the Northwest; he became a popular lecturer.

'He is a keen observer of man and nature, and is at home upon his theme – human nature. He was an early student of George COMBE and is a phrenologist of acknowledged ability. It is rare that one meets with a person endowed with so many gifts. As a public speaker he is humorous, pathetic, and forcible, as occasion may demand; and what is more, his whole life has been a constant endeavor to elevate the standard of correct living among those with whom he has come in contact. When the professor first arrived in western Iowa he was in great need of an overcoat, and having earned $20.50, purchased one for $20. He put it on and went to the post office, where he received a letter from his mother in England asking him to send her $20 to pay rent. He returned to the street, sold the overcoat, and sent her the money.'

GLENYS MARRIOTT glenys@bishopdale.demon.co.uk

35. Elizabeth ALDERSON from Swaledale to the homes of the nobility and finally back to Muker

Elizabeth Alderson
1844 – 1908

Elizabeth ALDERSON, known to her family as Betty, was born in Upper Swaledale in 1844, where her parents, John and Mary ALDERSON, farmed at Thorns. She was the fourth child of John and Mary, their eldest being Ann, who was my great grandmother and it was from her daughter, my grandmother, that I heard the beginning of this story.

Betty must have had a busy time growing up as her parents had ten children and, as was the custom in Victorian times, she would have been expected to help with her younger siblings. It is not known when she left Thorns. She was there at the time of the 1861 Census and she had left by 1871. She entered domestic service but where she first worked and in what capacity is not at present clear – we have not found her on the 1871 Census.

By the age of 37, Elizabeth was working as *housekeeper* to the Countess of Sandwich who, according to the 1881 Census, employed a further twenty one domestic servants at her house in Huntingdon.

Later she worked for the Duke of Beaufort at Badminton. The Duke was well known for his fox hunting parties and it was to one of these parties that Lord Derby was invited. As a result of his visit, Lord Derby offered Betty the position of *housekeeper* at Knowsley Hall in Lancashire.

When she left Badminton House in 1893 she was given a pair of large oval pictures and on the back of each is a printed note saying that they were a gift from the Duchess of Beaufort to Mrs ALDERSON. Although Betty was not married, like all housekeepers she was referred to as *"Mrs"* as a mark of respect for her position in the household.

Betty worked for Lord Derby at Knowsley Hall for fifteen years until her death in 1908. On one occasion in the 1890s Lord Derby was host to the Prince of Wales. On leaving, the Prince gave Aunt Betty a pearl butterfly brooch – apparently a common practice when Royalty stayed overnight with their friends. He visited Knowsley Hall again after ascending the throne as King Edward VII and, again, Betty was the recipient of another pearl brooch.

When Aunt Betty died, her brother travelled to Knowsley Hall to collect her belongings and to escort her coffin back to Swaledale where she was buried with her family in Muker Churchyard.

Her Will was duly proved and registered and her brother John, together with George FAWCETT the local *schoolmaster*, dealt with the numerous bequests. As she had no children of her own she left her brooches (including the one she described as *"the brooch the King gave me"*), pictures, watch and chain, silver inkstand, cushions and covers and her travelling clock to her nieces and great nieces.

My grandmother received one of Betty's pearl brooches and all her pictures. When my grandmother died, my aunt in England received the pearl brooch and the pictures. After my aunt died, my mother brought them to Australia. On my mother's death, I took over looking after them but as neither my brother nor I have any children, I have spent much time searching for a relative, preferably for one who was a descendant of someone mentioned in the Will.

Eventually I established contact with someone whom I knew as a schoolgirl before I came to Australia! Her grandmother married my grandmother's brother, which makes her my second cousin and also makes her the same relation to great great Aunt Betty as I am! Not only that, but my newly found cousin has seven grandchildren which makes me very happy as they will be able to treasure Aunt Betty's brooch and pictures.

Aunt Betty's Brooch – a personal history Life below stairs in Victorian England By Evelyn PEACOCK

Written in 2003 by Evelyn PEACOCK of Australia for the ALDERSON Family History Society Newsletter. Additional research by Alan GIBSON.

Updated by YVONNE ALDERSON

ALDERSON Family History Society www.afhs.org

Copyright ALDERSON Family History Society, printed with permission.

A group of people with an interest in the ALDERSON name formed the ALDERSON Family History Society in 1983. Now our membership is about 280 worldwide, with roughly two thirds in the United Kingdom and the remainder around the world including the United States of America, Australia, Canada, and New Zealand.

Members of the Society research and share information on all aspects of family history, particularly in connection with the ALDERSON name. Over the years a large database has been built up with over 140,000 records, grouped into families where possible, and available to members. We hold two meetings each year where members have the opportunity of getting together – in September a weekend at Muker in Swaledale, which includes our AGM, and a spring meeting at a different venue each year, usually at a place with an ALDERSON connection.

We are always pleased to welcome new members, whether experienced family historians or those newly interested in discovering their family roots. We are a friendly society with a lot to offer both from the information and research point of view, and socially. Details of how to join are on our website www.afhs.org

36. "To seek a better Livelihood" – The Yorkshire Migration to Nova Scotia 1772 – 1775 The GELDARTs of Coverdale.

On the morning of 11th Mar 1774 the Brig *Albion* set sail from the Port of Kingston-upon-Hull bound for Nova Scotia, British North America. The ship, burden of 150 ton and a crew of 9, had on board (sources differ between 184 and 188) passengers as settlers for available lands near Fort Cumberland in Nova Scotia. The ship's master was Thomas PERROT (or PORRITT).

The port of Kingston-upon-Hull was to become the main Port of Departure for the transports taking the families and individuals who had signed up for passage to Nova Scotia during the *"Yorkshire Migration of 1772-1775."*

Nathaniel SMITH, one of the passengers, in a letter to his brother Benjamin, and mailed before sailing, established the departure as 11th March. A subsequent letter from Fort Cumberland, dated May 29th, 1774 confirms arrival at Halifax after nearly grounding on Cape Sable Island and an outbreak of smallpox on board that resulted in the vessel being quarantined before permitted to land at the town. The passage took 8 weeks and included "…*three weaks of excessive stormes and dreadful horicanes…*"

The quarantine was soon lifted and the ship sailed on around the south of the Nova Scotia peninsula and into the Bay of Fundy. Fort Cumberland (now Fort Beausejour) is situated on a rise of land overlooking and at the head of the Bay. The passengers disembarked and were taken to the Fort and then on to their negotiated lands. Some were yet to purchase and searched for business deals with agents.

Among the passengers in the *Albion* was a party of five in company and listed as follows:
Joshua GILDART 48 years Husbandman
Robert LEEMING 51 years Husbandman
Robert LEMING 17 years Husbandman
John GILDART 19 years Husbandman
Eleanor HARRISON 48 years Widow

The spelling of family names was frequently different at every writing. GELDART is commonly accepted in Canada and in England and LEAMAN (and less frequently LEEMAN) is in use in Canada.

Joshua GELDART and Robert LEEMAN senior and Jr. reported reasons for emigrating as "*On account of grate advance of rents & in hopes of Purchasing*". John GELDART and the Widow HARRISON are "*To seek a better livelihood*". John is thought to be a nephew to Joshua. Civil listings registered soon after arrival record Eleanor HARRISON as Joshua's housekeeper.

Joshua acquired by purchase and by grant, land on both sides of the Petitcodiac River at the confluence of it and the smaller stream the Coverdale River near the present village of Salisbury. He soon made a purchase of 567 acres from George WORTMAN, one of the tenants of the land companies that formed the Monc(k)ton Township in 1766. Soon after, he applied for and received a grant from the Nova Scotia government of 181 acres on the south side of the Petitcodiac. It would seem that his residence was on his southern property and John worked there for his "uncle". Robert LEEMAN would not acquire title to land until receiving a grant from Government after 1800. It would seem that he and his son may have been part of the Geldart operation until they had selected and developed a piece of available land. The difficulties experienced by the new government of New Brunswick (after 1784) to process land settlement and convert holdings as developed by the previous government of Nova Scotia delayed application (by memorials) for, and the granting of, land titles.

Joshua's purchase was along the western boundary of the Moncton Township. His land extended from the low hills to the north and then south to the river. With the arrival of the six Yorkshire families in this area the river was called the "Coverdale" in deference to their Yorkshire homeland. The "Coverdale" name was to live on in the extended communities of Upper Coverdale, Middle Coverdale and Lower Coverdale.

Joshua returned for a time to Yorkshire to attend to family business. It would seem that John was left to look after his holdings during his absence. When Joshua returned, he found his land on the South side of the Petitcodiac that had been previously granted by the NS government in Halifax, had been re-granted to others as part of a large tract of land by the new government of NB. He managed to regain and retain his land, at least for sufficient time to sell the properties before returning to Yorkshire. He died there in 1801 and is buried in the Coverham Holy Trinity Churchyard.

John, whether by the loss of the land from under him or by preference, removed down river to Mud Creek in Lower Coverdale where he acquired a grant next to that of his new wife's family, that of James SMITH, a Londonderry Irishman and his three sons. John was later to sell this property and with his growing family removed up the Petitcodiac to Pollett River. His grant, on the opposite side of the river from the extended settlement now called "The Glades" became their new home. John and Mattie raised their family of five sons and six daughters. He is buried in "Burnt Hill" Cemetery.

His Will, dated 9 Mar 1830 and proved 7 Sep 1831 lists children as: "...*three sons, John, James and Charles already provided for... three daughters Ann Blakney, Margaret Sears and Martha Parkin... paid their portion ... son Jonathan ... dau Mary Crossman ... dau Sarah Babcock ... dau Mary Ann ROBINSON ... son Thomas GELDART.*" His wife Martha ("Mattie") survived him and was provided for in the Will.

The descendants of John and Mattie (Smith) GELDART have expanded across Canada and well into the USA. With very few exceptions, those bearing the Geldart name are their descendants. The exceptions are thought to be the phonetic interpretation by those who were unable to write and accepted another's spelling. Two other known lines include the Geldert family in Southern Nova Scotia that came with the Loyalists (United Empire Loyalists(UEL)) with the British army in 1783 and came from Sunderland, Durham. The other family spells the name as Gildart and trace their line from Coverdale through Liverpool and a migration to Southern USA and New York.

John's lineage in Yorkshire has not been proven. His father and mother John and Mary (Render) GELDART were married in Coverham Holy Trinity Church. The father John was from Carlton and the mother Mary from Little Scrafton. No further link is known. Little Scrafton appears to be a single farm complex which suggests Mary may have been a member of the household and perhaps not a permanent resident. The Geldart house in Carlton would seem to be Elm Tree House at the upper end of the village but it went to a descendant in New York and has since been (by 2007) divided into two cottages and owned by summer residents. A short conversation with the owner of Little Scrafton in 2007 adds some confusion refuting Elm tree House as the Manor house in favour of an unoccupied structure on the opposite side and further down the street that would seem to be well past repair. The same owner mentioned a difficult title search in his purchase dealings and a large transaction that included search difficulties concerning an interest by a Geldart descendant in America.

V. BING GELDART bingg@rogers.com

37. Matthew DINSDALE – The Circuit Rider

No publication about the people who left the Yorkshire Dales would be complete without mention of the book '*The Circuit Rider*'. Originally published in 1980 by Abigail CURKEET in America, it tells the story of John DINSDALE and his descendants. It includes a pamphlet summarizing many of the letters, known as the Matthew DINSDALE Chronicle.

The main body of material on Matthew DINSDALE's life was placed in the care of the Wisconsin State Historical Society many years ago by Abigail's grandmother, who was Matthew's daughter, Annie Dinsdale SWENSON. Another collection was left by Abigail's mother, Edith, Annie's second daughter. Her aunt Mary Swenson NORTH also preserved material which is included in the book.

Abigail records in the introduction that Matthew DINSDALE was one of many who came to the relative wilderness of North America seeking his fortune, leaving family, friends and the comforts of a civilized society for an unknown fate.

She asks why should the '*life of an obscure Yorkshireman be of sufficient interest to deserve preservation at all?*' She notes that he was surprisingly well educated for a person of his time and station. He was a keen observer and had a deep interest in all events of his time. His gift of expression was evident in his letters and journals. Through his eyes readers can see the society and circumstances of the relatively new land to which he went.

The DINSDALE family is an old one in Wensleydale, and Ivor was reputed to be the first head of a school founded by Elizabeth I in Askrigg. One was a famed stone mason, whose work survives him by a century or two. James, Matthew's father, became a trustee of the Askrigg School. Matthew was apprenticed to a firm of drapers in Richmond and stayed there until he was 21. At first Matthew planned to go to India but tales of America brought back by others, as well as letters from friends who had gone before determined him to seek his luck there also.

Matthew left England after the death of his father in 1843. He was the eldest of nine children born to James and Elizabeth THOMPSON. He planned initially to take a look at the land and if a better living was offered to take the rest of the family over. Many of Matthew's friends were preachers and he was ordained as a local preacher before he left England. The church did not pay at all in most cases so Matthew decided to do both – he became a Circuit Rider and also owned a general store.

A Circuit rider or saddlebag preacher was a popular (as opposed to official) term referring to clergy in the earliest years of the United States who were assigned to travel around specific geographic territories to minister to settlers and organise congregations. They travelled with few possessions, carrying only what could fit in their saddlebags. They travelled through wilderness and villages and preached every day at any place available. Unlike clergy in urban areas, Methodist circuit riders were always on the move. Many circuits were so large that it would take five to six weeks to cover them. This early frontier ministry was often lonely and dangerous.

Abigail's book includes numerous letters, maps, photographs, genealogical charts, indentures, poems, notes and glossary.

It is unusual to find a copy for sale, world wide, and we are grateful to Peter and Janet LEYLAND who loaned their copy to be displayed at the Upper Dales Family History Group 10th Anniversary.

GLENYS MARRIOTT glenys@bishopdale.demon.co.uk

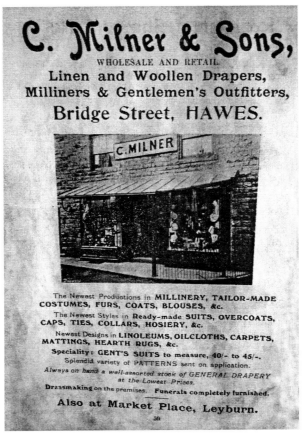

C. Milner & Sons, Hawes, pre 1900 advert

38. Dalesmen in New Diggings, Wisconsin

The Great Seal of the Territory of Wisconsin

The village of New Diggings in Lafayette County, Wisconsin, is located not far from the spot where the first white settlement in the lead section was made, in 1824. New Diggings is the oldest 'digging' in the state, and while the rest of Wisconsin was still a vast wilderness, with only two other settlements and an occasional trading post or mission to mark the approach of the white man, this little mining community, called Natchez, was the scene of feverish activity.

In 1822 the settlement at Galena, then called *LaPointe* or *January's Point,* consisted of about thirty people, engaged in prospecting, mining and smelting, or trading with the Indians. They lived in a few log cabins at the foot of the hill called *"The Point"* on the *Fever River.*

The list of burials at the Leadmine Primitive Methodist Church Cemetery, New Diggings reads rather like any village in Swaledale.

KENDALL Francis 1832-1876; wife Margaret 1830-1922 and I presume two sons.
BAINBRIDGE Eliz widow of Joseph died 22nd March 1884
ROWE George 1866-1932; Eliz 1863-1845
PEACOCK John H 1879; Hannah M
CLARKSON Henry died 5th June 1889 aged 74 born Swaledale; wife Margaret died 15th October 1886 aged 78 born Arkangathdale.
CLARKSON John H 1849-1926
PEDELTY George R; Joseph; Peter W
CARTER, Elmer; Nannie; Leonard M; Starle W; Fremont J.
HESLOP Margaret 1861 – 1938; Christopher 1868-1956
HARKER Joseph M; Mary
WHITE John L. 1847; Isabel; William C
COATES James 1842-1916; wife Mary; Charles O; Bertha O; Garfield
PRATT Mary J 1858-1948; Martin; Wesley; Nora E.
PRATT Edith

FOWLER Bernard 6th November 1824 – 24th August 1891; Elizabeth 12th May 1835 – 9th January 1936
FOWLER Anthony 12th June 1864 – 11th January 1936
PEDLEY Mary widow of William died 17th October 1880 aged 57 years
HARKER Joseph native of Yorkshire died 1st September 1862 aged 54 years; Simon son of Joseph and Mary;
BLENKIRON Thomas born near Richmond 31st March 1823 – 30th June 1886; Ann wife 18th January 1842 – 3rd September 1870
COATES Richard born Yorkshire 1st July 1821 – 20th July 1875; wife Jane born Durham, 22nd April 1827 – 8th April 1891.
ROWE Catherine; ROWE Michael; Jane; RAW Ann; Martin; ROWE John; James; Mary widow of John
PRATT Sarah A daughter of J. W and J
DENT Ann Pratt died 1904 aged 76 years
RAW Ralph son of Martin and Ann
CHERRY James died 1st February 1863 aged 31 years, native of Yorkshire
CHERRY/ANDERSON Ellen widow of Jas, and Thos ANDERSON born Yorkshire11th November 1827- 12th November 1910. CHERRY Nicholas.
BIRBECK Jonathan Turner died 7th October 1880 aged 55 years.
MILLER Catherine 1826-1912; Ralph born Gunnerside 1819-1888
RAW William, Mary J
PEDELTY John born Yorkshire 1820-1883, wife Margaret born Westmorland
NATTRASS Nanny Pedelty widow of Thos
WAGGETT Mary A, Robert
MILLER, Peter W, and family
BIRD....including a Mary born Swaledale 8th April 1838 (probably wife of Joseph R)

CHRISTINE AMSDEN camsden@mymts.net

39. Hugh STONES (1849-1909) a Mining Lad from Arkengarthdale

Arkengarthdale – Arkletown and Langthwaite

I always believed that my family was the first branch of the STONES family to live in Northumberland when we moved to Morpeth in July 1965. Family history has taught me that one should not assume anything.

From the England census of 1901, I discovered that my great, great grandfather's brother, Hugh STONES, lived in Ashington, Northumberland. Knowing that the family were from Arkengarthdale, my curiosity was aroused as to why he should be living in Northumberland; and so my research began into the life of Hugh STONES with a visit to the Swaledale Museum at Reeth

Hugh STONES was the fifth child of Edward and Elizabeth STONES and was christened at Whaw Methodist Chapel, Arkengarthdale on the 6th January 1850 aged 1 week and 3 days. He lived in Arkengarthdale for the next twenty years of his life.

In 1851 he was living at Mell Close with his father and mother, brothers John George (my great, great grandfather) and Robert, and sister Elizabeth. His father, like many men of the Dale was a lead miner. Sadly Hugh's mother died in 1857 when Hugh was seven years old. By 1861 the family was living at Low Faggergill and being looked after by a housekeeper.

In the same year Edward married his housekeeper Dinah TILBURN, who was also widowed, and began a second family. According to family hearsay this was not a happy period of Hugh's life, for his stepmother was cruel to him. This was maybe why, in the 1871 census, Hugh was not living with his father and new family at Seal Houses, but was a boarder with Mary ALDERSON at Low Faggergill. Could this have been a contributing factor to Hugh leaving the Dale?

Like his father and brothers, Hugh worked in the lead mines and records of him can be found in the *Arkindale Lead Miners Pay Book* working in Faggergill and Punchard mines. His last pay was drawn in August 1871. Could employment elsewhere be another reason for Hugh deciding to leave the Dale?

A happier time began for Hugh after this for in 1872 he married Jane HOULDEN, née READSHAW, a widow with two sons, at Middleton-in-Teesdale. The following year their daughter Elizabeth, known as Lizzie, was born.

In the censuses of 1881 and 1891, Hugh and family were living in Middleton-in-Teesdale where Hugh was still employed in the lead mining industry. Lead mining around Middleton ceased in the 1890s, but when and why Hugh moved and settled in Ashington is, as yet, a mystery. Ashington as a settlement did not exist until the discovery of coal. By the 1890s Ashington was an up and coming mining village and eventually became known as the largest pit village in the world. Families came from Scotland, Ireland, Wales, Durham, Norfolk, Devon and Cornwall and many other counties of England to work in the Ashington coalfield. According to the 1901 census, Hugh was the only one to have originated from the Yorkshire Dales.

Hugh's daughter Lizzie married Sam SNOW in Northumberland in 1899. On the 1901 census Sam and Lizzie and son Henry Cephas SNOW were living with Hugh and Jane at 16, Second Row, Ashington. The Rows were purpose built terraced houses for the miners. Between 1901 and 1907 Lizzie had a further five children, two of whom died in infancy and her family lived in the Hirst area of Ashington.

In 1906, Hugh had an accident whilst employed as a *wasteman* at the Carl Pit. Working in mines all his life appears to have taken its toll on his health. In 1909 Hugh succumbed to influenza and exhaustion and died on the 6th July aged 59 at 38, Putney Terrace, Newbiggin-by-the-Sea. I can only surmise that he was moved to Newbiggin to be away from the smoke and grime of the pit and that the bracing North Sea air might have aided a recovery.

Hugh, although a Methodist, was buried in the Holy Sepulchre Churchyard on the 10th July. His burial record stated that he lived at 16, Second Row, which was just across the road from the churchyard. His wife Jane died in 1913 and was buried near to him.

Today, Ashington is a thriving town, the colliery is no more, Second Row where Hugh lived is a modern housing estate, but it is good to know that a mining lad from Arkengarthdale and his descendants played their part in the history of Ashington.

ANGELA TEASDALE (née STONES) angela.teasdale@hotmail.co.uk

40.   James METCALFE in St Helena

Longwood, St Helena
(Photo courtesy of http://www.napoleonguide.com)

St Helena is a small mountains island situated in the Atlantic Ocean 1200 miles off the west coast of Africa. In January 1673 the Dutch captured the island but were ejected afterwards by a British Squadron. The recapture of the island gave rise to the question to the respective rights of the Crown and the East India Company. By a charter signed 16th December 1673 Charles re-granted the island to the Company in perpetuity. At that time nearly half the population were imported slaves but all the inhabitants were free by 1836. A count in 1820 showed nearly 8000 residents of which whites (3534), soldiers (2181) and slaves (1156) were the biggest groups. There were sizable numbers of Chinese and freed slaves and a small number of Lascars (East India sailors or soldiers). Apart from the execution of a small number of East India Company soldiers for robbery life seems to have proceeded very quietly until 15th October 1815 when the *Northumberland* arrived with the ex – Emperor of France Napoleon Bonaparte on board. He landed on the island on 17th October and took up residence at Longwood, a large house on the island. From 31st March the island was administered by the Crown.

The first METCALFE about whom I found information was James METCALFE who was buried on 22nd October 1826 aged 36 years. Several months later I found the following in the *"Who was who or a directory of the island during the Captivity of Napoleon"* published in 1919. James was a *carpenter* who often did repairs to the furniture at Longwood. In this capacity he was sometimes in the presence of Napoleon, particularly on 16th and 17th April 1822, when the dying emperor, from his bed in the drawing room, watched him finishing his work. After death it was METCALFE who made the coffin of the great emperor which now rests in Invalids. The subsequent history of METCALFE is unknown but his great grandson Mr. HANDS still lives in St Helena.

I found an 1827 administration of the estate of James METCALFE which stated *"A private soldier in the St Helena regiment lately deceased left a trifling sum of £3-18-11½d. Which will have to go to his relatives who are living in West Witton in Yorkshire."* However in 1817 a *Private* in the St Helena infantry Regiment was paid 8 pence per day, this was not such a trifling sum. The Muster Rolls revealed the following:

Private Thomas METCALFE (Mitcalfe) first appeared on 1st January 1791, then on detachment to India in March 1792 before being transferred to the Colonels Co. in 1796 and then to the Grenadier Guards in June 1799. He was discharged on 1st August 1801 and that was all that was recorded.

Private Robert METCALFE (Midcalf) appeared on 1st April 1796 in the Muster Roll and also for 14th February 1802 which gave more information. He arrived at St Helena in 1795, and his home Parish was given as Richmond. He was a private in the St Helena regiment aged 40. He was *"non effective"* from 1st April 1808 and discharged on 20th February 1809.

Private James Midcalf (Medcalf) was recorded on 1st July 1799. On 14th February 1802 Muster Roll he arrived in St Helena in 1798 from his Parish of Grassington, a *Private* in the 2nd Battalion St Helena Regiment aged 30. He was recorded as being *"non effective"* from 1st July 1807 and discharged on 1st August 1811.

Private James METCALFE arrived in 1815 aged 28 years, former occupation *labourer*, formerly of His Majesty 66th Regiment of Foot. He was discharged in India in 1821. He appeared in the St Helena Muster Rolls on the 1st May 1821. His age at burial was 36. All the other information was the same so there was little doubt it was the same man.

Gunner William METCALFE was also recorded with the 1st Company St Helena Artillery Regiment aged 29 years from the County of York. His previous occupation was as an *armourer*, enlisted on 11th March 1823 and he arrived in St Helena in 1823. He was in hospital on the 27th September 1822 and discharged in 1830.

When I worked through the St Helena birth, marriage and burial records I found the following entries:

Baptism   20th Sept 1779 Harriet Metcalfe daughter of James and Mary ADNEY
Burial   20th January 1781 a daughter of James ADNEY, schoolmaster
Baptism   26th Sept 1783 James William Metcalfe son of James and Harriet ADNEY
Baptism   26th Sept 1783 Cordelier Harriet Metcalfe daughter of James and Harriett ADNEY
Burial   10th Dec 1784 Cordelier Harriett Metcalfe daughter of James and Harriett ADNEY

From the records of the METCALFE Society James ADNEY married Mary METCALFE on 11th April 1767 at London St Olave. Mary was baptised on 8th September 1742 at Lincoln Inn Fields London.

I bought a copy of the Will of James METCALFE who died on the 8th December 1856 aged 71 years. James METCALFE was born in Coverdale. In his will dated 14th December 1854 he left his property at Willow Bank and Robinsons with *"all my property situated in Jamestown opposite the churchyard or burial ground"* to my adopted son James SMITH (who is now generally known as James METCALFE) the son of Mary SMITH native. The property was to be held in trust for his grandson Henry Geldart METCALFE and his granddaughter Mary Alice METCALFE was to inherit property called Richenbach's estate. Willow Bank in 1883 was described as *"quite the prettiest house in the locality"*. James had the distinction of making coffins. In 1817 he finished a large library table for Bonaparte then he was asked for the dimensions of an easy chair that the Governor Sir Hudson LOW had requested. In 1826 he also held property from the East India Company to the value of 10 shillings. James was employed at Longwood by George BULLOCK who operated from Tenterden Street, Hanover Square, London and was responsible for the furnishing of Longwood. It was likely that James had also been working in London.

Henry Geldart METCALFE the son of James and Lydia METCALFE was baptised on 12th November 1851. The Monumental Inscription (1903) of James describes him as *"late Captain, St Helena Militia, Willow Bank."* Henry died in Upper Norwood in 1915. Probate was granted to Grace Lucretia MORRICE. It was common on St Helena for couples not to get married owing to the cost of the wedding.

The HANDS family lived on St Helena for almost 70 years when John Compton HANDS was born in May 1842. He went to train at St Augusta College Canterbury and became Deacon and Curate of St Matthew's on St Helena in 1868. He was ordained in 1874 and became vicar in 1875, looking after the whole island for 14 years until 1885. On 30th March 1869 he married Mary Alice METCALFE, the organist at St Matthews, and described as of *Willow Bank*. They had two sons and two daughters. Mary died on 21st July 1905 whilst her husband died some 23 years later on 25th November 1928.

GEORGE BUXTON g_buxton@talktalk.net

41.   John HARKER from Arkengarthdale to Knottingley

The launch of *Glaisdale H at* **Knottingley on 12th July 1961**

John HARKER was born in Arkengarthdale in 1846, the son of a small *farmer* who was also the village *overseer of the poor.*

In the census of 1851 the family was living at the Gill, Arkengarthdale. Ralph HARKER aged 34 was a *lead miner* born in Arkengarthdale whilst his wife Mary was just 27 years old with five children. Thomas was their oldest child aged seven, followed by Tabitha aged five. John was the middle child aged four with two younger siblings James aged three and Ann just ten months old.

Ralph died four years later. John started his working life at the age of eight, on a neighbouring farm. By 1861 the family was living at Arkle Town, and John was recorded as a 14 year old *lead miner.*

He then moved to Bradford, where he worked for some time on the railway and in the mills. John married Jane FAWCETT in Bradford in 1867. Around 1868 at the age of 21 he started work for a firm of tar distillers trading as Messrs STAINSBY and WALSH at Bolton Woods near Bradford. By 1871 in Idle, also near Bradford, John and Jane had two young children James W. aged three and Margret Ann aged one year.

In 1875 STAINSBY and WALSH suffered two misfortunes, firstly the death of Mr WALSH and secondly a large part of the works was destroyed by fire. Mark STAINSBY approached John George LYON and eventually persuaded him to come into partnership. It is possible that Mr LYON moved to Shipley around this time, but it was decided not to reconstruct the damaged works. A new factory designed by John George LYON was built at Knottingley, known as *"The Aire Tar Works"* and thus Messrs STAINSBY and LYON came into existence in 1877 when John HARKER moved with the company to Knottingley. He was appointed a *foreman* by one of the co-founders, John George LYON.

The 1881 census records John and his family in Low Green, Knottingley. He was now a *chemical labourer.*

Jane was recorded as having been born in Leeds. James now aged thirteen and Margret aged eleven were both *scholars,* with two younger siblings in the family. Martha J. aged nine and Isabella aged four had both been born in Bradford.

In the early days the company operated three open wooden vessels which were towed by horse along the inland waterways. Mr LYON gave John HARKER the privilege of operating the lighterage side of the firm. This was the loading or unloading of a ship, or transportation of goods, by means of a lighter, or barge and was carried out in Knottingley with five barges towed along the canals, first by horse, and later by steam tug.

John and his family had moved again by 1891 to Racca Green, Knottingley, where he was recorded as a *"chemical works foreman* from *Arkengarth Dale."*

In 1893, when the firm became a limited company, he became a shareholder and was then appointed a *Director.* John HARKER became a prominent member of the community, being elected as a councillor on the Urban District Council, later serving as Chairman. He died on 9th April 1911 in his 64th year.

After his death, the business was continued by his son James W. HARKER, and his son-in-law James William KIPPING, who had married John's daughter Isabella. KIPPING started his working life as a *junior clerk* with STAINBY and LYON. His father, William KIPPING, was the local *police sergeant,* born in Eton. Family stories say that William KIPPING ran away when he could not get on with his step-mother.

Crude tar was brought to Knottingley from gas works at Bradford, York, and other towns, in open barges. Here the tar was refined and pitch was then exported via Goole to Northern France and Belgium. Oil was exported in barrels via the port of Hull. In 1918 STAINSBY and LYON purchased the HARKER/KIPPING business and formed a company under the title John HARKER Ltd and Kipping continued as *general manager.*

By the mid 1930s the company had continued to grow and operated more than 30 vessels. In 1936 a new holding company was formed, incorporated under the title Lyon and Lyon. The former STAINSBY and LYON went into liquidation with shareholders receiving cash in addition to shares in the new company. The name of JOHN HARKER was retained for the shipyard and barges.

The naming of ships followed a pattern of naming them after family members or people connected with the company, but by the mid 1930s they were quickly running out of names. A competition was held amongst the employees for suggestions as to how the ships could be named, and the winner was a young secretary, Alice PEARSON, who suggested that they should be called after the Yorkshire Dales, with a suffix "H". Perhaps it was because John HARKER had been born in Arkengarthdale, this suggestion was a popular choice. The first dale barge *"Darleydale H"* was built and launched on 26th May 1937; at that time she was the largest vessel of her type, capable of carrying 280 tons. Undergoing trials in the River Humber, she was designed for service in the Severn estuary between Avonmouth and Worcester, working with a dumb barge *"Arkendale H"* which had been built at RICHARD's Ironworks in Lowestoft. In 1948 *"Darleydale H"* was cut in two at the Gloucester shipyard and a 20 foot midships section inserted thereby increasing her capacity to about 70 tons, and taking around four months to complete. At the same time *"Arkendale H"* was lengthened and converted into a self-propelled vessel by having a 150 bhp Crossley engine fitted.

On 21st December 1958 near Stourport on the Severn *"Darleydale H"* struck the Haw Bridge and tragically the skipper, Stanley EDWARDS, was killed by falling girders and masonry as he dashed out of the wheelhouse. She was sold in 1963.

RON GOSNEY 18 Downland Crescent, Knottingley, WF11 0EH
rongosney@knottingley.plus.com wrote the original history of John HARKER which was
edited by MARION MOVERLEY moverley.lyons@virgin.net

42.   Arkengarthdale Church of England School

Arkengarthdale School 1885

Arkengarthdale School was founded in 1659 by Dr John BATHURST, the physician to Oliver Cromwell and Lord of the Manor. He left an endowment of £20 per annum; £16 of which was to pay a schoolmaster to teach all the children of the tenants of the Manor of Arkengarthdale in reading, writing, accounts and the rudiments of Latin and English grammar. The remaining £4 was to be used for a boy to be apprenticed to a handicraft trade at York or London, who had to be able to read and write. In the absence of a boy, a young girl was to be given the same opportunity.

This endowment, the rebuilding of the school in 1813 by George BROWN Esq., the later extension and the purchase of the school in 1935 by the Arkengarthdale Parochial Church Council when it became a Church of England School all paved the way for a thriving school.

The school has survived in the dale despite the constant fluctuating numbers in its earlier days due to children working the land and working at home, outbreaks of scarlet fever and diphtheria, the huge decrease in numbers in the late 1800s due to the decline of lead mining and the near closure in 1968 due to a very low number on roll.

Today the school has 40 children on roll and this is the highest it has been since the war years. Evacuees from the north east of England helped swell the numbers even further.

In 2009 Arkengarthdale Church of England School celebrated 350 years of its existence and long may it continue to exist and thrive in this beautiful, small dale. We are pleased to support the Upper Dales Family History Group exhibition to enable more members of the public to see examples of the school archives.

MARY HUTCHINSON Headteacher mary@swaleview.me.uk

43. Gateshead Mercers and Drapers Guild Admissions 1645-1819 and The London Apprenticeship Abstracts 1442-1850

A number of dales boys were enrolled in the *Gateshead Mercers and Draper's Guild*:

John ROBINSON, son of Wastell ROBINSON of Spennithorne. Master Robt. HENDERSON, trade *Mercer* apprenticed 25th March 1678.

Anthony CAYGILL son of Matthew CAYGILL of Askrigg. Master William MOORE. Apprenticed 17th August 1686

George FORSTER son of Jon FORSTER, *hosier*. Master John ROBINSON, *merchant*. Apprenticed 20th August 1688.

Henry JACKSON son of Henry JACKSON of Ridding. Master Edw. FAWCETT, *grocer and chandler*. Apprenticed 2nd February 1688.

Jon LONSDALE son of Willm LONSDALE, *gent* of Richmond. Master Mark SHAW *grocer*. Apprenticed 9th November 1689.

One of the largest Guilds was that of the Vintners' Company which admitted the following dales boys:

ARRUNDELL Anthony, son of James, of Grinton, to John SEDGEWICKE 2nd Oct 1610
ELLISONNE Henry son of John, of Wensleydale *yeoman* to John SEDGEWICK 6th June 1614
MALLABY Richard son of James of Coverdale *yeoman* to Andrew PEAST 1st Dec 1630
BOUSEFIELD Robert son of Stephen of Richmond *yeoman* to Christopher PHILLIPPS 3rd March 1634/5
HELMSLEY George son of Peter of Marrick *yeoman* to Francis PALFREYMAN 5th Oct 1641
HUTCHINSON, Matthew son of Rowland of Richmond *yeoman* to Richard TIBBETTS 7th May 1644
HUTCHINSON, Henry son of Rowland of Marske, *gentleman*, to Ralph HUTCHINSON 5th May 1657
HUTCHINSON, Humphrey son of Rowland of Marske *yeoman* to Hugh STEDMAN 6th March 1659/60
HUTCHINSON, Thomas son of Brian of Marske *yeoman* to Matthew HUTCHINSON 6th Dec 1664
THORPE, William son of Gervase of Marske *clerk* to Matthew ROYDEN 3rd Sept 1650
BARKER, Thomas son of William of Richmond *tanner* to Thomas HUTCHINSON 4th Feb 1655/6
CLASSON John son of William of Marske *husbandman* to Matthew HUTCHINSON 3rd Feb 1656/7
HARRISON, Robert son of William of Ellingstring *yeoman* to George JONES 6th Oct 1663
RAYNE Robert son of Robert of Richmond *yeoman* to Thomas PAULSON 2nd July 1661
RAYNE James son of Robert of Richmond *yeoman* to Thomas PAULSON 6th July 1669
CLARKE John son of Thomas, of Crakehall *husbandman* to John JOHNSON 2nd Feb 1668/9
KELLEY Ambrose, son of Thomas, Richmond, *yeoman*, to Thomas ALLEN 5th Dec 1671
ARCHER Joseph, son of William, Richmond, *fuller*, to Martha FOWLER 7th Mar 1681/2
HOPPS John son of John of Richmond *draper* (deceased) to Thomas MERRETT 4th July 1682
GUY Francis son of Christopher of Askrigg, *smith*, to John DOWSE 7th July 1685
PINKNEY Henry son of James of Richmond, *cordwainer* to Matthew FOWLER 7th Nov 1688
PICKERSGILL Robert son of Simon of Ellingstring *yeoman* to Esther WELLS 6th July 1692
PICKERSGILL Richard son of Simon of Ellingstring *yeoman* to Esther WELLS widow 2nd Nov 1692
BOWES Thomas son of John, of Aysgarth, *yeoman*, to John CLARK 20th June 1693
BOWES George son of John of Thoralby, *yeoman*, to Thomas WELLS 4th Dec 1695
DINSDALE James son of Edward of Askrigg *mason* to Joseph GREEN 5th April 1693
GRISEDALE Arthur son of Henry of Richmond *cordwainer* to William FOWLER 5th Dec 1694
DAVIS John son of Henry of 'Halagh' *husbandman* to John WOODWARD 3rd Oct 1710
PRESTON Robert son of Robert of Masham *farmer*, to John ADAMS 2nd April 1729

SHEILA HARRIS hsheila10@yahoo.com and KATHLEEN BOWErevkmbowe@aol.com

44.   Three Cambridge Alumni from the Dales

St. John's College Cambridge

James INMAN of Garsdale Foot, Sedbergh

Born in 1776 at Garsdale Foot Sedbergh, the son of Richard INMAN and Jane HUTCHINSON his education initially was at Sedbergh Grammar School and he entered Cambridge University in 1794. He graduated in 1800 as Smith's prizewinner and Senior Wrangler. A Wrangler was a student who had completed the third year (called *Part II*) of the Mathematical Tripos with first-class honours. Until 1909, when the class list ceased to be published in rank order, the highest-scoring student was named the *Senior Wrangler*, the second highest-scoring student the *Second Wrangler*.

Initially he intended to go to Syria as a *missionary* but could get no further than Malta due to the Napoleonic War. He stayed there for a while learning Arabic. On his return he was appointed *Astronomer* to Captain Matthew FLINDERS' ship surveying Australian waters in 1803 -1804. On his return to England aboard an East Indiaman he was present at the battle of Pulo Aura when a French Naval Captain was tricked into losing an easy prey. It is said that he commanded some *pikemen* during this battle but this cannot be confirmed.

He was ordained on gaining his MA in 1805 although he never took up a clerical position. In 1808 he was appointed *Professor of Nautical Mathematics* at the newly renamed Royal Naval College at Portsmouth. He remained in this post for 30 years until he retired in 1839. In 1810 the Admiralty, on his suggestion, created the School of Naval Architecture and he was made its *Principal*. He became a Bachelor of Divinity in 1815 and a Doctor of Divinity in 1820. He published several books on Seamanship and Naval architecture and was instrumental in many improvements during these years. He is also credited with having been the first man to apply science to shipbuilding.

He married Mary WILLIAMS in 1807 in Oakham, Rutland. They had four sons James Williams INMAN, Henry, Matthew and Richard and three daughters, Mary, Frances Sarah, and Jane.

After his retirement he remained in Portsmouth until his death on 7th February 1859.

Inman Harbour and Inman River in Canada and Cape Inman in Tierra del Fuego are all named after him

Christopher NAYLOR of Grinton

Christopher was baptized in 1738 at Grinton the son of James NAYLOR and his wife Martha MACHELL. James was a *farrier*, but we suspect with help from Lord BATHURST, he sent his son to school in Canterbury and thence to St John's College in 1758. He obtained his BA in 1761 and was ordained a *deacon* in September of that year. He became a Priest in February 1763 and married Mary BRAMBLE in December of the same year. In 1768 he was living in Turnham Green. Whether this was when he was tutor to Lord ARDEN and his brother the Rt. Hon Spencer PERCIVAL is not clear. At least one of his sons was born there.

Between 1772 and 1777 he was *rector* of Llanaber, Merionethshire and then *curate* of Burnsall between 1778 -1779. In November 1779 he was appointed *vicar* of Roxby cum Risby in Lincolnshire, a post he held until his death in 1816. He must have been an absentee vicar for much of the time because in 1780 he was appointed *Second Master* at Kings School Canterbury and he became *Head Master* in 1782 holding this post until his death. He also became *rector* of Scremby in Lincolnshire in 1788.

A manuscript book left to St Augustine's College, Canterbury, by the Rev. Canon George GILBERT states: *'The Rev. C. NAYLOR was a dignified looking man, but with much severity of aspect and disposition.... The rod was his great dependence on all boys but those in the first class. He was a good scholar and apt at versification.'*

Cambridge Alumni (Venn) states that he died on 11th April 1816 and was buried in Canterbury Cathedral Cloisters. The Clergy of the Church of England database however states that he died on 7th May 1816. He did leave a Will which was proved in Canterbury on the 7th Oct 1816. In this Will he states that he wished to be buried as simply as possible alongside his daughter Mary Anne who was already buried in Canterbury Cathedral Cloisters. He also named in the Will his daughter Caroline Le GRAND wife of John, and sons Robert, George and Christopher Bramble.

John PERCIVAL of Carperby

Born in Carperby on 3rd April 1863, the son of Elizabeth PERCIVAL he went to St John's College Cambridge in 1884 where he gained an honours degree in parts I and II of the Natural Science Tripos.

He spent the next few years lecturing on agricultural topics at universities in East Suffolk and Surrey. When the South Eastern Agricultural College was founded at Wye in Kent he was appointed *Professor of Botany*. He remained there until 1902 when he moved to the University of Reading becoming the Head of the Agricultural department. He was appointed *Professor of Agriculture* in 1907 and in 1912 *Professor of Agricultural Botany*, he continued in this appointment until he retired in 1932.

By the time of his death, his book on *Agricultural Botany*, first published in 1900, had been translated into many languages and was in its eighth edition. His main field of interest was wheat and he studied many thousands of different varieties from around the world to produce the monograph *"the Wheat Plant"* published in 1921. Right up to the time of his death he continued to be involved in research on seeds and germination.

He had married Ethel Elizabeth Houston JOHNSTONE in Aysgarth in the autumn of 1896. In the 1901 census they were recorded living in Wye in Kent with their son Alan Vivian. Ten years later in 1911 Ethel and Alan were in Reading but John was not with them.

He died on January 26th 1949 in Reading leaving his widow and son.

John's obituary said he was a fine *linguist, artist and musician*. He had an encyclopaedic knowledge of Agriculture and was a great teacher but could be aloof at times. He loved nothing more than to be in wild and lonely places on field trips and he spent several months living with the Laplanders. He returned time and again though to *"his beloved Dales."*

SHEILA HARRIS hsheila10@yahoo.com

45. YEOMAN of Coverdale – William (1801), Timothy (1836) and Christopher (1883)

Chris YEOMAN

In 1800 there were a number of YEOMAN families living in or near Coverdale. Many of them were related and they also had large families. In the next 150 years almost all had moved away. This is a brief story of one family who moved to the south of England and then one son and his family migrated to Western Australia.

William YEOMAN was born in Braidley, Coverham to parents Christopher YEOMAN and Mary (SPENCE) in 1801. William married Mary SPENSLEY in 1831. William and Mary baptised their first three children William, Mary and Timothy at Askrigg while living at Nappa Scar and Woodhall where William worked as a farm hand. By 1837 they had moved to Coverdale and lived at the Ashes near Caldbergh. They had ten children with two not surviving infancy.

In 1850 William, the eldest son aged 16, died after three weeks of typhus – *"Erysipilas Typhus."*

Timothy was 14 yrs old and not long afterwards moved away to work on other farms all in the dales area. He married Mary Ann WALLS (1843) in 1860 at the Northallerton Registry Office. Timothy and Mary Ann registered the births of five children at Redmire, Richmond, Downholme, Dalton and Appleton. In 1875 they had left the dales and had a son Arthur (1875) and daughter Margaret (1878) at Egerton Lancashire. In 1881 the family was in Poynton Cheshire when Edith was born. Christopher (1883) and Minnie (1885) were born in Woodham Ferrers near Chelmsford Essex.

By 1891 Timothy, Mary Ann and the youngest five children were in Essex at Saffron Waldon. Their eldest daughter Mary Elizabeth married Charles EATON at Chelmsford and stayed there. Timothy Jr. and Alfred were in Horsham in Sussex whilst William was married and living in Southampton. The family continued this drift south with Timothy senior and younger children all in Sussex by 1901.

Christopher and his brothers all worked at various farming jobs such as *dairyman, farmhand* or *farm bailiff* like their father. Christopher married Ellen HOWARD (1881) at Patcham Sussex in 1904. Three daughters were born at Brighton Sussex Helen (Dolly) in 1905, Bessie in 1907 and finally Christine 1908.

Christopher served in the Royal Naval Volunteer Reserve at Hove while living in Sussex. Christopher emigrated to Western Australia arriving in Fremantle on the *Ophir* on 3rd May 1910 with his wife Ellen and three daughters.

On arriving in Fremantle Christopher applied for a virgin block of land and was granted land seven miles from Merredin approximately 165 miles from Perth. The family built a house from bush wood and hessian with a corrugated iron roof. It was extremely hard to feed a family in this situation so Christopher left his land and took a job with the railways. Later they moved to work on Duff's farm.

In 1912 whilst living and working on Duff's farm, Ellen was pregnant with twins. Together with her three young children and her sister Edie she moved to Cottesloe in Perth until the twins were born on 23rd February 1912 and named Isobel and Christopher. In April the family was living back on the farm in very poor conditions when baby Christopher died. He was buried on Duff's farm as recorded in *"Lonely Graves of Western Australia"* by Yvonne and Kevin COATE. Aunty Dolly reported that the death was very hard for the whole family.

Another son Arthur was born 1914. In July 1915 Christopher enlisted in the Army and served in France as a *Lance Corporal/Driver*, serving in 11th Battalion 3rd Brigade in World War I, not returning until June 1919. Arthur was five years old when his father returned from the war. While he was away Ellen and the children moved to the city and the older children were able to go to school. Christopher survived the war physically unscathed and on his return again went to work at South Kumminin and again on new uncleared land. They built a weatherboard house with a wood stove in the kitchen. The kitchen had a dirt floor but the other rooms had floor boards. Christopher named his farm Mouquet Farm after a place he been during the war in France. William (1920) and Mary (1924) were born after the war. After 6 years the family left the wheat belt area of Western Australia with its dry hot summers and cold winters and travelled for a week to Pemberton. The Western Australian government of the day was offering Land Settlement schemes in the south west.

The family moved to Pemberton where they found very large trees and land they had to clear by hand. The climate was cold and damp, not unlike southern England. The farm was near the town of Pemberton so the children were able to attend school walking 2 miles each way. The family also moved to a Land Settlement place at Manjimup but eventually moved to the city.

When World War II started Christopher saw his two sons Arthur and William (Bill) both enlist so he recorded his age as five years younger and joined also! He served at Head Quarters Detail Camp for a period of 250 days when he was discharged at his own request. Christopher was unwell and died of stomach cancer in December 1943 aged sixty. Everyone who had known him spoke well of him and he was very good with animals. Taking care of horses during the war was his job in the army.

Farming during the early years in Australia was extremely hard work with many not succeeding.

DOROTHY YEOMAN Western Australia Dorothy@yeoman.com

46. MORLAND of Hawes in Wensleydale and RAISBECK of Langthwaite in Arkengarthdale

Thomas MORLAND Margaret (née RAISBECK) with children
Thomas Wilfrid, Vivian and Margaret c. 1886-88

My grandfather used to boast (with a twinkle in his eye) that he was a Liverpudlian. I couldn't understand this as we lived in South London and, as far as I knew, his childhood had been in Surrey and Worcestershire. Thomas Wilfrid Raisbeck MORLAND (1876-1968) was proud to have his mother's maiden name, just as I am to have my mother's as a middle name. His father, Thomas MORLAND (1843-1904), was the twelfth child of Leonard MORLAND (1786-1868) who worked as a *farmer/ corn miller* in Hawes. Leonard was born in Dent and probably inherited his trade from his father since there were several mills in Dent valley in the 18th century. The site of Leonard's mill (now the Conservative club) is still visible by Gayle Beck in the centre of Hawes and the builder's stone dates it as 1831. Leonard had four children by his first wife Hannah SCARR: George, Ann, Phebe and Hannah. His second wife Hannah HOLME bore him ten children: Joseph, John, Leonard, Nancy, Matthew, Abraham, Robert, Thomas, Esther and Sarah.

My great-grand mother, Margaret RAISBECK (1848-1889), was born into a lead-mining family in Arkengarthdale. Margaret grew up in the Old School House at Langthwaite (across Arkle Beck from Scarr House) with two brothers and four sisters. At that time there were several Raisbeck families living in Arkengarthdale and there is also a connection to the Isle of Man. RAISBECKs gradually departed from Arkengarthdale and probably the last survivor was 92 year old Mary RAISBECK who died in 1985. My great-great-grandparents William and Margaret are buried in the churchyard at St Mary's, Langthwaite. The discovery of their substantial headstone was my first tangible link with my dales heritage.

The connection between these two dales families is strengthened by the fact that not only did Thomas marry Margaret but an older brother, Abraham, married her sister Elizabeth. It was these liaisons which eventually gave the clue to the Liverpool connection. In 1864 Abraham and Elizabeth married in West Derby and Thomas and Margaret were married there in 1875. This was the beginning of the migration of the MORLAND sons. By 1851 the eldest son George was married and had set up in Hawes as a *flour dealer*. A decade later John, now 30, was working as a *book-keeper* in Everton, married to Jane, a Liverpool girl. Younger brother Robert had also moved to Tranmere, Birkenhead and was working as a *measurer of ships' cargoes.* As a master stevedore he employed others and lived in fashionable Toxteth Park with his Lancashire wife and seven daughters, two of whom became *school governesses.* Matthew had probably left home by 21. He turned up in Everton working as an *earthenware dealer,* married to a Scotswoman, Margaret, by whom he had a son Frederick. By the turn of the century he was recorded as a *coal agent* in West Derby where four daughters had been added to the family: Frederick was a *hosier's shop assistant,* Margaret a *butcher's book keeper,* Janet a *milliner,* Alice *an apprentice to a draper,* and Agnes was still at school.

In the 1861 Census patriarch Leonard, aged 74, was described as an *agricultural labourer* as was 18 year old Thomas. I imagine my great-grandfather would have learned to work with animals during this time, giving him the grounding for his later career. Father was perhaps just keeping his hand in since sons Joseph and Abraham are named in that year as *corn millers.* Abraham however soon made his way westwards and established himself in the Liverpool docks, eventually becoming a *master stevedore* and setting up home in West Derby. Leonard died in 1868 and I have a sense that once he was gone any attempt to maintain a family business had finally collapsed. Although Joseph carried on alone, living now in Townfoot in Hawes, a decade later he too had joined the others in Liverpool. There was still a tenuous link: he worked as a *baker and flour dealer* in Everton, living with wife Alice and sons Leonard and John.

By 1867 Abraham and Elizabeth had two daughters, Margaret and Anita. Clearly Elizabeth and her sister Margaret were close and spent time together. Whether Thomas and Margaret had already become acquainted back in the Dales or whether their courtship developed through visits to Liverpool is not known. What is certain is that my great-grandfather turned out to be the most adventurous of all the sons. At the age of 28, Thomas was living at 137 Marine Parade, Brighton, Sussex, employed as a *servant-coachman.* In the same year Margaret RAISBECK was living in Everton with her sister Ellen who was married to greengrocer and fruiterer John THACHWAY. Four years on Thomas married Margaret in West Derby, presumably supported by his brother Abraham, sister-in-law Elizabeth, and others of the Morland family now permanently established on Merseyside.

My grandfather was born a year later (1876) at 17 Clifton Road, West Derby, the home of Abraham and Elizabeth. On the birth certificate his father Thomas is described as a coachman, though whether he was working as such in Liverpool is not known. Only two years later Elizabeth was dead at the young age of 38 and by 1881 Thomas had returned south and set up home at Barrowhedge Farm, Carshalton, Surrey with Margaret and young Thomas and the addition of my great uncle Vivian and great aunt Margaret both of whom I remember well. Thomas continued to work as a coachman and they later moved to Pull Court in Upton-on-Severn, Worcestershire. My grandfather often told me how he walked several miles across the meadows to the Abbey School in Tewkesbury. His mother Margaret died at Upton in 1889 aged only 41. Young Thomas worked as a *gardener* at Goodrich. His father re-married and had two more daughters by Emma DRINKWATER who were born in Bushley, Gloucestershire and Mudiford, Hampshire. The family eventually settled in Lancaster Mews, Richmond, Surrey, where father Thomas had risen in status as a *riding stable master.* Great uncle Viv followed in his father's steps and became a *riding school master.* Much later he became chairman of the Royal Richmond Horse Show. Grandfather became a qualified *surveyor* and worked for the London County Council apart from 1917-19 when he went into the Royal Engineers and was posted to Palestine. His Dorsetshire wife, Louisa Sarah, died four years after his return from the Great War. He never remarried but had an active life as a sportsman and horticulturist. At heart he was a countryman. Although he never went to Wensleydale, something of that rural way of life was an essential part of him.

COLIN MORLAND NASH 11 School Cottages, Church Road, Crockenhill, Kent BR8 8JY
nashcol@googlemail.com

47.   Ninion THWAITE from Mossdale Head to Liverpool

Ninion THWAITE, son of James in West Derby, Liverpool

Ninion THWAITE was baptised on 17th January 1863 at Mallerstang, near Kirkby Stephen. Ninion was the fourth child of James THWAITE.

His father had grown up at Mossdale Head, near Hawes, marrying the girl from the farm next door, Elizabeth METCALFE, when he was 23. James's brother, Simon, married Elizabeth's sister. (I have a feeling they didn't get out much!)

James moved to Mallerstang to run his own farm and proceeded to produce six children – Agnes, Isabella, Simon, Ninion, James and Alexander.

Ninion's forename is an unusual one. He was named after his maternal grandfather, Ninion METCALFE. Ninion is definitely a "METCALFE" name. Many with this unusual Christian name in Yorkshire and Lancashire seem to be descendants of Ninion METCALFE.

James farmed at Compston Hill in Mallerstang until 1872 when, for some unknown reason, he decided to auction off his farm stock and move to Liverpool. Why did he go? Was the farm failing to thrive? Did the proximity of the railway lure him to the city? Did he believe there was a better living to be had in Liverpool? Whatever the reason, James auctioned off his belongings for the sum of £408 and transferred his family to the city.

James set up as a *cow keeper* in West Derby, Liverpool. Many dales men moved to the cities at this time to make their living as cow keepers. Milk had been turning sour on its journey by rail to Liverpool, and keeping cows in yards in the city seemed a much better idea.

I do not know how James and his children found their new life; whether it was everything they had hoped for. James must have had some regrets however, when, less than two years after moving to the city, three of his children, Agnes aged 18, Isabella aged 16 and James aged only nine all contracted typhoid and died within the space of a week. They were all buried at Hardraw, the family's home parish, Isabella on the 19th April 1874, and Agnes and James five days later. Although I know there are many examples of infant deaths among my ancestors, I do believe that the death of three children that were so much a part of this family must have been devastating. This must have been a very difficult time for the family but they chose to remain in West Derby, continuing to keep cows.

Ninion, James' son, followed in the family tradition, choosing to work with animals. He continued to live in West Derby and became a *coachman*. I have several photos of Ninion sitting proudly on the driver's seat of his coach. He married Martha TOMLINSON and had two daughters, Mary Elizabeth in 1898 and Agnes in 1906, before his wife died prematurely in 1908 at the age of 36, leaving Ninion with the care of two small girls.

Ninion died in 1930 without returning to the dales. In later years he worked as a *domestic gardener*, staying true to his family's farming roots. His brother Simon (known as Tom) became a *shepherd* in Whiston and Tarbock, just outside Liverpool.

Mary married the boy next door John Philip SMITH. Mary Elizabeth THWAITE developed a strong sense of family loyalty and interest in her dales roots. She diligently kept records of her father's baptism, her parents' marriage certificate, old photos (unfortunately not always labelled) and notes she had written about her father's family. She kept in touch with her cousins (Simon's descendants) and also more distant cousins such as Ninion THWAITE, a second cousin, who was known to us as *"Uncle Nin"* and lived just outside Liverpool. I have happy memories of collecting apples on his farm as a child and climbing on the hay bales in the barn. She kept lists of names of another THWAITE family, headed by Richard THWAITE, who ran a dairy in Liverpool and to whom she was sure she was related. This was correct, albeit it a distant relative.

She also had a very old postcard sent by a *"cousin Simon"*, who, it turned out was actually a cousin of her grandfather, James.

Mary Elizabeth THWAITE passed the name Ninion to her son. It is my uncle's middle name and he is often asked about the origin of his unusual name. Ninion THWAITE, James and their descendants did not return to the dales to live, but those of us who have managed to visit agree it is a beautiful place and we are proud of our dales roots.

GILL HOLMES holmgilli@aol.com

48. METCALFEs from Ivelet Heads, Swaledale to Stainmore

One of the many METCALFE families in the dales was that of George and his wife Ann (HARKER) living at Ivelet Heads in Swaledale in the early 1800s. Their eldest daughter Jane, baptised in 1808 when George and Ann were living at Heights (about a mile east of Gunnerside) was my great great grandmother. Of George and Ann's eight children, two moved to Stainmore farms and they and their growing children quickly took over South Stainmore. The eight were:

1. Jane 1808-1892 married *gamekeeper* James SPENCELEY (1838 Coverham);

2. Thomas 1811-1848 married Mary PRATT 1835;

3. Robert 1813-1868 an unmarried *schoolmaster*, lived at Calvert Houses with his widowed sister Elizabeth.

4. Elizabeth (Betty) 1814-1888. Before her marriage to *miner/farmer* Thomas DUNN in 1849 she had a son John (b. 1840). See Chapter 49 for Betty's story.

5. Rosamund (Rosey) 1817-1879 married Calvert Houses *farmer* John COATES 1841 moved to Stainmore.

6. George 1819-1887 married his brother's widow Mary 1849;

7. Margaret (Peggy) 1824-1863 married *lead miner* John FAWCETT 1852; Peggy died in 1863 and John children went to Wisconsin in 1865 (see chapter 71).

8. Mary Ann 1821- a *straw hat maker* in 1851, married *lead miner* (but later *landowner and farmer*) William BUXTON in 1844;

In 1838 Jane married James SPENCELEY, a twice-widowed *gamekeeper* born in 1799 at Feetham Holme, son of James and Rosamond SPENCELEY (née MASON, of Hardraw). James and Jane spent much of their married lives at Widdymans in Coverdale, where James worked for Sir William CHAYTOR. His appearances at the local magistrates' court, prosecuting poachers, were reported in the local newspapers. As well as James' two daughters from his previous marriages, they had four other children: Ann who died as a child, William Mason who became a *policeman*, Ann who married Isaac WINTER, and George who went into service. He retired to breed horses in Harrogate, having first been *valet* to a future Prime Minister and subsequently *butler* to close friends of the Prince of Wales.

Ann died in 1881, leaving seven young children – including my grandfather James Spenceley WINTER (1871-1938). In 1883 Isaac married Ann's cousin and Jane's niece Ann BUXTON (another granddaughter of George and Ann METCALFE). James SPENCELEY had died in 1878 and when Jane finally died in 1892 Isaac and his second Ann moved to Otterburn Hall near Gargrave. Isaac (1844-1901) and three of his unmarried children Wilson (1869-99), Isaac (1878-99) and Rosamond (1880-95) were buried together in Kirkby Malham churchyard. Isaac and Ann's surviving children were John Francis (1875-1916), an unwilling schoolboy, truanting young poacher, and keen ornithologist, whose experimental incubators eventually enabled him to send healthy pure-bred chicks by rail around the country from his Craven Poultry Farm at Bell Busk; Mary Jane (1873) who married *farmer* Charles RICKARDS of Bell Busk and Annie (1876) who married Joseph WHITELL in Clitheroe, 1912.

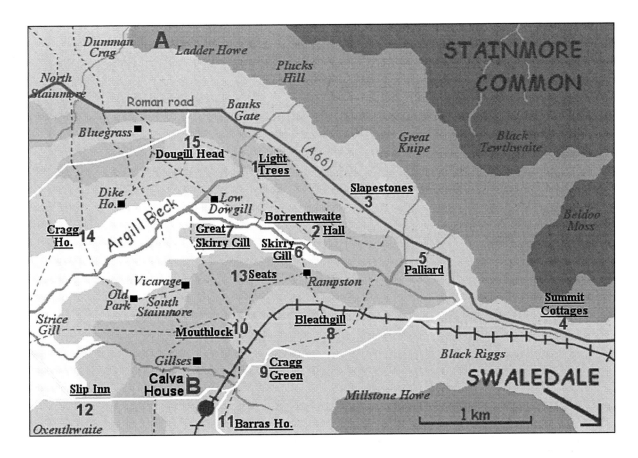

This map shows the neighbourliness of these families on Stainmore between about 1860 and the 1900s. Our editor's ancestral Cumpstone House is at A. My ancestral home of Calva House is marked B, where *farmer* William WINTER's family included son Isaac, who later married two of the METCALFE girls.

In the list below I have identified everyone by their relationship to Jane METCALFE or her son-in-law Isaac WINTER.

1. Light Trees. Margaret Ann (b. 1837 Ivelet Heads, daughter of Jane's brother Thomas METCALFE and Mary) and her husband *farmer* Isaac TALLENTIRE lived here from 1866 to 1892, when Isaac died. By 1901 Margaret had moved to live with her brother George at Little Musgrave.

2. Borrenthwaite Hall (later Barrenthwaite) was where 16-year-old Ann SPENSLEY was a *housemaid* in the 1861 census. Evidence suggests that she was my great-grandmother-to-be Ann SPENCELEY, daughter of James and Jane, born at Widdymans in 1845 and niece of Jane's sister Rosamond COATES, long settled at Palliot farm, half a mile away. This Ann was the only one born in Yorkshire of the right age in that census, and this was the only way in which she could have met Isaac WINTER of Calva House. Isaac's father was a *farmer*. In the early 1860s Isaac was working for the new railway company that had just built the line – including the infamous Belah viaduct and Barras station, just up the hill from Calva House. Isaac and Ann married in 1868.

3. Slapestones was the home of *farmer* William COATES (b. 1870 at Stainmore, grandson of Jane's sister Rosamond) and his wife Ada from about 1895 to 1901.

4. Summit Cottages close to the railway summit, was where Ann (b. COATES 1845, daughter of Jane's sister Rosamond) and her husband John BOUSFIELD lived from 1865. In the 1871 and 1881 censuses John was a *platelayer and Methodist lay preacher*. By 1891 the family had moved to West Derby (Liverpool), where John was a *cow keeper* with premises at 21 and 23 Albert Street.

5. Palliard was called Palliott in the early censuses. The farm of Jane's sister Rosamond (Rosey, b. 1817 Calvert Houses) and her *farmer* husband John COATES, from about 1861 to 1880, then of their son *farmer* George COATES (b. 1850, Stainmore, m. Nancy WHITELL of Low Oxnop 1882) from 1880. Some time after 1891 George and Nancy moved to a farm at Orton.

6. and 7 see below

7. Skirry Gill and Great Skirry Gill. One of these farms was home to Jane's brother *farmer* George METCALFE (b. 1818 Calvert Houses) and his wife Mary (who had first been married to George's brother Thomas) from about 1858 to 1887, when they both died. By 1891 their son James Robert had taken over one of the farms and Thomas METCALFE (George's stepson) was at the other one.

8. Bleathgill was the farm that Ann BUXTON wrote about to her cousin Ann FAWCETT out in Iowa (see chapter 49). Ann's father William BUXTON moved there from Ivelet Heads with Ann and her two *farmer* brothers William and George some time around 1881.

9. Cragg Green was the first local home of Isaac WINTER's sister Annie (b 1847 Stainmore) and her husband James HALL in 1881, when James was also a *railway company employee*. William WINTER, father of Isaac and Ann, lived with Ann and James until he died there in 1885.

10. Mouthlock was where Mary (daughter of Isaac's sister Annie HALL) and her husband Robert CLEASBY, *cattle dealer*, lived in 1901.

11. Barras House was the home of *farmer* Richard BRUNSKILL (b. 1832 Stainmore) and his two sisters. Richard married Isaac WINTER's sister Jane in 1874, when Jane was 44. Jane had spent much of her adult life visiting and caring for her mother's sister, the unmarried and wealthy Jane WILSON. Jane died in 1889 and by 1891 Richard was a *carter*, living with his farming sisters at Slip Inn.

12. Slip Inn By 1901, this was the third local home for Isaac's sister Annie and her husband James HALL, still a railway signalman.

13. Seats was possibly the home of the younger Thomas METCALFE between 1881 and 1891 (see Ann's letter), and certainly the second local home of Annie and James HALL in 1891, when James was a *signalman and farmer*.

14. Cragg House home of *farmer* Christopher COATES (b. 1842 Calvert Houses, son of Jane's sister Rosamond) and his wife Margaret (WILLAN b. Stainmore) from 1869. They had moved to Dufton.

15. Dougill Head was the home of Elizabeth (b. COATES 1847 at Stainmore, daughter of Jane's sister Rosamond) and her *farmer* husband Joseph NICHOLSON.

MARION HEARFIELD, Stroud, Gloucestershire
marion@hearfieldresearch.com website: http://www.johnhearfield.com/Marion.htm

49. Correspondence between two granddaughters of George BUXTON (born 1780) and Ann (HARKER) (born 1786) of Calvert Houses

Ann BUXTON in Gunnerside to Annie FAWCETT in Iowa.

Letter from Ann BUXTON

Ann BUXTON was the daughter of Mary Ann METCALFE born 1821 at Ivelet and William BUXTON born in 1815 at Gunnerside (transcript from John Winter, cousin of Marion Hearfield.) Ann BUXTON married widower Isaac WINTER of Stainmore in 1883. They lived at Calva House, the WINTER family home on Stainmore, and then moved to Otterburn Hall. Isaac's first wife was Ann SPENCELEY, daughter of gamekeeper James SPENCELEY born in 1799 in Grinton and Jane METCALFE born 1806 at Ivelet Heads. One of their children – James Spenceley WINTER – was my great-grandfather.

Ann SPENCELEY had married Isaac 1868 in East Ward, Westmorland. She was working at Borrenthwaite Hall in 1861. In 1871 she was having her second child in Dodworth, near Barnsley at the "mysterious great clan gathering" of the Spenceleys. The fact that she married at East Ward and not Coverham suggests that the Spenceleys had already left Widdymans in Coverdale before 1868. Other brothers of James, Richard and Mason, had emigrated to the USA. In the 1871 census James and Jane SPENCELEY were briefly in Dodworth, living near his coal-miner brother Thomas who had left Swaledale much earlier. They soon returned to live with their son-in-law Isaac at Calva House, and both died there.

"Ivelet Heads October 27th 1880

Dear Cousin,

We are all well except Father – he is not strong. Perhaps you will know that Cousin Mary Jane SUNTER (daughter of Rosey COATES née METCALFE) is dead. She died soon after Christmas, also Uncle John COATES [husband of Rosey née METCALFE] is dead. He died last June so you see what changes there is in the family. Old Jeffrey and Jeffrey Thomas THEAKSTONE [some THEAKSTONE mining neighbours in Ivelet but no Jeffrey] are dead. I think we shall be leaving Calvert Houses in the spring.

We have taken a farm on Stainmore near Uncle George [METCALFE, Jane's brother]. We have taken about 300 sheep this fall belonging to the place. We shall perhaps milk 9 or 10 cows and bring up a good few young calves. Also Cousin John METCALFE [Betty's son] has taken a larger farm, will be leaving in the Spring. They have taken his wife's mother's farm [at Ellerton Abbey], perhaps will milk 16 cows and bring a good few of calves up – also Cousin John and Robert COATES [sons of Rosey née METCALFE] has taken another farm further down Westmoreland.

Cousin George COATES [Rosey's son] is staying on Palliet Farm. They are going to divide themselves also Cousin Thomas METCALFE [Thomas's son] has taken a farm nearer to Uncle George. I think he will have a house keeper to hire so we shall be all away from the old place. We had sister Hannah [now wife of Edward SUNTER] from Liverpool a few weeks ago. We had Uncle and Cousins here from Stainmore this Fair. Brother William is on Stainmore at present. I think they are all well. Aunt Betty is all well. She has two little boys, and is in a fair way for another little one [I can't identify who this is, unless Ann means her Aunt Betty DUNN who had two grand-sons with another baby due – she did look after them. I do not think Hannah's father had a sister called Elizabeth]. John HARKER has been very poorly but is going about again. John HARKER's brother William [there was more than one such pair of brothers in the 1871 Swaledale censuses] is coming to Aunt Betty's farm and George ALTON is coming to ours in the Spring [Was this the Heights neighbours George and Rosamond taking over the BUXTON farm at Calvert Houses?]

Aunt Betty's farm they have taken is called Ellerton – about four miles below Reeth [I think Ann means that her aunt Betty DUNN is going to be at the same farm as her son John METCALFE and his wife Annie née BELL, who are in the later census for Ellerton Abbey]. John's wife's mother, sisters and brothers is going to a very large farm not so far off London How is John and George [Ann's brothers?] getting on. Oh how I should like to see you all again. Whether that will ever be or not I cannot tell but we may all meet in heaven where there will be no parting again that will be the best meeting.

Father Brother's joins me in love to you all from your Cousin Ann BUXTON"

Letter from Annie FAWCETT

Annie was the daughter of Margaret [Peggy] METCALFE born in 1824 at Ivelet Heads and John FAWCETT born 1826 at Gunnerside. Peggy died in 1863 at Calvert Houses. John and the children emigrated to Wisconsin in 1865. The children were John FAWCETT born 1853, Ann FAWCETT born 1855 and George Metcalfe FAWCETT born 1860

"Alexandria December 20th 1880" [USA – there is an Alexandria in Missouri, just south of the Iowa state border]

"Dear Cousin Ann.

I received your unexpected letter some four weeks ago. I had given up ever hearing from you again if I were to follow your example I ought not to answer this before 18 or 20 months, if I am not mistaken but I hope and trust you will try to do better this next time to your orphan cousin out in the territories. No I had not heard of cousin Mary SUNTER's death it is news to Uncle John COATES and me is dead to. I would like to have one of their cards each if it is convenient to you and send me one. We are all well at present and hope these few lines will find you the same. Time makes lots of changes even in a little place like Ivelet Heads if I were to come back I would find some changes I suppose. I can tell you the 20 months we have been out here is a good many changes we had to go six miles to town for a while but at first sixty-four miles. Now we have just as good a town two miles from us the name of it is Alexandria. The railroad comes in and brings the mail twice a day, and we have a first class market to.

We all like to hear it out here very well so far I think some of you had better come out here and get some farms of your own, then you would not have to rent and pay the rent. But it is selling up real fast around here and the land is good out here and grass is good, stock does well. We have 31 head of cattle and 6 head of horse we are getting along as well as can be expected of us. Will send you a picture of my new sowing machine I got this spring. I don't know if it is anything like yours or not we are having nice weather at present it was quiet cold in November. I don't know theses few lines will be interesting to you or not for I can't think of much to write you. I would like very much to hear from you once in a while and the old place. Remember me to any that may think of me if there be.

As ever your affectionate cousin A FAWCETT

> *Wherever you go may contentment be your lot*
> *And fortune like Ivey encircle your plot*
> *May each rosy morning be dressed in mantles of peace*
> *Bring light to thy dwelling your gladness increase.*

Is the wish of your cousin in the west Please write soon if this letter is worth answer. Wishing you all a merry Christmas and a happy New Year so I must come to a close for this time. Annie"

These letters have been reproduced thanks to George Buxton, who originally sent me the transcripts and agreed to their inclusion.

MARION HEARFIELD, Stroud, Gloucestershire
marion@hearfieldresearch.com website: http://www.johnhearfield.com/Marion.htm

50. Two PEACOCK cousins from Swaledale

1. Harker PEACOCK Grinton to London 1838 – 1898

Harker was born about 1838 in Reeth and was the illegitimate son of Elizabeth PEACOCK. In the 1841 census, Harker was living with his grandmother Jane PEACOCK at Providence Cottage, Grinton. By 1851 Harker and his grandmother had moved into the Woodyard at Grinton.

Harker is not recorded on the 1861 and 1871 census but he does remerge in Chelsea, London for his marriage to Fanny NOYES on the 8th February 1871 at St. Saviours Parish Church, living in St Martin's parish. His occupation was recorded as *valet*.

Harker was a *publican* living at 18a Clarence Road, Camden when his daughter Adelaide was baptised on 7th July 1872. He had moved down the road by the 14th Dec 1873 to 41 Clarence Road when his second daughter Fanny was baptised. Harker was recorded as *a licensed victualler* living at that time. His third daughter was baptised on 27th Sept 1874 when Harker was a publican at The Victory on Clarence Road.

In *The Book of Household Management* by Isabella Beeton, 1861 she gave a description of the duties of a valet – they received orders from their master, dressed them, accompanied them on all their journeys, they needed a polite manner, modest demeanour and a respectful reserve. The average yearly wage of a valet in 1861 was £25 – £50 when not found in Livery, or when found in Livery £20 – £30.

In 1881 Harker became a widower looking after his three daughters Adelade aged nine, Fanny aged eight and Florence aged six. Harker seemed to do well for himself as a *licensed victualler* and the family was living at 20 Fetter Lane, St. Dunstan in the West, Middlesex, London. Living with the family was Alice JACKSON a *nursemaid* whom I presume was there to look after his daughters, plus a *cook* Edith JACKSON.

Harker continued as a *licensed victualler* but as *manager/servant* living at 79 Grosvenor Square, St George Hanover Square in London in the 1891 census. Harker died on the 21st September 1898 and was buried with his wife Fanny at Norwood Cemetery, Lambeth.

2. William PEACOCK Reeth to Bacup, Lancashire 1865 – 1906

William was born about 1865 in Reeth and was the eldest son of Horn PEACOCK and Margaret GILL. His brother John was a year younger than him.

In 1871 William, his widowed mother and brother were living in Reeth. The family was still in Reeth in the 1881 census when William was recorded as a 15 year old learning the trade of a *blacksmith*. The *Victorian Times* describes a blacksmith taking up to six years to learn his trade, resulting in the skills to make and repair farm tools and other household items. The blacksmith worked in a hot and grimy smithy and remained independent. In the early 1880s the blacksmith was considered as "the master of all trades."

In 1891 William had moved to 3 Rochdale Road, Spotland, Bacup, Lancashire and was lodging with the BREEMAN family. He was then 25 years old and his apprenticeship as a *blacksmith* was over. In 1891 William married Ellen GILLDUFF. The couple moved to 6 Quarry St, Bacup, in 1901 with their four children and William's occupation on the 1901 census was *blacksmith shoeing*. William died at the young age of 43 in the autumn of 1906.

NAOMI APPLEBY naomi.appleby63@btinternet.com

Editor's note: Naomi has embroidered a sampler for the exhibition showing these PEACOCK cousins. See page 113

51. The HEBDEN family from Wharfedale

The HEBDEN family today certainly enjoys a rich mixture of bloodlines, including Saxon and Viking, and the ancestry is complicated and incomplete. Variations of the name include: Hebdon, Hebdin, Hepden, Ebden, Ebdon, and Epton. The name HEBDEN is made up of two components "Hep" or Hip – for a Wild Rosehip and "Denu" – Old English for a wooded valley. Hence Hepden means "a valley where rosehips grow".

The actual name is tied to the location of Hebden, a village in Wharfedale, North Yorkshire. The variations in the name occur largely because of local accents and recording before standardised spelling became the norm in the late 19th and early 20th centuries.

The HEBDEN name has been linked to the Wharfedale area since earliest times, and over the years offshoots of the family have grown up in Burnsall, Conistone, Cracoe, Appletreewick, Stalling Busk and many towns and villages in the area. Most HEBDENs living today will have some connection with one of these early family lines.

The Mediaeval family took their name from the manor of HEBDEN now a village in Wharfedale, which they had been granted. They were of Saxon descent, marrying well and acquiring property in Lincolnshire.

Two main descendants have been found from Ripon in the late 16th Century, the first via Hampsthwaite, Appletreewick, Lofthouse in Nidderdale and London to New South Wales and Queensland in Australia.

The Grimwith line, first mentioned as tenants of Bolton Abbey were at Grimwith above Burnsall until 1841 when Grimwith was sold by John HEBDEN who moved to Dublin. He intended his only son, another John, for the law, but he became ordained instead. After working in Cheshire and Macclesfield he emigrated to Australia.

My own family was in Raydale from 1690 until the late 19th century, having come over the hill from Oughtershaw in Langstrothdale. My grandfather, Joseph was the youngest of five surviving boys of 13 children, who all left at various times for Burnley.

The eldest was Robert, who started a business there called HEBDEN Brothers, a major car dealership which is now sold.

John moved to Batley on joining the West Riding Constabulary, rising to *sergeant*.

Joseph started a grocery business after the woman he wanted to marry said she would marry a grocer but not a grocer's assistant. They later sold bicycles, toys and motorcycles.

Back in Langstrothdale, other lines moved to Dent, via Ravenstonedale to Preston.

Before Parish Registers, the 1538 Muster Roll of Craven and Bowland, the 1524 Lay Subsidy Roll of Buckden and the 1499 Langstrothdale Rental showed the presence of HEBDENs from the 15th century.

A further line went from Conistone via Cracoe and Rylstone to Padiham, Blackburn and Bolton.

All the families before the 19th century had an individual naming pattern of Christian names, which is a useful guide to research.

JOHN HEBDEN hebden@one-name.org

52. Across the 'Gert Dub' – The LAIDMAN family from Redmire to Canada

The LAIDMAN family

Thomas LAIDMAN, born 1729 in Bowes, Yorkshire, married Ann BELL of Middleton in Teesdale, Durham in 1763. They had nine children; their third child born in 1768 was a daughter Martha, who was also known as Matty. Martha gave birth to an illegitimate son Samuel LAIDMAN who was baptized in Bowes on the 30th January 1790.

In Redmire, Wensleydale, Elizabeth PICKERSGILL, daughter of Richard and Margaret PICKERSGILL, was baptized on the 17th of February 1788. Richard was a *joiner* by trade.

In March 1795 Thomas LAIDMAN, who had by then moved from Bowes to Wanleys, a farm in West Witton, died, followed the next month by the death of his sixteen year old son, also named Thomas. Thomas senior had written his will on January the 29th 1795 in which he refers to himself as *'but sickly and weak as to my body'*. He notes lands and property he still owned in Bowes and among the bequests he leaves twenty pounds and *'furniture sufficient for a room'* to Martha.

Wanleys, now known as Wanlass, lies on the south bank of the river Ure. Redmire is on the north side and it is possible to cross the river at various points by the way of fords. There are two adjacent farms in West Witton overlooking the river – High and Low Wanlass.

Martha LAIDMAN and her brother Mark were recorded in Edmund PEACOCK's book on *Methodism in Wensleydale* as members of the West Witton Methodist Society in 1808. Mark was the leader of the West Witton group and was instrumental in setting up meeting houses in West Witton and Aysgarth.

Martha's son Samuel married Elizabeth PICKERSGILL from Redmire on the 14th of May 1812. Their first child Thomas was born in 1813; Marmaduke followed in 1814 and Mark was baptized in Bowes in 1816. The family then moved to Wensleydale because their fourth child Joseph was baptized in West Witton in 1819. Over the next few years five more children, Samuel, Margaret, Martha, Richard and Elizabeth were born at regular intervals.

In 1830 Samuel and Elizabeth LAIDMAN, then tenant farmers in West Witton, made the life changing decision to sail across the 'gert dub' to Canada with their nine children. In 1825 a total of 8,741 like minded British subjects emigrated to the North American colonies and by 1830 the numbers had risen dramatically to over 30,500. In the Dales incomes from lead mining suffered due to the importation of cheaper lead from Spain. Between 1826 and 1832 the price of lead dropped to £12 per ton – the price had been as high as £27 a ton after the Napoleonic Wars ended. Many miners from Swaledale emigrated in 1830. With poor prospects for the future livelihood of his large family the move to a land of plenty was hopefully a prosperous and successful one for the LAIDMAN family.

The ship set sail from Liverpool to New York on the 8th of August 1830 with the LAIDMAN family on board. The journey of 2,980 nautical miles took over forty days and finally they berthed in New York on the 20th September 1830. Despite the risk of disease and death the LAIDMAN family all survived the journey. The American writer Ralph Waldo EMERSON is quoted as saying 'The road from Liverpool to New York, as they who have traveled it well know, is very long, crooked, rough, and eminently disagreeable'

After arriving in New York the family made their way north to Lake Ontario where they spent their first winter on the Elijah Secord farm at Mount Albion. In June 1831 Mark LAIDMAN in West Witton wrote a letter to his nephew Samuel in Canada. It began 'Your long expected letter dated March 22nd arrived 28th April.' We can only imagine the concerns of the family in Wensleydale not knowing what was happening to their loved ones so far away. Samuel's mother Martha was living with her brother Mark at this time and there is talk in the letter of her wishing to join the family in America.

Samuel bought land at Binbrook from the Canada Company on Lot 25, concession 7. The land was cleared for building and crops and a log cabin was built to house the LAIDMANs. John Edward, a seventh son for Samuel and Elizabeth was born at the new homestead in Binbrook in 1833.

The LAIDMANs worked hard in Binbrook establishing a good life for the family and became respected members of the community. They were active Methodists as they had been in Yorkshire. Samuel and Elizabeth were keen to ensure that their children had a good future and that the land would provide employment. They understood also the importance of education. There was a receipt made out to Samuel LAIDMAN, 'July 8, 1837 to July 8, 1838, £4-15-0 for tuition for 3 children'. LAIDMAN descendants were teachers in schools in Binbrook into the 20th century.

A new homestead was built in 1848 near to the original log cabin. It is said that when Elizabeth LAIDMAN was an old woman she could stand out on her yard in the morning and look across the landscape and see the smoke coming from the chimneys of the homes of all of her ten children. It is also recorded in the family archives that Elizabeth had a rose bush growing by her front door that she had brought from her home faraway in Wensleydale. Subsequent generations of the LAIDMAN family enjoyed its fragrant blooms for over 100 years. Elizabeth LAIDMAN died on 6th of December 1862 and Samuel died four and a half years later on the 14th of April 1867. The intrepid pioneers from Wensleydale are buried in the Auld Kirk Cemetery, Binbrook, Ontario as are more than fifty other LAIDMAN family members.

In the Bowes Parish Register Samuel's illegitimate birth was recorded in 1790. His father's name is also recorded – James SAYER. If Samuels's parents had been married would there now be a Sayer Road in Hamilton, Ontario rather than Laidman Road which can be seen now?

Acknowledgements to Neil LAIDMAN, Nick Michael and the LAIDMAN family website. www.laidman.org and Maureen STONES

LIZ KIRBY lizkirby@hotmail.com

53. Thomas HOGG, Bandmaster

> The judge awarded the prize in this contest to Mr Thomas Hogg, conductor of the 4th Durham Artillery Volunteer Band, and assigned Mr Sydney and Mr Ramsey to the second and third places:
>
> Of Mr Hogg's playing the judge said that his style and quality of tone were very rich, the former being of a high order, and his phrasing being very correct, which carries no mean compliment. He also expressed himself as particularly pleased with his articulation, and his performances throughout he described as being of a first-class character.

The Northern Echo, 1874. The judge at this contest in Stockton, the publisher of the *Champion Brass Band Journal*, awarded Thomas HOGG the cornet solo prize for his playing of *Weber's Last Waltz*.

My great-uncle Thomas HOGG, born in Leyburn in 1845, was apprenticed to his father Thomas as a *carpenter* (see chapter 67), but was something of a child prodigy as a musician. He would have been twelve when in 1858 the *Ripon and Richmond Chronicle* said in a report on the Leyburn Brass Band: '*The most promising is a youth named Thomas HOGG, who is a perfect master of his instrument.*'

The following year, in a report on a band contest in Northumberland, *The Newcastle Courant* stated that '*The Leyburn Band......numbered only eleven performers, some of whom were only youths, but their taste and precision were much admired. It was confidently asserted that they would carry off some of the prizes; an assertion which was fully verified by the decision of the judges.*' They won the 3rd prize of £5, no mean sum 150 years ago and worth £215.80 in 2010. Then in early 1861, when he was just 15, the *Chronicle* reported that Thomas had risen to the dizzy heights of leader: '*The Leyburn Saxhorn Band commenced their summer evening playing on Friday last by performing a programme under the leadership of Mr T. HOGG.*'

Around that time he and his older brother John got another mention in the paper: '*Mr COOPER of the Agricultural Inn, Leyburn, gave his annual ball on Wednesday last.....The programme contained 21 dances, the musical part of which was executed in good style by Mr BLENKINSOP, Mr THEAKSTONE and Messrs. J. and T. HOGG, who each volunteered their services on this occasion.*'

In August 1863 the *Leeds Mercury* reported on a contest in Alexandra Gardens, Leeds. Leyburn Brass Band came 2nd among a long list of competitors, though the same month they were also-rans against 20 other bands at the Crystal Palace in London. The patronising reporter for *Lloyds Weekly Newspaper* found the musical invasion from towns he'd probably never heard of a terrible trial:

'*A brass band contest seems to demand judges with brass ears. To anyone not thus endowed it must be confessed that the incessant performances of more than twenty bands is apt to become monotonous...... although a host of provincials, fired with interest in the cause of their county or their town, patiently listened to the longest "selections."*'

At some point in the 1860s Thomas followed the example of his older brother John, his fellow band member at the ball in Leyburn, and moved to West Hartlepool. By the 1871 census he had become a *tobacconist* in Church Street, the main thoroughfare, where he lived with a *housekeeper*, Jane SUNTER, who was eleven years his senior. A few years later she was to become his wife. A Durham county directory gave Thomas the unusual job description of '*cigar importer and professor of music*'.

His musical career was indeed blossoming. The *Northern Echo* advertised to '*the Nobility, Clergy and Gentry of Darlington and neighbourhood*' his appearance as solo cornettist at a '*Grand Evening Concert*' in the Central Hall. Soon he was appointed *conductor* of the 4th Durham Volunteer Artillery Band. His younger brother William had joined him and was the band's *lead cornet player*. In July 1873 the *Northern Echo* reported that bands from Yorkshire, Durham and Northumberland competed at Stockton under the patronage of the local Licensed Victuallers' Association: '*The weather was extraordinarily hot and the rush to the only refreshment tent on the ground was continuous throughout the entire afternoon*'. As well as '*listening to the bands, eating buns and drinking liquors*' the thousands of spectators were offered added amusements, such as shooting galleries, archery, Aunt Sallies, fruit stalls and ice cream stands. More importantly Thomas HOGG and his band won the 1st prize of £20, of which some was no doubt spent in that refreshment tent and at the *al fresco* ball that followed.

In September, over on the west coast at Whitehaven, the bandmaster of the Royal Horse Guards gave Thomas 1st prize in the solo cornet competition for his playing of Arban's *Carnival de Venise*. The following year *The Era*, a national weekly paper covering the theatre, reported that Thomas's band '*enlivened proceedings*' at Barnard Castle Horticultural Show. Then in September Thomas won first prize in the solo competition at a contest on his home ground, playing Weber's *Last Waltz*. Noting his brother William's rendition of *My Lodging's on the Cold, Cold Ground* the *Northern Echo* described '*each air being accompanied with variations more or less florid.*'

But there was the occasional squall. At a West Hartlepool Council meeting Councillor TWEDDELL complained that, while the Durham Artillery Volunteers were in church, the band had spent the Sunday morning drinking in a public-house in Hartlepool. It seems probable that its conductor was in the pub with them, but happily for Thomas the complaint got nowhere. The Mayor didn't seem particularly shocked about it, ruling Mr TWEDDELL out of order for not giving notice that he was going to raise the matter.

In July 1875 bands from all over north-east England competed at West Hartlepool for a top prize of £20, owing to '*the enterprise of Mr Thomas HOGG*'. The following month at the West Hartlepool Flower Show the band '*performed a choice selection of music, including pieces by several of the great masters. Mr Thomas HOGG, the talented conductor, favoured the listeners with a solo on the cornet, which was heartily applauded. Indeed the musical performance, in the estimation of most persons, formed one of the great attractions of the occasion.*' In December Thomas '*gave selections on the cornet-à-piston*' in aid of the Hartlepool Hospital. But the following April he advertised no fewer than 15 times in the *Northern Echo* that the band, '*having resigned their connection with the Corps, have taken their original name, viz., Old Operatic Band, West Hartlepool*'. When the Artillery Volunteers later held a shooting contest a Mr BURNETT conducted the corps band, but Thomas's own band played as well (evidence of no ill-feelings over his departure). The weather was atrocious, but '*as one compensation, the ears of many people were regaled with some capital music*'.

The Old Operatic was soon in action at a Gala and Sports meeting near Darlington, '*contributing to the enjoyment of all under the able bandmaster, Mr Thomas HOGG*'. By August however, the *Northern Echo* reported a setback for the '*talented and enterprising conductor*'. He had organised a large-scale band contest, but the weather was against him, only four bands showed up, the public stayed at home and '*the venture, we are sorry to hear, will entail a loss to the promoters*'. Undaunted, later in the month he carried off first and second prizes in a contest at Seaham, conducting both the Old Operatic and another band.

Then in October 1880 Thomas moved to the far south of England. The *Hampshire Advertiser* stated that he had been appointed bandmaster of Southampton's 1st Hants Artillery Band: '*We understand that Mr HOGG, late bandmaster of the South Durham Artillery Militia, is a very fine leader, and, besides being a judge at many brass band contests, he is an eminent solo cornet player, having gained no less than sixteen cornets in single-handed contests. We congratulate the corps and town upon obtaining the services of so proficient a musician*'.

Disappointingly, apart from the 1881 census that is the last trace of Bandmaster HOGG and his family that I have found. I can only think they must have emigrated – a story in waiting.

JAMES HOGG JmsHogg@aol.com

54. SPENSLEY of Swaledale to Barnsley and the American Mid West

The hamlet of Feetham Holme, Swaledale, showing the three cottages

In the years immediately before their departure from Swaledale two branches of the SPENSLEY family lived in a hamlet called Feetham Holme, part of the large parish of Grinton in Swaledale. One of the branches was headed by James SPENSLEY, who had been born in Whitaside, the township in which Feetham Holme was situated, in either late 1772 or early 1773. His wife, Rose, had died in 1824, a year after giving birth for the fourteenth time (six of her children did not survive infancy).

Not all of James' sons and daughters made the move to the Barnsley area. His eldest son, James Jr., married in 1829 and may have already moved from Swaledale to nearby Coverdale before 1830. For a time he was a gamekeeper to Sir William CHAYTOR on his Coverdale estates. The second son, John, remained at Feetham Holme as a lead miner, the only member of either branch to do so.

The first member of James's family to be recorded in the Barnsley area was one of his younger sons, Thomas, whose marriage to Mary SHAW of Stainborough took place at Silkstone Parish Church in 1833. He lived for a time at Crane Moor Nook, between Wortley and Thurgoland. Eventually, with one of his sons, he settled in the expanding village of Dodworth, where he remained until his death in 1881. He was my great-great-grandfather.

William, Thomas's youngest brother, also migrated to the Barnsley area, possibly in 1832. Richard, much older than William and already married with a young family, remained in Swaledale until at least April 1835. At some point after that, he migrated to Stainborough, where he was certainly living in 1837 since one of his young sons died there at that time. As for William, he too migrated to Stainborough, possibly accompanied by his father, James, and sister, Margaret.

These three were recorded in the 1841 census at *'Dikeses', Stainborough,* two miles south west of Barnsley. In the SPENSLEY household James, then aged 68, was described as a *coal miner. 'Dikeses', or 'The Dykes',* as it was usually called, stood a few hundred yards to the west of Stainborough Fold (marked on modern large-scale maps) and a few hundred yards to the east of Stanhope Silkstone Main Colliery. It was a rectangular building, divided apparently into three, at the centre of a rectangular enclosure of half an acre and surrounded by small enclosed fields. There were five households at The Dykes at this time, with coal miners in four of them and a labourer in the other.

Two years before this census Richard had already emigrated from Stainborough to the United States. During the four years he had spent there, he had done well for himself if we can believe what his American biographer said about him:

> "…. one of the pioneers of the lead-mining region (of Iowa), was born in Yorkshire,… His early life was spent in the lead and coal mines of his native county, and for several years he held the responsible position of banksman in the famous Barnsley coal mines in that county."

His career in America was very successful – he purchased a lead smelting furnace near Galena, which he ran until his retirement.

Not long after they were recorded at Stainborough in the 1841 census, James, William and Margaret also emigrated, making their way to Dubuque, Iowa. James died there some five years later; Margaret settled in California after her marriage to a 'Mr RICHARDS', and William lived in South Dakota. Another son, Mason, also went out at about this time (1841). He married late in life, some years after his emigration. Some seven years after arriving he was able, jointly, to purchase 160 acres of land from the Government, and he too had a successful career in lead smelting. He also farmed in Grant County.

The second SPENSLEY branch living at Feetham Holme before 1830 was headed by George SPENSLEY. If the details on his burial record are correct he must have been born in 1772 or very early 1773. How George was related to James, the head of the other branch, is uncertain. He may have been the George, son of Jane SPENSLEY of Stubbins, Swaledale – no father is mentioned – whose baptism is recorded in 1778. If so he was a second cousin of James, sharing the same great-grandfather. This is the only possibility which has any support in the Grinton parish records.

This branch, which consisted of George, his mother-in-law, his wife Margaret, their three sons and at least two of their daughters, also migrated south to the Barnsley area. In 1833, the year in which not only George but also his mother-in-law and his youngest daughter all died, the family was living at Clappers or Claphouse, a group of connected cottages formed from what may originally have been a single building. It was a quarter of a mile south of Crane Moor Nook, and only a mile, as the crow flies, from The Dykes, where the other Spensley branch lived. By 1841 only three were living there: Margaret, George's widow and two of their unmarried sons. A son and daughter had married and moved a short distance away and another daughter had died when still a child. All three sons were to make a living as *coal or ironstone miners* in the immediate area. George briefly lived and worked at Pitsmoor, north of Sheffield, but later returned to the Wortley area. The lives of some of this branch are recounted by local historian Phyllis CROSSLAND in her book *Years of Grace: A Biographical Story of Life in a Rural Area of England, 1850-1973*, (Bridge Publications, 1985).

None of the above information about the migration of the SPENSLEYs from Swaledale to the Barnsley area in the 1830s appears to have been known to my father (born in Dodworth in 1907). He spoke, however, of some family tradition that certain Dodworth SPENSLEYs had gone north in search of work at some time in the second half of the 19th century. Having discovered the migration south from Swaledale in the 1830s, I initially thought that the tradition of which he spoke was simply a back-to-front version of what had actually happened in that earlier period.

Then I discovered that Thomas and his family had been joined in Dodworth in the 1860s by three close relatives from the north. They were his brother, James (the one who married three times), his third wife and their adult son. The two men had worked for a few years in the mining industry, James as a *coal leader (carter)* and his son as a *hanger-on* (the employee who hung containers on the rope at the pit bottom or pushed tubs of coal into the mine shaft cage). All three had later returned north. Was this return the source of the family tradition which my father recounted?

This is an abridged story and slightly amended version of one recorded in *"Moving Lives: Stories of Barnsley Families"* published by Barnsley Family History Society and reproduced with the permission of the author:

RON SPENSLEY ronspensley@lineone.net

55. The Descendants of Peter and Barbara BERESFORD of Raisgill in the Parish of Arncliffe

Peter BERESFORD 1826-1892 christened at Hubberholme on 1st October 1826
Hannah PALEY 1834-1906 christened at Stalling Busk on 5th January 1834
They were married at Stalling Busk in 1854

A note in an old family bible states that Peter BERESFORD moved from Beresford Dale in Derbyshire to Beggarmans (later known as Beckermonds) in Wharfedale in 1796 to work a lead mine as an employee of the Duke of Devonshire's Estates. The lead mine soon failed and Peter BERESFORD purchased Raisgill and commenced farming there.

Information about the origins of the BERESFORD family and trees, which are not all complete, showing the descendants of Peter and Barbara BERESFORD, who were married in 1797, have been produced by Malcolm McCALLUM. Whilst there is a little information about the descendants of their eldest son, Mark BERESFORD, who married Jane MITTON, most of the information available relates to the descendants of the youngest son, George BERESFORD and his wife Mary SLINGER.

The earliest photograph in existence is one of the sons of George and Mary BERESFORD, Peter with his wife Hannah, believed to have been taken at some time between 1890 and 1892. A visit to Hubberholme Church will confirm the strong presence of the BERESFORD family in Wharfedale. Many descendants remain farming in Wharfedale and Wensleydale, but some did have to find work elsewhere, some as cow keepers in the large Lancashire towns, some on the railway, but most who did leave the dales moved to Lancashire and can be traced to the Burnley area where they worked in the cotton mills.

The booklet *Beckermonds in Langstrothdale* by Florence Foster Brook is a fascinating history of the FOSTER family and the property originally known as Boggermont and later as Beggarmans, and includes references to many Wharfedale families, amongst them BERESFORD, LODGE, HIRD, THWAITE, BANKS, ROBINSON, SLINGER, METCALF, RUTHERFORD, COATS, STAMP, HEBDEN, BALDERSTONE, CHAPMAN, TENNANT.

From the incomplete family tree which accompanies the booklet, it can be seen that the author did know that one member of the family had emigrated to Canada and two others had emigrated to New Zealand.

Malcolm McCALLUM, Hunters Lodge, Bowling Green Lane, Manfield, Darlington DL2 2RL
malcolm.mccallum2@btopenworld.com

56. SPENSLEY of Raydale to Old Ing – a short but challenging local migration

Old Ing

Many members of the Upper Dales Family History Group will remember the late Alan SPENSLEY who was so generous with his research. One of the items he passed along to me was a memoir of the migration of his grandparents. Although local and covering the grand total of only 25 miles, the journey was nonetheless challenging. The Jim SUNTER he mentions moved to Hill Top Farm at Leyburn and many locals will know him and his son, also Jim.

The story as told to Alan SPENSLEY by Jim SUNTER of Raydale who had it passed down to him from his father who was John SPENSLEY's nephew:

"The SPENSLEY family John, Isabella, and their two oldest children James and Isabelle moved from their home at Hill Top near Kearton in Swaledale to Old Ing Farm, near Horton in Ribblesdale, a distance of some 25 miles. This must have taken place during the winter of 1898/99 as there was snow on the ground and their next child William was born at Old Ing in Oct 1899.

All their belongings were loaded onto horse and carts, the only means of transport in those days. They set off travelling to Low Whita and over Whitaside Moor dropping down into Askrigg and crossing the river at Yorebridge before taking the Cam High road out of Bainbridge.

Unfortunately for them, when they reached the north gate, they found that it was blocked by a huge snowdrift. As they had no means of shifting this they were left with no alternative but to find an alternative route. This they did, by going down Sleddale to Hawes then travelling up Widdale towards Ribblehead before branching off and taking the track to Old Ing.

This diversion increased the distance by some ten miles. They arrived eventually at their destination Old Ing Farm, a wild desolate property high on the hillside looking across to Ribblehead.

To make matters worse on arrival the horses were sweating profusely and there was not sufficient stabling available to put them under cover. This meant that they had to retrace their steps until they could find stabling. By the time everyone got back to Old Ing it was the small hours of the next day."

CHRISTINE AMSDEN camsden@mymts.net

57. Michael METCALFE from Muker to Bradford

Michael METCALFE was my great, great, great grandfather. He was born in Muker on the 26th December 1787. He was the son of Robert METCALFE, born in Thwaite in 1767, and Jane HARKER, born in Crackpot in 1766. He arrived in Bradford via Leeds with strong Preston connections. The mystery of when Michael left the dales has however eluded me through years of research.

On the 1st June 1818 he married Ellen SLEDDON at St Peters Church in Leeds. Ellen was born on 6th April 1798 and baptized two months later on 3rd June 1798 at Preston. She was the daughter of John SLEDDON of Quernmore, Lancashire and Ann WILSON. The witnesses to the wedding were William MILNES and Robert HARGREAVES. At this time Michael would have been approximately 31 years old, which poses the question as to whether he had previously been married.

Michael and Ellen's first child was John, my great, great grandfather, born in July 1818 at Meadow Lane, Leeds and baptized at Leeds Parish Church on 25th December 1819. Michael's occupation was given as *woolcomber*. Their second child was Adam METCALFE born in 1828 and baptized 15th October 1828 at Bradford. Whilst most of the stories in this book recount successful research, the ten year gap between the birth of John METCALFE and Adam METCALFE remains a mystery, as does much of his life.

According to the census for 1841 and 1851, the next three children, Francis 1831, William 1833 and Ellen 1836 were born in Bradford. No birth or baptismal records have been found. The sixth child, Michael METCALFE however, was born on 3rd August 1838 at Great Georges Street, Preston and baptized on 2nd September 1838 at St Johns, Preston.

According to the 1841 census, Michael METCALFE senior had returned to Bradford and was living with his family at Back Bowling Lane; in 1851 they were at 412 Mount Street and by 1861 were residing at 125 Myrtle Road. His occupation remained as a *woolcomber* until 1861 when he was listed as *"blind"*.

Ellen, his wife died on 12th December 1867 and was recorded as living at 15 Lancaster Street. She was listed as *'wife of Michael METCALFE, woolcomber'*, not as his widow. This would seem to be the last reference to Michael because I have found no further information about him. I have not been able to find him on any subsequent census, death certificate or burial record.

One further mystery is, despite Michael and Ellen METCALFE having numerous descendants, (John and Ellen alone had eleven children) I have been unable to find any contacts in the Bradford area related to them.

So, in conclusion, the absence of facts surrounding Michael METCALFE includes:

- When he left the dales.
- If there was a previous marriage
- Where was he between 1819 and 1828?
- Why he arrived in Bradford
- Was he still alive when his wife died?
- Why are there no death or burial records?
- Why are there no other descendants in Bradford?

I welcome any details which might help solve this persistent and nagging genealogical conundrum.

DIANE GREEN dgreenfh@btinternet.com

58. Professor Robert (Robin) PEDLEY (1914 – 1988) of Grinton

Robin PEDLEY was the fourth of five children born to Edward PEDLEY and Martha Jane PEDLEY (née HIRD). Edward PEDLEY was a *stonemason* and his wife was the *postmistress* at Grinton. Robin was born on 11th August 1914 in Grinton. His sister Elsie, his elder brothers William Hird and Edward and his younger brother Francis Harold all attended Fremington School until the age of fourteen. Robin transferred to Richmond Grammar School for his secondary education at the age of fourteen and he attended there from 1928 – 1932. In 1932 he won an Ellerton scholarship to Durham University where he read history and economics. The Ellerton Scholarship, to the value of £200, is awarded annually on the same basis as the University of Durham Unnamed Scholarships for Students in Residence. All other things being equal, preference is given to candidates from North Yorkshire and in particular those who have received their education at Richmond School.

His university education and his subsequent career in education saw his departure from the dales. On graduation he joined the education department of Durham University where he was awarded his teacher's certificate in 1936 and he was elected a fellow of the university between 1936-8. He was awarded his doctorate in 1939 for his study of the political and economic history of the northern Pennines.

During World War II PEDLEY was a conscientious objector and taught in schools in Yorkshire: from 1938 at the Friend's school, Great Ayton and from 1943 – 46 he was the senior history master at the Crossley and Porter school in Halifax. In 1946 PEDLEY moved to London where he became a lecturer in education at the College of St Mark and St John, Chelsea. A year later he moved to the University of Leicester as a founding member of the department of education. PEDLEY married in 1951 to Jeanne Lesley HITCHING and they had a son and a daughter.

PEDLEY remained at Leicester for 16 years and it was here that he developed his outlook on educational policy and practice. An early and leading proponent of comprehensive education, PEDLEY developed his thoughts in a series of papers that were published in the late 1940's. His first major work to gain attention was *Comprehensive Schools Today: An Interim Survey* (1955) and this was followed the following year by *Comprehensive Education, a New Approach*. Pedley's proposals were for a two tier, non-selective system of secondary education with a division at age fifteen. This was a change from the existing 'all-through' schools which catered for pupils from eleven to nineteen. PEDLEY argued the new model had several advantages. It could be implemented in existing buildings with the current secondary modern schools taking pupils between the ages of eleven and fifteen and the grammar schools taking those over fifteen. Both types of schools could be developed as community schools. Both sets of schools could be maintained at a 'reasonable size'. Finally, separation of the older pupils allowed them to be treated as their increasing maturity required.

The Ministry of Education encouraged an experiment to test PEDLEY's proposals and Leicestershire Education Authority announced a two tier, comprehensive plan in 1957. In 1963 PEDLEY published *The Comprehensive School* which offered interested parties, especially parents, an overview of country-wide plans for educational reform. This book was reprinted for several years. The book's publication coincided with the government's publication of the Newsom Report which presented a highly critical picture of the state of secondary education at that time.

It was in this year (1963) that PEDLEY accepted the position of director at the Institute of Education at Exeter University. He did not forget his origins in the dales. In March 1968 the then North Riding Education Authority announced the intention to close the school in Arkengarthdale. PEDLEY provided *"weighty written support"* to the locals who opposed the closure and against all the odds the closure was prevented. He was appointed Professor in 1970. He was Head of the School of Education and Dean of the Faculty of Education for four years from 1971 – 75. The following year he became Head of the Department of Education until his retirement in 1979. He was appointed Professor Emeritus at the University of Southampton in 1979. His last book was *Towards the Comprehensive University* (1977). This developed the themes that had been articulated earlier in that decade by bodies including the Association of Teachers in Colleges and Departments of Education and the National Union of Students supporting a federal model of universities on regional groupings. The ideas propounded a 'parent' university that would oversee, develop and validate awards and courses delivered by bodies including polytechnics and teachers' training colleges. As with many innovative ideas the approach met with mixed reactions but by the end of the 20th century most tertiary educational establishments had become part of just such a federal grouping.

Following his retirement PEDLEY lived at Brockenhurst, Hampshire. He died in Salisbury on 20th November 1988 of pneumonia, following several years suffering from Alzheimer's disease.

This famous dales-born man left his mark on the education system in England and his achievements are recorded in the Oxford Dictionary of National Biography, Who's Who 2010 and Who Was Who. His inclusion in this publication was suggested by Keith JACKSON.

BLAIR SOUTHERDEN blairsou@globalnet.co.uk

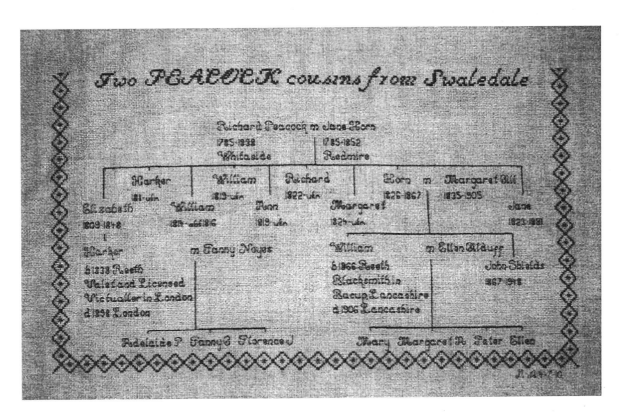

This new sampler has been designed and embroidered by Naomi Appleby for the exhibition and refers to her family in Chapter 50

59. Christopher (Kit) PRATT from Gunnerside to Bradford

Christopher and Jane PRATT and family

William PRATT settled with his new wife Annas in the tiny hamlet above Melbecks Moor after their marriage at Grinton Church in April 1799. She was the 18 year old daughter of Thomas and Agnes METCALFE. Thomas, a former *stonemason* was landlord of the King's Head Inn at Gunnerside.

Christopher, known as Kit, was their ninth child, born at Bent's House on the 10th February 1819. He was only five years old when his father died at 45 years of age – the average for a Swaledale miner. Annas was a widow at 42 with seven children, the youngest being four month old Jane.

Following the end of Napoleonic wars in Europe, demand for lead fell and the industry went into decline. Annas's eldest son James, like many others, had emigrated to America and became one of the founding fathers of Dubuque in Iowa.

Annas's brother Leonard METCALFE, a *stonemason*, had settled in Bradford with his sister Ann and their father where they were building houses. After a disastrous bank failure and Thomas's untimely death, they persuaded Annas to leave Gunnerside to live in the old man's house in George Street, off Leeds Road. A woman of exceptional character and strength of purpose, Annas faced up to the new situation, making the journey with her seven youngest children. The younger children, including eleven year old Kit, went to the Eastbrook day school, and her older sons, William and Robert, found work with their uncle Leonard who had, by now, a successful building business. They were working in North Parade, building a showroom and workshop for Joseph NUTTER, an enterprising *cabinet maker* who was well established in the town. He offered young Kit a job as *errand-boy* and he later served his time as *cabinet maker* under this master craftsman.

William and Annas had been loyal members of the chapel in Gunnerside, and in Bradford Annas and family attended the new Eastbrook Chapel where her brother Leonard was *class leader*. It was here that Kit met his future wife, Jane CHEESEBOROUGH of Snape near Bedale. She had come to Bradford to keep house for her brothers who were involved in the wool trade. They were married in Well Church on the 15th April 1842. He was now *foreman* for Joseph NUTTER. In 1845 Kit started his own business in Brummitts yard.

Jane's uncle, John CHEESEBOROUGH and cousin William ranked amongst the wealthiest woolmen in the town at that time.

Five years later Joseph NUTTER retired. Kit joined Thomas PRINCE, a former *carver*, in acquiring his stock and plant at North Parade, and together they leased the premises under the name of PRATT and PRINCE.

The firm prospered and expanded. Kit and Jane settled in Eccleshill and eventually had Highcliffe House built to suit the needs of their growing family of four sons and four daughters. For varying periods all four sons assisted their father in the business. In 1880 a partnership was entered into, and the name changed to Christopher PRATT and Sons.

In his public life Kit served the community in Bradford's new town hall, first as *overseer*, then as *town councillor* for six years from 1883. He held office in connection with the East Morley Savings Bank and the Board of Management of Bradford Royal Infirmary. He was a Freemason, being a founder and the first Master of Eccleshill Lodge. A lifelong Wesleyan Methodist, he was a tireless worker and faithful member of Eastbrook Chapel and Circuit.

In the mid 1870s Kit returned to his native Gunnerside to lay a memorial stone for the Literary Institute. He contributed to the cost and sent four dozen chairs from Bradford by rail via Richmond, to be used at the opening ceremony in January 1878.

Some time after his retirement from the firm, Kit leased the house called Holly Hill at Well, near Bedale. The devoted couple were well cared for by their two unmarried daughters, Elizabeth and Ruth. In her 78th year Jane was taken seriously ill and died. Kit lived another five years and died in January 1903. They were both buried in the family grave in Bradford's Undercliffe Cemetery.

1904 saw the unveiling of Bradford's statue of Queen Victoria who was born in the same year as Kit and died two years before him. Like many worthy characters who lived through her glorious reign, Christopher PRATT was honest, enterprising and hardworking.

A caring family man, he never forgot his humble beginnings in the lead mines of Swaledale.

This is a personal tribute by his great grandson.

DAVID PRATT Hunterland, Turner Lane, Addingham, Ilkley, LS29 OLF

60. Arthur William CLOUGHTON and Margaret HESELTINE from Wensleydale to Idaho

Arthur William CLOUGHTON and Margaret HESELTINE

My grandfather, Arthur William CLOUGHTON was born at Askrigg but lived at Keld Gills Farm, High Abbotside, with his parents George and Eleanor CLOUGHTON née ROBINSON. He had six brothers and one sister. By the age of 16 he was working on his own as a cattleman for the Stockdale Farm in Worton in Wensleydale.

He decided that he needed to emigrate to the United States and in 1906 he left his homeland. According to relatives in England he and William HESELTINE and ten others left together on the *SS Baltic* from Liverpool. They arrived at the port of New York on 5 May 1906. He had a cousin Sarah MYERS who lived in Santa Pablo, California so he struck out for that area. I was able to piece together some of his travels in the United States. I found one of the postcards he sent to his sister Maggie DAYKIN, née CLOUGHTON, had a sender's address of Egbert, Wyoming. Egbert is in Laramie County, Wyoming.

He saved his money and by 1914 he and Margaret HESELTINE were married in Hailey, Blaine, Idaho. They made their home on 160 acres of land that they proved up at Homesteaded West of Hailey, Idaho. They had their first two children there on the homestead. By 1920 they bought eighty acres on what is known as the Glendale Area South of Bellevue, Blaine, Idaho where four more children were added to the family. By the 1940's my grandpa had added more land adjacent to the 80 acres and built a new house for him and grandma. She lived in that house for about two years before her death in 1943.

Arthur and Margaret had some trials along the way going through the Great Depression. I'm sure they wondered where they would wind up in those tumultuous times. Grandpa would always say *"we had to save our money so we wouldn't end up in the poorhouse."* After reading about the Public Workhouses in England I can see his reasoning. His obituary was recorded as follows:

"CLOUGHTON Is Laid to Rest Here Oct. 15 Retired Stockman is Called Sunday Night: Came to Area In 1912. The many friends of Arthur CLOUGHTON paid him last tribute Wednesday afternoon at funeral services held at the Hailey Community Church. The Rev. Charles SHIRK officiated at the services and gave the dedication at the graveside. Mrs. Jo ASTORQUIA sang "The Garden of Tomorrow" and she and Mrs. Harold BUHLER sang as a duet "The Old Rugged Cross." They were accompanied by Mrs. Ralph ANDERSON at the piano.

Pallbearers were T.W. WALKER, Henry WURST, John BROWN, Fred SHIPP, R. G. BROWN and Thomas FICA. The many beautiful floral offerings were taken care of by Miss LoRene LARSEN, Mrs. Lena HARRIS, Mrs. Joe ASTORQUIA, and Mrs. Dorothy POVEY.

Burial was beside his wife in the Hailey cemetery, under the direction of the McGoldrick funeral home. The 68-year-old prominent sheep and cattle grower passed away Sunday night in the Hailey Clinical Hospital following a lengthy illness. Arthur William CLOUGHTON was born July 30, 1884 at Askrigg. He and Miss Margaret HESELTINE were school day sweethearts. When he was 19 years old he came to America to seek his fortune. He stayed for a time in Wyoming, coming on to Idaho in 1912. He homesteaded on Rock Creek and purchased some sheep and in 1914 felt he had established a home which he could ask his sweetheart in England to share with him. She arrived in Hailey on July 22, 1914 and they were married here. As the years rolled by Mr. and Mrs. CLOUGHTON purchased a ranch in Glendale and moved there to live. They enlarged their sheep holdings until Mr. CLOUGHTON became known as one of the county's leading sheepmen.

Mr. CLOUGHTON was confirmed in the Episcopal Church when a boy in England. Mrs. CLOUGHTON preceded her husband in death on Nov. 15, 1943. He is survived by two sons, Mathew and William, who have been associated with him for several years in the stock business; three daughters, Miss Catherine CLOUGHTON, who has kept house for her father since her mother's death; Mrs. Wayne (Margaret) MYERS of Venice, Calif., and Mrs. Verne (Mary) LUTHER of Moscow, Idaho; one sister, Mrs. Margaret DAYKIN of Askrigg, England; four grandchildren; a cousin, Sarah MYERS of San Pablo, Calif.

Mrs. MYERS and Mrs. LUTHER had come home to be with their father several weeks before his death. Other out of town relatives and friends who attended the services were Mr. MYERS, Mr. LUTHER, Mr. and Mrs. William ROBERTSON, Mrs. Dora WILKS, Mr. and Mrs. Floyd HOLLOWAY, Twin Falls; Mr. and Mrs. Vernon (sic) (Verlin) WILLIAMSON, Castleford; Russell GRIFFITH, Jerome, and Mr. and Mrs. Sam BRADFORD, Boise".

I didn't have the privilege to ever knowing my grandma Margaret CLOUGHTON, née HESELTINE as she died before I was born. Everything I have heard about her leads me to believe that she was a sweet, kind, and gentle person though. My mother, Ila CLOUGHTON, née HOLLOWAY, always spoke of her in a loving and respectful way. Margaret came from a large family of ten children. I have inherited a number of family photos which reflect a happy childhood. Margaret was closer to her sisters Eleanor (Nellie), Mary (Molly) and Catherine (Kate).

The HESELTINE children appeared to have experienced a Christian upbringing as Marilyn PETTINGILL née MYERS, and I both have child storybooks that were presented to Grandma CLOUGHTON by the Thoralby Wesleyan Methodist Chapel. Grandma CLOUGHTON was trained as a baker and there is a picture of her standing in front of the Heap Bakery in Lancashire. She gave Aunt Molly, (Mary SHEPHERD, née HESELTINE), money and helped support her so that she could become a nurse.

Grandma CLOUGHTON emigrated to the United States of America in 1914 and married my Grandfather, Arthur CLOUGHTON in Hailey, Idaho. She sailed from Liverpool on 7th July 1914 on the Laconia. She landed at the Port of Boston in Massachusetts

On the Manifest of Alien Passengers for the United States it states that her nearest relative was Kit HESELTINE whose given name was Christopher. Her last address was recorded as Burnley, Lancashire. It also stated that she had thirty dollars for her trip by train to Hailey, Idaho. This was quite a lot of money for that time, but her journey was vast, and a train ride across almost the whole United States with so little money would have been arduous. Grandma CLOUGHTON appeared to be a tall woman in her photographs and was quite striking with her dark hair and medium skin colour. Her build was medium boned and she probably weighed between a hundred and fifty pounds to maybe a hundred and seventy pounds later in her life. She wasn't very old when she died by today's standards of life expectancy, but in one of her last pictures she looked as though she did not feel well and she looked very tired. She died as the result of a massive stoke. My mother always quoted her saying, *"you have to eat the skins of the baked potato, because that was where the potash is."*

ELAINE (CLOUGHTON) MYERS hmyers@northlink.com

61. Bernard Tennant CLOSE from Bishopdale to Manchester

Ann and John Close and family

My grandfather, Bernard Tennant CLOSE was born at Ribba Hall, Bishopdale on 11th November 1883. The eldest of seven brothers and with one older sister his parents were John CLOSE and Ann (Tennant) CLOSE.

John CLOSE was born on 5th November 1853 at Soulby, Westmorland, one of nine sons. His parents were tenant farmers at various locations in Westmorland including Tarn House Ravenstonedale, Aisgill Mallerstang and finally at Wythop Hall, Bassenthwaite, Cumberland.

Ann TENNANT was born on 12th August 1853 at Heaning, Thoralby, one of a family of eight children. The family lived and farmed in the Thoralby and Cray areas.

The 1871 census recorded John and his family living at Aisgill, whilst at a neighbouring property, Helgill, was Richard TENNANT a farmer and his sister Elizabeth TENNANT his housekeeper. Richard and Elizabeth were siblings of Ann and this is probably where John met his future wife.

John and Ann married at Hubberholme on 10th February 1881 and the census recorded them living at Wythop Hall with John's parents. Their first child, Isabella was born there on 8th December 1881. By the time my grandfather was born in 1883 they had moved to Ribba Hall and went on to have six further sons:

Joseph Longstaff CLOSE (25.12.1885)
John Edmund CLOSE (29.3.1888)
Christopher Richard CLOSE (6.5.1889)
George Robert CLOSE (20.5.1892)
Thomas Victor CLOSE (11.6.1897)
Septimus James CLOSE (12.10.1898)

The 1891 and 1901 census returns recorded the family still at Ribba with my grandfather described as a '*scholar*' and then, at 17, a '*farmers son*'. However by 1911 he was living on his own account as a '*Butcher (shopkeeper)*' living at 105 Beech Road, Chorlton-cum-Hardy, Manchester. Also with him was a housekeeper,

Sarah GOULD aged 45 born in Masham North Yorkshire. Two of Bernard's brothers, John Edmund and Christopher Richard, were also *'own account butchers'* living in lodgings in Northenden, Manchester in 1911. At some point they both returned to the dales. At about the same time some of the TENNANT relatives were also setting up as butchers in the Manchester area and I remember one of these, Jimmy TENNANT being a regular visitor to my grandparents in Flixton.

The 1911 census also records Ethel CLAYTON living with her brothers George and William at 101 Beech Road, Chorlton. The brothers were *'own account Fishmongers'* and Ethel was their housekeeper.

Bernard and Ethel were married at Chorlton on 15th January 1912 and lived together at 105 Beech Road. John Edmund CLOSE was one of the witnesses at the wedding. This raised the query as to whether or not the Bishopdale family attended the wedding. I know my grandfather was always closest to his brother Joseph and I feel sure had Joseph been able to come to the wedding he would have been witness.

Bernard and Ethel went on to have a daughter, Ena, born on 8th December 1912 at 105 Beech Road. By 1916 the family had moved to Malt Kiln Farm, Flixton, Lancashire and had two sons, Bernard Kenneth CLOSE (my father) born 16 August 1916 and Norman CLOSE born 18th November 1919. Norman died in 1932 and I have two very moving letters sent to my grandparents by their family doctor.

My grandfather returned to farming in Flixton firstly at Malt Kiln Farm and later at Acre Gate Farm. My parents lived at a nearby farm and my father and grandfather farmed about 250 acres between them. I was born in 1946 and my earliest memories of my grandfather are of him in a striped shirt, bib and brace overalls sitting on an upturned bucket in the middle of a field paying a long line of people who had been potato-picking. He loved the traditional ways of farming and it was a real treat to sit with him behind his working horses at hay time. He was very proud of his dairy herd and modern shippon although they were not very profitable and eventually had to go. He was a very fair man with a quick wit. One story my father told me was that during the war, because my father and most of the farm workers were in the army, there were several land girls working on the farm. My grandfather realised that one of these girls was stealing milk by hiding it in a pocket of her coat which was hanging up in the barn. He didn't want to cause a fuss and lose the girl but at the same time didn't want to let her think she had got away with it, so one day when there was no one about he took a hammer, went to the barn, and broke the two bottles of milk while still in her pocket. She never took milk again but was really the loser because, had she asked, I'm sure he would have let her have as much milk as she needed! He was also a very sociable man and my father spoke of a very happy childhood and wonderful New Year's Eve parties at Acre Gate! However he was a lifetime teetotaller and I have his Temperance Pledge signed in 1897. The nearest neighbour to Acre Gate was the Bird in Hand public house and he would have been horrified if any of his family had dared to enter those *'dreadful'* premises!

My grandfather missed the dales and he took my grandmother to Ribba on at least one occasion and she was apparently terrified by the narrow lanes and ford they crossed with a pony and trap. She was a Manchester girl and had never been away from the town before! I believe she was equally terrified of his mother, Ann, who, I am told, was a rather daunting lady. I wonder if it was because of this that he never returned to live in the dales. My grandparents were a very devoted couple. My grandmother was a tall, statuesque, quite elegant lady and grandfather never wanted her to work outside. Towards the end of 1958 we swapped houses with my grandparents so that my father could take on running the farm but their retirement was short-lived and my grandfather died in August 1959.

I am happy to say that my grandfather's love of farming, horses and the dales still flourishes in our family and I now live in the small fell-side village where his grandparents lived and married in 1850.

LINDA CLOSE lindaclose@btopenworld.com

62. The HESELTINE family and Riddings Farm, Thoralby, Bishopdale

The Riddings, looking over Bishopdale and Walden

The house and its setting

When the first HESELTINEs began farming on the slopes of Bishopdale more than 300 years ago the hillside looked very different from the way it looks today. For the name they gave to their farm, the name it still bears, was Riddings, or probably in those early days Ryddinges, meaning a clearing in the forest. The hillside, as well as the spelling, has changed down the centuries – today there are few traces of the woodland which must once have clustered thickly around the farmstead. The house is surrounded now by fields, their outlines traced by the traditional stone walls of the dales. The farmstead faces south towards Penhill and the Heights of Haseley and from their home the HESELTINE farmers could track the clouds and the gales and the winter snows as they stormed into Bishopdale from Kidstones Pass at the head of the dale. For more than 200 years until the 1960s the house and its barns protected its inhabitants, both human and animals, against the harsh dales winters.

The HESELTINE family at Riddings – 1697- c. 1870.

The HESELTINE family lived at Riddings Farm from 1697 until the late 1860s working on 43 acres of steeply sloping fields around the house. While most were farmers, several were described as coopers; one became a stonemason and built the market cross at Askrigg; his initials are also carved on the archway of a cottage in West Burton, across the valley from Riddings Farm. In the 19th century members of the family moved further afield but Riddings remained the family home for over 150 years.

The first HESELTINE believed to have been born at Riddings Farm was Leonard in around 1697. He married Elizabeth METCALF in 1722 at Aysgarth and they had four children. The last head of the HESELTINE house was Leonard's grandson William. William was a farmer and a cooper; he and his wife Margaret had nine children, all of whom were born at Riddings Farm. William was 75 when in 1867 he fell in the field below the house, was discovered bleeding by his son in law, William ROBINSON, and taken back to the farmhouse where the local surgeon operated on his skull. The operation was unsuccessful, and William died; a report of the inquest held at the Volunteer Inn in Thoralby appeared in the local newspaper at the time.

"Inquest on view of the body of William HESELTINE, 75 years, of Thoralby 12 Aug 1867 To Thomas GEE, constable of Thoralby...at the house of Roland FAWCETT known by the sign of the Volunteer Inn in Thoralby. Verdict. Fracture of the skull from an accidental fall. Farmer Jurors Thomas FAWCETT, Roland FAWCETT, James THWAITE, James FAWCETT, Joseph UDALE, Thomas SADLER, John DUCKITT, Thomas DIXON, Jeremiah METCALFE, Francis RIDER, William MILNER, John NEWTON, Thomas GEE. Witnesses William ROBINSON, Matthew WILLIS I hereby give notice that the body of a man aged about 75 yrs is lying dead at Riddings, Thoralby, name Wm HESELTINE, Time of death 10.20 pm 10 Aug 1867. Persons present at time of death, John FAWCETT, John HESELTINE The deceased fell off a lime kiln and fractured his skull at 8 a.m. the same day and was found bleeding by his son in law William ROBINSON. The deceased lived from 8 a.m. 10.30 p.m., attended by Dr. WILLIS and 3 other medical men. Signed Thomas GEE. Police Constable no 104 stationed at West Burton. Sworn statement of William ROBINSON of Riddings, Thoralby, farmer On Saturday morning last the deceased and myself set out to mend a stack, when he went down the field .... I came along the lane and saw him lying on the ground trying to turn himself. I got off my horse and went to him where I found that he was lying in a pool of blood which had come from a wound in his head. I spoke to him saying that I thought he had killed himself. When he replied "Oh no, I shall get better". I was present when he died the same night. Wm. ROBINSON Sworn statement of Matthew WILLIS of Aysgarth, surgeon. I was called to see deceased on Saturday last when found him suffering from symptoms of concussion. I examined his head and found a wound there and upon further examination I fount fracture of the skull. I got the advice and assistance of 2 of my medical friends and we decided to trepan the skull. We found a fracture of the .... of two inches over the Temporal and...... regions with depression the portion lying upon the brain. This we carefully removed and found several fragments and two fisures. He died the same night, death being the result of the injury. Matthew WILLIS, M.D."

Riddings Farm from 1870 to mid 1900s.

After William's death there are no records of HESELTINEs at Riddings Farm. By 1871 William DINSDALE and his wife Eleanor were living there with their four children and farming the 43 acres. Ten years later the occupants were Edward BOLLAND his wife Sarah and their young son and daughter.

The Riddings from the 1960s until the present day.

The house continued to be inhabited until the 1960s, though in an increasing state of dilapidation. After the last occupant died it quickly became derelict and local people still recall seeing cows, having struggled up the stone staircase, gazing out of the upstairs bedroom windows. In 1983 most of the land was sold, leaving just over three acres remaining with the property. A new vehicle track was created from the Aysgarth to Thoralby road – for centuries access had been across the fields down to Eastfield Lane and even today, in dry weather, the outline of this track can still be seen.

Renovation of the house began in the early 1980s and has been continued by subsequent owners. The last major work in the early 1990s was the rebuilding of the barn attached to the house, possibly predating the house itself. It was during this work that a pair of ancient ice skates was discovered at the foot of a wall in the barn. They were a touching reminder of those long ago HESELTINE farmers and their many children enduring the long cold winters on their isolated hillside. Those rusted skates, attached to wooden soles with leather straps for binding them to boots, evoked poignant images of the families skating to Thoralby along a flooded and frozen Eastfield Lane below their home and brought their distant lives into sharper perspective.

MAUREEN HORROX maureenhorrox@yahoo.co.uk

Editor's note: Maureen and Keith HORROX owned and lived at The Riddings from July 1994 to September 2007. This chapter by Maureen illustrates the long standing connection between dales houses and the families who lived in them, often for well over 100 years. See chapter 5 for further information about The Riddings and the Heseltines who lived there.

63. Letter to "Mrs Mary ALDERSON, Faggergill, Arkingarthdale, Near Richmond, Yorkshire, England" from her son Edmond ALDERSON

Letter ZSC 5-3-1

This letter forms part of the ZSC collection at the North Yorkshire County Record Office. The collection is on film number 1160. Whilst the letters are readable from the film the quality is not sufficiently good enough to print. We are grateful to Keith Sweetmore and his team for making the originals available to us to enable them to be transcribed. The ink is very feint, and the paper is not white; some of the paper is quite yellowy, and one, the worst, is written on blue paper.

Council Hill Township is one of twenty-three townships in Jo Daviess County, Illinois, USA. Its name changed from Scales Township on December 6, 1853.

"Counsilhill 29 June 1841

Dear Mother I take the preasant opportunity of answering your letter I received your letter on the 19th June and I was sorry to hear of the death of my grandfather and grandmother you said that I was to wright back as soon as possible to let you know what had left for me in his last will so now I will let you know how I have managed it I have given power of attorney to William CALVERT of Thwait in the parish of Muker to draw the money of the said executor that is my unkle Jonathan of Eskelith who is as it was said in your last letter was the sole executor William CALVERT. As son of the said William CALVERT which is living at Counsilhill which I am well acquainted with A young man that came into this country at the same time when I came here and we have agreed that he was to pay me the sum of two hundred dollars and that my unkle Jonathan has to pay the said William CALVERT of Thwait to whome I have given the power of Attorney to the said sum of £40 pounds and this power of Attorney will come to the said William CALVERT of Thwait in A letter from his son And I hope you will have no Objections to Pay the Money any time as it will be all right and we are both writing together but the letters perhaps may not both reach you at A time.

And if there be any Misunderstanding Concerning the Money that is left to me by My Grandfather I wish you to wright back to me Quick. Dear Brother you said in your letter that my uncle Jonathan thought if I intended to return to the old sod that I had Better set it to be Put into some Bank and to run Interest upon interest But I think I can make more of it hear by A great sight in this Part Money will fetch from eight to twelve Percent and some More and more than that when a man has money by him he often sees chances of making a bargin that he can make twenty or thirty Percent on money So I thought I would make it so that I Could Receive it at this time, As My Companion William CALVERT wanted to send money As to his parents As he has two of his brothers living at home and he wished to have the Pleasure of getting them Each some trade as the rest of them out of six Brothers has got Each a trade which I Believe he has started in his own letter so I thought that I might as well fixed the way that I have done As it is a great deal Better for us Both And I did not see any other way of getting it or so lickly as this and so safely As I dont here that Any of you has any notion of Coming to this Country and if there had been any body coming to this Country it woud not A been so safe as the way that I have fixed it so I think that I Could A done no better with the money that is left to me.

By this way of doing some of you may be apt to think that I dont intend to Return Back Again But I do intend to come and se you all once Again But I dont Belive that ever I shall come to stay any time As this is the Country for A Poor (now)ing man in this Country A man Can get a better living with working half of his time than he can do in the Old Country with working all the time, and he can get himself a Parcel of Land at A Low rate of One dollar and a quarter pr. Acre, and then he can Raise his own grain and other things within himself so as they wont cost him more than his own Labour and he can keep all Kinds of stock as many as he has A mind to, and No body will say them horses or them cows has got into my Pasture But times is rather duler

At Present than they have been some time back Lead is lower at this time than it has been for three months but we expect it getting up after A while it is now worth about two dollars and eighty cents pr hundred Pounds and the Miners Can get from 14 to 15½ dollars pr thousand of our Pounds And the Miners wages is from sixteen dollars to thirty pr month and found and some can get More for one month or two but the Englishmen in General had rather work for themselves as they generaly make more money and Another thing they are there own boss they Can work when they Please so Now dear Brother if you have any notion of Coming to this Country I hope you will take the opertunity of writing Back to me and let me know whether you will Come or not and let me know if there be any body Elce that is Coming but I am afraid you are all too faint hearted and dear Brother A faint heart will never gain a fair lady

Dear Brother, remember me to Ruben ATKINSON and tell him if he is still living that I is enjoying the Blessings of good health thank the Lord for it but I am sorry to hear of his sicking but I hope he will take a turn and get Better Again, Give my kind love to John AKⁿ, and wife and Ann A And tell them that there Brother William is well and working About thirty Miles from me with Wᵐ PEACOCK and I losed his letter at the Post About five weeks ago and sent it out to him and has not seen him since,

Give my love to Jonathan RAIN and Thomas RAIN I am sorry for him Remember me to Thomas WINTER (2½ lines crossed out) in this Part Dear Mother give my love to my sisters Ann and Betty

Next time you wright to me let me know who my sister Betty is living with Remember me to all my uncles and aunts and I hope to meet them once again and the next time you write to me let me know how my uncle James and family is getting on give my love to Cousin George and family Give my Kind love to All Enquiring friend and my Old Aquantances so No more from your dear son Edmond ALDERSON"

There is a post script written across the border of the letter:

"Dear Broth when you write to me again let me know how all the young men and women is getting on and who is married and all Peticulars"

**SUE NEALE nealesl@iinet.net.au transcribed this letter and the others in the set on behalf of KEITH SWEETMORE, County Archivist, archives@northyorks.gov.uk
North Yorkshire County Record Office, Malpas Road, Northallerton, DL7 8TB.
Tel. 0044 1609 777585.**

Editor's note: The Upper Dales Family History Group is indebted to Keith and the staff in the Archives for their support and enthusiasm, not only in this our 10th Anniversary year, but throughout each year. Keith's encouragement for our research, his local knowledge, and his deep understanding of the importance of sound family history research has encouraged us to use this collection of stories as the basis for a Dales Migration Archive.

64. George Frederick ATKINSON (1882 – 1961)

George Frederick ATKINSON (r) at the opening of the Hodder Water Supply Scheme by Prince Albert, Duke of York, before he became King (centre)

George Frederick ATKINSON was the youngest son of Octavius and Esther ATKINSON. Octavius was born and brought up at Gownleyfoot (now called Gollinglith Foot), but left the dales. After working as a *gas fitter* in Bradford, he set up a *blacksmith* workshop in 1873, in Tower Street, Harrogate, just before he married. His mother, Esther was the daughter of George RAYNERD born at Kirkby Malzeard in 1809 and Esther GRAHAM born at Ellingstring about 1812.

George Frederick, known as Fred, was born on 5th November 1882 in Harrogate. He appeared on the 1891 census for Bilton with Harrogate living close to the Tower Street works, aged eight. In 1901, he was 18, living with his widowed mother and siblings at 25 Robert Street, Harrogate employed as a *pupil, civil engineering*.

When he married Dorothy ALLEN in Bilton, Harrogate in 1909, he was working for the Fylde Water Board, Blackpool, where he became Chief Engineer in 1924.

During the three years after his appointment to the Fylde, two Bills of major importance were negotiated through Parliament and Fred was responsible for the execution of almost the whole of the works authorised by these two Acts of Parliament. They included the service reservoir and water tower at Warbreck, and the Hodder Supply Scheme, which comprised Stocks reservoir and filtration plant, the Hodder aqueduct which was 28 miles long and the Westby service reservoir.

His son, Peter, who worked in the same industry, wrote a biography of his father and I am indebted to Peter's daughter for a copy of this. Peter wrote:

> *'My father, George Frederick ATKINSON, known to his friends as 'Fred', was a distinguished Civil Engineer who held the post of Engineer to the Fylde Water Board from 1924 until he retired in November 1947. During his period of office GFA was responsible for major reservoir and pipeline construction work for the water supply of Blackpool in Lancashire, and the surrounding area known as the Fylde. His achievements were recognised by the Institution of Water Engineers (IWE); he was elected to the Council in 1933 and held the office of President for the year 1942-43. Shortly before his death in 1961 he was elected Honorary Member in recognition of his engineering achievements and his service to the Institution, a rare distinction.'*

MARGARET HAWKINS snikwahrm@hotmail.com

The Burgoyne Hotel & Restaurant
Reeth, Swaledale

A part of Reeth's history since 1800, this historic house is now the premier hotel of Swaledale, offering luxurious accommodation, beautiful fresh food & the very best of Yorkshire hospitality

Why not spoil yourselves?
Relax & be cosseted ~ See for yourselves
(01748) 884292 www.theburgoyne.co.uk

65. The Journey from the Yorkshire Dales to Bradford – Jeffrey HESELTINE born 1816

Great grandad John HESELTINE born 1857 (nickname Gussy) son of Jeffrey (1816)

This is the story of my great great grandad Jeffrey HESELTINE born in 1816, Thoralby, Bishopdale. Jeffrey was the great great grandson of Leonard HESELTINE born 1698 and Elizabeth METCALFE who lived at The Riddings, a 17th century farmhouse in Thoralby. Jeffrey was one of 13 children born to Leonard HESELTINE (1789) and Alice GRAHAM. Jeffrey's father was a stonemason and the book *Yorkshire Village* by Marie HARTLEY and Joan INGILBY, cites Leonard HESELTINE as *"an Askrigg man"* who received £21.2s 5d for building the present village cross at Askrigg in 1831 and building and encasing the present village pump in a handsome stone casing in 1849. There are several references to the work carried out by Leonard in the *Trustees Market Toll Book of Askrigg* held at the Hawes Museum detailing monies paid to Leonard for *stonemason work*.

The Riddings was the ancestral home of the HESELTINE family for at least 145 years and possibly longer. The first recorded birth at The Riddings was that of Dorothy in 1722, the first of four children born to Leonard HESELTINE and Elizabeth METCALFE. Records show HESELTINEs continued to live there right up to William HESELTINE who died at The Riddings in 1867. By 1871 there were no HESELTINEs recorded as living there.

Life was hard and at least four of Jeffrey's siblings died young. By 1844 Jeffrey was married with two young children, having married Mary CLARK of Coverham in 1839. It was the time of the industrial revolution and no doubt the draw of a better standard of living in Bradford for his wife, Mary and young family was the reason for his move to the textile manufacturing town in the West Riding of Yorkshire. Bradford was booming and more mills were being built. People flocked there for work and houses needed to be built to accommodate them. This was a great opportunity to find regular work as a stonemason.

Jeffrey's parents along with other members of his family also moved to Bradford. The Askrigg 1841 census recorded Jeffrey as a *stonemason* and his second child Isabella was born in 1844 in the village. It appears Jeffrey moved to Bradford between 1844 and 1847 and their third child was born in Bradford in 1847. They had three further children and lived in a terraced house in the Bowling district of the city. By 1861 he was a *road surveyor* in Bradford. This was the start of this line of the Bradford born HESELTINEs and six more generations were to follow.

John born in 1857 at 39 Well Street was the youngest of Jeffrey and Mary's six children. He found work at the age of 14 as a *carter* working at the Exchange Railway Station. In 1870 his father Jeffrey died. On the 1871 census John was living with his brother Leonard a *stonemason* aged 22 and was recorded as *head of household* living at 40 Sloane Street with his mother and two older sisters, Elizabeth (24) and Mary Ann (16) and niece Mary aged seven.

The photo shows John with his horse, of which he was very proud. Shire horses were used on the railways due to their power and capacity for pulling large, heavy loads. John, who also had the nickname of *Gussy*, married twice. His first wife died and by the time John was 24 he'd met and married Hannah, the girl who lived with her mother and young daughter Ann Elizabeth in Warwick Street, Bradford, the same street where John lodged. Hannah worked as a *worsted weaver*.

From this marriage came four children, Ann Elizabeth born 1879, Mary born 1885, Thomas Henry born 1886, and John Heseltine born 1888. Tom worked alongside his father John as a *carter* at the railway station. By 1908 both of Tom's parents had died, his mother at 44 and his father dying just a short time after Tom's marriage to Bertha YOUNG in 1908. Bertha was a Leicestershire girl who had moved to Bradford to live with her sister Emma.

Tom and Bertha were publicans at *The Old Waggon & Horses & Commercial Inn*, Bradford and had two children, Thomas Henry born 1918 and Hilda born 1922. Whilst many of my HESELTINE ancestors were *farmers* and *stonemasons* it was surprising to discover how many were *innkeepers*, often combining more than one of these trades at the same time. As well as my own grandfather and grandmother, Tom and Bertha, there were many who were inn keepers in the Yorkshire Dales.

World War II broke out and Tom joined the 50th Division of the Northumbrian Light Infantry. The very next day, following his marriage, he left his young bride Lillian living with his parents and travelled to Market Bosworth where he was stationed, later to be posted to Dunkirk. In 1940 Tom's sister Hilda died suddenly after contracting TB, an epidemic sweeping the country at that time.

When the war ended, Tom returned to Bradford having been away for seven years. He and Lillian started their married life together living in a little stone built back-to-back house in the Bradford Moor area. They were very happy in their first home and had very good neighbours. Lillian's sister lived just a few doors away but the house soon became too small for their growing family and they moved to a larger house. They had six children, eleven grandchildren and six great grandchildren.

Tom worked in the textile mills, mainly in the dyehouse. Before his retirement Tom worked at Lister's Mills in Manningham, the largest silk factory in the world with floor area covering 27 acres. Wherever you were in Bradford you could always see Lister's chimney. At its peak, Lister's employed 11,000 men, women and children manufacturing high quality textiles such as velvet and silk. During WWII the mill produced vast quantities of parachute silk, flame-proof wool, khaki battledress and parachute cord for the armed forces. They also supplied 1,000 yards of velvet to Westminster Abbey for the Coronation of George V in 1911 and even velvet for curtains in the White House in Washington.

Tom and Lillian spent many happy times with their family on holiday in Bridlington, on the East Yorkshire coast. On his retirement Tom fulfilled his dream of moving to Bridlington where he died in 2002, aged 83. Allan their fifth child has moved recently from Bradford to live in one of the lovely quaint villages of the Yorkshire Dales, going full circle and returning to the roots of the HESELTINE family tree.

CHRISTINE (HESELTINE) SCOTT silverdalejrts@btinternet.com
1 Georgian Mews Bridlington YO15 3TG

66. WINTERSGILLs of Healey and Fearby

Fearby, old postcard.

The surname WINTERSGILL originates from the place-name Winterscales, a tiny hamlet not far from the famous Ribble Head Viaduct near Ingleton. However, those bearing the name WINTERSGILL today are, with very few exceptions, all descended from the WINTERSGILL families who were well established by the early 16th century in Fearby in the parish of Masham in Wensleydale.

Several of the early families were Roman Catholics and were excommunicated from the Church of England and unfortunately do not show up in the Parish Registers. However other detailed documents do survive so we know of their existence even though the ancestral line cannot be proven. Upwards of 1000 entries of WINTERSGILL and its many variant spellings appear in the Masham Parish Registers but today there is only one family still living in the parish although there may well be WINTERSGILL descendents no longer bearing the name.

So where did they go?

There are now more people bearing the name WINTERSGILL in Canada than there are in Yorkshire. These are mainly in Saskatchewan and British Columbia. In the UK, the borders of Durham and Northumberland top the list, followed by the northern end of North Yorkshire around the Middlesbrough area. Almost certainly these are descended from the Fearby and Healey WINTERSGILLs and not the early entries in the Egglescliff (Durham) or Ingleby Greenhow parish registers both of which lines had died out by the early to mid 17th century.

My own line begins with Thomas who was the first to be found in Healey, the adjoining village to Fearby, at the time of his marriage in 1646. It is mainly this line that produced the bulk of those who went to Durham and Northumberland and Middlesbrough. Others who went further afield became natives of New Zealand and to a lesser extent, Australia and America.

Most of the WINTERSGILLs to go overseas are not descended from my line but from Thomas WINTERSGILL (born c1730) and Mary JACKSON (both of the parish of Masham) who married in Masham in 1755. They are scattered about the globe in huge numbers, mainly in America and Canada and more recently in France.

Not all the WINTERSGILLs may have left of their own free will. John WINTERSGILL born in Fearby in 1741 married Letitia SMITH in London in 1765. The following year he was back in Masham where his first son, also John, was baptised in 1766. This birth was followed by Marmaduke who died soon after and Jane baptised in 1770. Nothing is known of them until 1785 when, at the age of 19, John Jr. and his father make an appearance in court at the Old Bailey.

John Jr. was charged with theft and his father of receiving stolen property. John senior was a saddler in Westminster, London and his son a *journeyman saddler*, servant to Robert GIBSON in Coventry Street, Haymarket. John lived with his parents and sister at their shop in nearby Swallow Street. John had enticed another employee of Robert GIBSON, one William SINCLAIR to steal goods for him as *"it was easier for him as he lived on the premises"*. John Jr. then put them on sale in his father's shop while the latter was away. The court decided that John senior was innocent as he had been unaware of the situation and that his son was the receiver, the more serious of the crimes and William SINCLAIR the thief. John Jr. was sentenced to seven years transportation in 1784.

Offenders were no longer sent to America but were not yet bound for Australia. Many prisoners spent their whole sentence on a hulk ship. The hulk ships were notorious places and mortality was very high. No records of John have been found however on hulk ships or lists of transported convicts. No death or marriage or any other record has been located. However, at this time, convicts were being shipped out to Bermuda and Barbados. Although we have no evidence to suggest that John had been sent to either of these places, records show that there was an Edward WINTERSGILL married in Barbados in 1802 and a Dorothy Ann WINTERSGILL in 1812. So who were their parents? Could these be the children of John? Or had an earlier member of the WINTERSGILL family also been sentenced to transportation? Further research is ongoing but unless an early death is found for John they could be his descendents.

John's sisters, Jane and Nancy Letitia were the joint beneficiaries of their grandfather's estate in his Will drawn up shortly before his death in January 1794. Jane was obviously educated and signed a good clear signature, unusual for a female in Masham at this time, but probably consistent with living in London. Both her and her grandfather's addresses were given as Spelderbanks (Fearby). Had she returned from London to look after her ailing grandfather? I am not aware of any other record being found for Jane or any other members of the family. None of them appear again in the Masham Registers. They just vanished.

Was John Jr. ever transported? Did his parents John and Letitia and their daughters Jane and Nancy Letitia emigrate as a result of the shame of the Old Bailey trial or perhaps just for a better life? Perhaps one day a descendent will claim this family.

A full account of the Old Bailey trial can be found at www.oldbaileyonline.org. Masham and other parish registers, wills, maps and other documents relating to Masham were consulted at the North Yorkshire County Record Office and West Yorkshire Archives, Leeds. Masham parish registers have now been transcribed and indexed by the Yorkshire Parish Register Society.

BRENDA GREEN www.yorkshireancestors.com brenda@yorkshireancestors.com
Studley House Farm, 67 Main Street, Ebberston, Scarborough, North Yorkshire, YO13 9NR

Tan Hill Coal Mine
Photo courtesy of Dr. Christine Hallas

Miner's tools
Photo courtesy of the Richmondshire Local History Museum

67. HOGGs who left Wensleydale

This photograph was taken in my great-grandfather Thomas HOGG's front garden at Downholme House, West Hartlepool. Seated were Thomas, born West Burton in 1813, and his wife Jane (Walker) HOGG, born Constable Burton in 1829. Standing were my grandmother Laura HOGG, my great-aunts, my grandmother's brother and my grandfather James HOGG.
My grandfather and great-aunts were all born at Leyburn.

The first HOGG reference I know of comes in a Latin document from 1465 concerning Thomas HOGG, the reeve of Thoralby. I can't prove I descend from Thomas, but since my 18th century HOGG ancestors came from Aysgarth and the name Thomas recurs among them, it is not impossible. The HOGG surname continued locally over the centuries and after the Rising of the North in 1569 three HOGGES of Thoralby were among those pardoned.

My forbears were variously described as *carpenters* or *joiners*. Great-great-grandfather Thomas HOGG was born in Aysgarth in 1778, but before my great-grandfather Thomas was born in 1813 he had moved to West Burton. The first HOGG migrant was Thomas senior's brother John, who became an *innkeeper and stone merchant* and later returned to the district in grander circumstances than when he left. He kept the Fleece Inn at Wakefield, and then in 1811 took over the Rose and Crown in Briggate, Leeds. From there he ran daily stagecoaches to Liverpool and other centres, while the stone business was nearby at Rodley. John's son, yet another Thomas, was thus born into a well-to-do family, unlike his cousins back in the dale.

Having prospered in Leeds, John HOGG sent his sons to boarding school at Spofforth, near Wetherby, and one of them, Thomas, kept a journal of his mini-Grand Tour to France, with amusing descriptions of his journeys. In the 1820s John bought Littleburn, a handsome house in Thoralby, and when he died Thomas inherited the house and his father's money and settled into the life of a gentleman. A collection of letters written to him in 1840 when he was courting the sister of one of the correspondents shed light on the way young men of that era advised each other (sometimes quite bluntly) on the business of getting a wife.

Oral history handed down to Thomas's great-granddaughter, Barbara ROOCROFT of Gayle, described how he fell in with the racing men at Middleham and squandered his inheritance. Littleburn and most of its fine contents were sold (a newspaper report listed the items) and to earn his living Thomas became landlord of the Lady Bab Inn, Coverham, then of the Commercial Inn (now the Richard III) in Middleham. Thomas's son John became a *coach-painter* and migrated between the West Riding and Chesterfield. Eventually his grandson Albert, who'd been born in Middleham, achieved his dream of moving back to Wensleydale.

Meanwhile back in the 1830s my great-grandfather Thomas, first cousin of the Middleham innkeeper, married Mary Ann SIMPSON and caught the migration bug. Before their first child (another John) was born in 1839 they had moved to Bradford where Thomas is recorded as a *carpenter*. The move was not a success, because by 1843 they had resettled in Leyburn. By 1851 however, Thomas, a *carpenter employing one man and two apprentices*, was widowed, with five children and his mother acting as housekeeper. In 1854 he remarried at Wensley. His bride Jane WALKER, 14 years his junior, had been born in Constable Burton, with forbears buried in Spennithorne churchyard. Together they had six children, the last being my grandfather James HOGG, born in Richmond Terrace, Leyburn, in 1869.

By 1861 the family of ten, plus one of Thomas HOGG's apprentices, was crowded into a house in Peter Gate, Leyburn. Thomas was by then a *farmer of four acres and a carpenter* employing one man, his oldest son John, and two apprentices. The next son, Thomas Jr., was the second apprentice, but was also making his mark in music (see chapter 53).

Eventually John HOGG decided to strike out on his own by pioneering the family's migration to the new port of West Hartlepool. He set himself up as a builder and like his Uncle John before him in Leeds, he prospered. A newspaper article of 1876 described how '*Lynn Street keeps moving, now slowly and anon by bounds, in a southward direction. Mr HOGG and others have lately erected about 100 houses......*' John advertised in the local papers for six joiners, sometimes ten joiners. He became a member of the West Hartlepool Improvement Commission, which ran the town until it achieved borough status, and after his first wife died he quietly broke the law by marrying her sister, Mary Bell from Grinton, in 1873.

Just before then he had been joined by the rest of the Leyburn family, his father and brother William as *joiners*, Thomas as a *tobacconist*, and Francis Stephen also heading his own building company. When F.S. HOGG became a Liberal town councillor his election address boasted of his familiarity with drains! The HOGGs did not forget their roots, and named one house they built Leyburn House. Others were called Downholme House and Ellerton House, in both of which they lived themselves.

Meanwhile another HOGG migration from West Burton had taken place. My great-grandfather Thomas's brother Stephen had taken over a timber mill, on the north bank of the Tees at Wycliffe. His sons later took over the mill and two of them saved a boy from drowning when the river was in spate. They were given Humane Society awards for their efforts.

In West Hartlepool there was sorrow in the family when Francis Stephen HOGG's son Algar died suddenly at 16. His first name occurs nowhere else in the family, but I found that the Lord Bolton of the day was also Algar. I suspect that when the HOGGs were in Leyburn they may have done some work at Wensley Hall and sought a little reflected glory by associating themselves with their noble employer.

My grandfather James HOGG worked for the FURNESS family's produce business and later for the Union Cold Storage Company in Riga, then part of Russia, where my father spent most of his childhood. The family got out before the Germans invaded in 1917, but my grandfather stayed on and was interned near Berlin. After the war he settled in London and never again lived in West Hartlepool. My father became a *surgeon*. I have not yet traced any descendants of my HOGG great-uncles, but I have not given up hope of one day finding more cousins from this old Wensleydale family.

JAMES HOGG JmsHogg@aol.com

68. Matthew COOPER, Saddle-maker to Kings

m. COOPER. The Proprietor.

Matthew, the son of James COOPER and Margaret WARD, was born at The Red Lion, Reeth, on January 24th 1814. He was educated at Fremington, and sent to work in the lead mines from age 11 to 14. He then went to live with Dr BOWMAN in Ripon as his *page boy*. However, the doctor found him too light, but very kindly recommended him to the Rev. Mr GREEN, Bishopston Grove, who kept a Boarding School. Having learnt the basics of the leather trade from his father, who was a *shoemaker*, he went as an apprentice to John ATKINSON, *saddler*, Leyburn in 1829. During this time they spent a great deal of time going out to work at farmhouses, often walking up to seven miles, doing a day's work and walking home again. They had tan pits to dress their own white leather, and in order to get skins, Mr ATKINSON bought old horses, which they had to skin, which was not a very pleasant piece of work, especially if the horse had been dead a day or two. Matthew's master used to attend different fairs with his goods. In addition, Mr ATKINSON's son took on the contract to carry the government mail between Leyburn and Askrigg, and from Leyburn to Bedale and Leeming Bar, and then on to the New Inn in Leeming Lane, a distance of 18 miles. Matthew used to start from Leyburn at 20 minutes to five in the afternoon, sleeping at the New Inn, and returned at 8.20 the next morning, and then worked at the bench until it was time to start again. This he did both summer and winter for some time, saying that in the summer the duty was very pleasant, but in the winter quite the reverse. He felt it gave him *"a thorough knowledge of and liking for the horse, both of which, I contend, every saddler ought to possess"*.

In February 1835 at the end of his apprenticeship, Matthew moved to York and found work with a *piece master saddle maker* named Mr GUILDERTHORPE. He worked for him only a fortnight, as it was agreed he would have no wage. He then went to Malton and got work with Mr SCOTT where they went out to work at farmhouses. Anxious to work at saddles whenever he could, he made several for the different saddlers in Malton leaving that town in September 1835 to go to Stamford Bridge where he finished both cart collars and saddles for Mr WALLACE, *saddler*. He went to York, then worked in Leeds. In September 1839 he was invited to come back to York to commence as a *piece master saddle maker* in the place of Mr GUILDERTHORPE, who had just died. He continued in that capacity until 1851.

In 1850 Matthew heard about Prince Albert's plan for the Great Exhibition of 1851. He says: *"By then I had 11 or 12 years experience from 1839 in the saddle making, and as I had never seen anything from London any better than my own, and as all were invited, I thought I would let them see what York, could do, as such I applied for space and got it, and although I was then living in a small cottage of £12 per year rent and having a small family to keep and no capital, I set to work with a full determination, to accomplish the task set before me. This was at the latter part of 1850. As it was* *looked upon at that time that goods such as had never been seen before were to be exhibited, I fixed upon making a side saddle, introducing a quantity of Berlin wool work in the centre of the seat, heads, safe, flaps and skirts, the edges of the hog skin attached to the wool work are all turned in. I also made a Military saddle with Berlin wool work introduced in the seat, besides these two, I also made a hunting saddle, somerset saddle, quilted all over and a race saddle, and I had a mahogany case made with flaps all round which cost £35. The value of the case and all in it was estimated at £100. This only shows what can be done with perseverance and industry as in the month of October 1850 when I started of my exhibition work, I had no capital and had a family of six to provide for, and all my private work as a Piece Master as well and by the month of March following I had my work ready, and I may here remark that I never saw any other man, make either a Side Saddle, Military Saddle, Somerset Saddle, or a Race Saddle, but myself....I am, what was named at the time of the exhibition of 1851 was opened, a self taught man. When my case, and goods had to be sent to London, I could not spare either the time, or money, to go myself but fortunately I had a brother-in-law living in London who undertook to see the case and goods properly placed in the building, then came the opening on May 1st 1851, and before the exhibition had been opened a fortnight it was given in by all the leading workman in London, that the York saddles were the <u>best in the building</u>. The first time I was ever in London, was on Saturday July 30th 1851 when a cheap trip was run from York, return tickets 5/-, Monday morning August 1st was the first time I had been in the building, and knowing that Mr KIDD, of the firm of WILKINSON & KIDD, was an associate to the jury, to assist them in their judgement, I called upon Mr KIDD, when this old shop was at the corner of Park Lane and Oxford Street. Mr KIDDs remark to me was, well Mr COOPER, I must congratulate you, on having such a case of goods as you have in the exhibition, there the race saddle in particular is the prettiest piece of workmanship I ever saw in my life, this was said in the hearing of all his men in the front shop, amongst whom was the late respected Mr CHAMPION, who was side saddle hand with the old firm."* The Illustrated London News of 6th Sept 1851, reviewed the exhibition: *"Racing Saddles:; Several are shown, but for form, workmanship, and weight, nothing can exceed the one exhibited in No. 50 by Mr COOPER of York, the whole case is highly credible, and the racing saddle has been pronounced by one of the leading members of the Jockey Club the best he ever saw....His Somerset saddle is also a piece of right good workmanship."* This success was the forerunner of many others. He won medals at London and York in 1862, Dublin 1865, and York and London in 1866, in fact everywhere that he exhibited.

The 1851 York Directory shows Matthew had set himself up with a saddler's shop and manufactory, first at 25 Swinegate, York. By 1872 he was in more prestigious premises at 18 Railway St, where it remained until 1900 initially trading as M. COOPER and later as M. COOPER & Sons. It then moved to 4-6 Railway Street, where Matthew continued to work until his death on 3rd June 1903. In 1911 the firm merged with RYMERS in Stonegate, a successful venture owned by Mr ROBSON who had been Matthew's employee for about 15 years and the two firms became known as Messrs. ROBSON & COOPER. Matthew PHILLIPS, Matthew's grandson was the COOPER representative and they moved into newly purchased premises in Lendal.

As well as being Church Warden in the Parish Church of St. Martin-cum-Gregory, Micklegate, for over 25 years, Matthew was also one of the key originators and committee member of the "The Yorkshire Gala." Amongst the many attractions was a balloon ascent every year, and as one of the balloon committee, he made 18 ascents, three times going above the clouds. He was also a longstanding member of the Eboracum Lodge of Freemasons and at one time, Grand Master. Matthew was instrumental in saving two lives; one a boy who was drowning in the river Swale near Muker, in Swaledale; and another time, when following the Bedale Hounds, in 1832, a short distance below Wensley Bridge, he saved a man named Bryan THOMPSON from drowning in the river Yore, in Wensleydale in the presence of the whole hunt.

When the Volunteer movement was first brought forward, he was among the earliest to join the Yorkshire Corps. This was in 1859, and at that time the volunteer had to find his own outfit, including rifle which together cost about £12. He served in the 1st Company for about 12 years, rising to the position of Colour-Sergeant. For forty years Matthew enjoyed an international reputation as a saddle maker. Among his patrons during that period were the King of the Belgians, the late Czar of Russia, Prince Albert Victor, Prince Francis of Teck, the Maharajah of Baroda and several other European royalties as well as Indian Princes. He was one of the first makers of racing saddles.

Carolyn McCartney – one of Matthew's great, great, great, grand-daughters.
carolyn.mccartney@btinternet.com

69. George BROWNRIGG (alias ROBINSON) of Askrigg 1856–1905

George BROWNRIGG was a dalesman, a cavalryman using a false name and a hero of Darlington.

A yellowed, faded newspaper cutting from 1905 tells the following story.

SUDDEN DEATH OF A WELL-KNOWN DARLINGTONIAN

The news of the sudden death of ex-Sergeant George BROWNRIGG will be received with great regret by his many friends in this neighbourhood. Deceased had for twenty one years served in the 9th Lancers – over ten years of which were spent abroad and he was in receipt of a pension. He saw active service in the Afghan campaign of 1878-80 for which he received the Afghan medal. He also received a silver medal for long service and good conduct and was in possession of a certificate for education. Deceased left the army some 12 or 13 years ago, when he was appointed timekeeper at Clifton Mills, Halifax, which position he held until his death. Ex–Sergeant BROWNRIGG's end was most painfully sudden. He had for some time complained of pains in is chest, but still continued to fulfil his duties. Last Thursday he reached home shortly after noon, and after speaking to his wife, went into another room for his dinner. On his wife's arrival a few minutes later deceased had fallen from his chair dead. The cause of death was heart failure, brought on by walking uphill during excessive heat.

Ex-Sergeant BROWNRIGG will be best remembered by Darlingtonians for the heroic services he rendered during the Kinross-street fire 16 years ago, when several lost their lives. The untiring manner in which deceased rendered first aid to the injured made the people of Darlington proud of their hero, and resulted in a public testimonial being promoted, and at the Railway Tavern Sergeant BROWNRIGG was presented with a riding whip and a silver watch, suitably inscribed, for his services. Alderman HARDING, who was Mayor of Darlington during that period, made the presentation, and spoke in the highest terms of the way Sergeant BROWNRIGG had conducted himself. The late sergeant, who was 49 years of age, leaves a widow and four children.

The people of Darlington were unaware apparently of a mystery surrounding George BROWNRIGG. Why did he enlist in the army as George ROBINSON? An examination of his life may shed a little light on this but there is no hard evidence.

He was born in Askrigg in 1855, the son of John Heavey BROWNRIGG and Ellen ROBINSON. His parents were married on 18 January 1855 at Askrigg Chapel and their story is told in chapter 24. His grandparents were James ROBINSON, a grocer, chemist, postmaster and registrar and Margaret KETTLEWELL.

At the time of the marriage, John H. was a *Private* in the Royal Sappers and Miners. He must have left the army within a few years, as by 1861 he was a *civilian land surveyor* in Buscott, Berkshire. George's siblings were Margaret, born in 1858 at Brough, Westmorland, John, born in 1868 in Hexham, Northumberland, and James Robinson (my grandfather) born in 1872 in Darlington, County Durham. 1861 is the only census that shows John H. and Ellen together at the same address, so perhaps he had many short-term jobs and Ellen did not always go with him. Since his surveying work required frequent travel, it is possible that George saw little of his father.

George appeared in the 1871 census in the household of his grandfather, James ROBINSON, in Reeth. He was a 15 year old *student*. His grandfather was living in Hill House (now the Burgoyne Hotel) which belonged to his nephew, George Alderson ROBINSON, a wealthy property owner. George's mother, Ellen, was living a few doors away with children Margaret and John but without her husband. Had George perhaps lived with his grandfather for many years and come to be known as a ROBINSON rather than a BROWNRIGG? This could be reinforced by his father's absences from family life.

On 14 April 1873 George enlisted at York in the 9th (Queen's Royal) Lancers as George ROBINSON. His records show that he was 18 years old, five feet eight and a half inches tall, with greyish blue eyes and light brown hair. He is described as a *labourer*. He gave as next of kin his father Jack ROBINSON of 18 Powlett

St, Darlington This was his mother's address in the 1881 census. Of course, his father's true surname was BROWNRIGG.

After some home service, he sailed to India on *HMS Euphrates* in 1875 and was deployed in Sialkot. After ten years of service in India and Afghanistan he returned to England on *HMS Crocodile* and was based there and in Ireland. He was promoted to *Corporal* in 1888 and to *Sergeant* in 1890. He was discharged on 16th April 1894 after the *"termination of his second period of limited engagement."*

It is surprising that he wanted to sign on for a second term, as his foreign service was distinguished mainly by illnesses including tonsillitis, sprain of foot, fever, ague, jaundice, ulcer, boils, fever again, tape worm, dengue, synovitis, and piles. The cause of his many illnesses was often stated to be the climate.

Eventually officialdom caught up with him when it was discovered by unknown means that he had enlisted under a false name. In January 1885 he signed this declaration:

> *"I George BROWNRIGG do solemnly & sincerely declare that I was enlisted on the 14 April 1873 under the name of George ROBINSON which name I now declare to be incorrect. The name of George BROWNRIGG contained in the accompanying certificate of birth I now declare to be my true name and I make this solemn declaration conscientiously believing the same to be true and by virtue of the provisions of an Act made and passed in the sixth year of the reign of His late Majesty King William the Fourth chapter 62 entitled 'The Statutary (sic) Declaration Act 1835'. I have also been warned that if the above declaration be false or untrue in any material particular I am liable to be indicted for perjury. George BROWNRIGG Pte 9th Lancers."*

So after nearly 12 years in the army, he owned up to his real identity. There is no evidence to explain why he rejected his father's name and used his mother's maiden name. Was there a quarrel with his father? Did he resent John H.'s frequent absences? Was his grandfather a surrogate father? Both his brothers later joined the 9th Lancers but they used their true surname. When his brother John enlisted in 1885, he named his father as John BROWNRIGG of London, address unknown.

After his discharge from the army in 1894, George went to Halifax, where he became a timekeeper at Clifton Mills, Hipperholme. In 1895 he married Sarah Ann LOCHHEAD (or LOCKHEAD) at Halifax. She was a 34 year old widow with a five year old daughter. George and Sarah Ann had three children, Robert Brier, born 1896, Ellen, born 1898 and Margaret, born 1904. BRIER was Sarah Ann's maiden name.

In spite of 21 years in the army, he must have spent a good deal of time in Darlington in order to have *"many friends in the neighbourhood"*.

There are BROWNRIGGs in Halifax and I have tried to contact one of them but with no response. Perhaps his descendants could explain the mystery of the false name.

ALLAN BROWNRIGG, great nephew ambrownrigg@optusnet.com.au

70. Missing Fathers – a 20th Century Migration

My great-grandfather and namesake, John WHITTON who was born in Bainbridge in 1789, was imprisoned (later transported) when my grandfather, George was only 7 years old. George left the Dales for about 30 years but returned to Bainbridge, re-married and my father Thomas was born. George died when Thomas was only eleven years old. Thomas became the *farmer* at Manor House in Bainbridge and married when he was 45 years old. I think of myself as being from Bainbridge but actually I was born in Sedbusk at the home of the district nurse. My earliest memory is of looking out of Manor House window at the V.E. celebration (Victory over Europe May 8th 1945) with my father who was very ill and I had the measles. My father died shortly after that and the farm was sold. I moved with my mother, Connie and my sister Margaret, to a house that overlooks the village green near the old Bainbridge School.

If my father had lived a few more years there is no doubt I would have become a farmer like him. I attended Bainbridge School and even though the school was right across the road from my house I was often late! I enjoyed playing football and cricket on the green and in winter sledding down the hill. During the severe winter of 1947 I was hit by a sled and taken to Northallerton Hospital. An overnight stay turned into 2 weeks as I could not get back up the dale because of snowdrifts.

In 1951 I went to Yorebridge Grammar School near Askrigg and stayed for the next 7 years. I continued to play football and cricket but developed a love of fly fishing on the Rivers Bain and Ure. My real passion was billiards and from the time I was about 13 years old I played nearly every day, sneaking in on Sunday when the Village Institute was officially closed. In 1958 in my last full year in the dales, I was the youngest player and Upper Dales Individual Billiards Champion. My strengths at school were physics and math but I did not have sufficient qualifications to get into University. I found a physics' research training programme with Associated Electrical Industries in Rugby, Warwickshire and that is where I went in 1958 and I have since only had short stays back home in the dales. The company had a large home named Coton House, for about 300 boys and men who were apprentices. I was there about three years and made friends that I still keep in touch with 50 years later. I attended Rugby Technical College one day and two evenings a week and eventually received a Higher National Certificate in Applied Physics. In 1961 I was accepted into the Physics programme at University College of North Wales, Bangor. I think I spent too much time partying and not enough studying, but I graduated with a BSc Honours degree in Physics in 1965.

I then went to work with MEL Co. LTD in Crawley where one of their products were Linear Accelerators used for Cancer Treatment. 45 years later I am still working with these machines. I enjoyed exploring the London area over the next three years but it was a time of recession and in advance of impending lay-offs, I decided to emigrate to Canada. My flat-mate, Mel, had gone the previous year and was settled.

Canada was still offering assisted passages and I sailed from Liverpool on the *Empress of Canada* in April 1968. It was the first sailing of the year and it took about six days. The last day and night you could hear the crunching of the sea-ice. We first landed in Quebec and then went down the St Lawrence to Montreal where we left the ship and continued on to Toronto by train. I stayed with my friend Mel and his wife and baby, for about one month while I looked for employment. Then I had my big break, as I was offered entry into a Medical Physics programme at Princess Margaret Hospital, part of the Ontario Cancer Institute. This is the largest cancer treatment facility in North America and my instructor, Dr Jack Cunningham was (and is) a world renowned medical physicist, so I received excellent training which led to a long career.

I did not know it at the time but I have a lot of distant WHITTON relatives in Ontario, Canada.

Shortly after I arrived in Canada, Robert Kennedy was assassinated in Los Angeles on June 5th 1968. I was also in Toronto on July 21st 1969 when Neil Armstrong first walked on the moon. We watched it happen on a large screen television that was set up near the city hall. It was in Canada that I learnt to ski, which I still enjoy.

Near the end of my two year programme I met a doctor from Milwaukee, Wisconsin who was studying the Canadian way of cancer treatment. He offered me a job as the medical physicist at two hospitals where he was starting a cancer treatment programme. I jumped at the chance and obtained my "green card" and went to Milwaukee in mid 1970. Wisconsin is also home to many of my distant PRESTON relatives.

We built a new cancer treatment centre and installed the first high energy linear accelerator in the Milwaukee area. That was where I met my wife Philomena BARI of Sicilian descent. We married in 1975 and we left for California as I had been offered a job at Stanford Medical Centre in Palo Alto. We stayed about two and a half years and took time out to see all the beautiful areas such as Yosemite, Monterey, Giant Redwoods and of course Disneyland. We also took a trip to Hawaii.

In 1976 I passed the American Board of Radiology exam in radiological physics, which is the qualification needed to practice medical physics in the USA. In 1977 my previous doctor colleague in Milwaukee offered me my job back with more responsibilities and an increase in pay. My wife was also offered a position to start a school for radiation therapists (radiographers in the UK) so we returned to Milwaukee. We stayed there for the next thirty years and that is where our two children Derek Baynes and Amber Bari were born.

I continued to ski during our long cold winters and started to play golf in earnest during our warm but short summers. Over the years I lost interest in English soccer and cricket and began to follow American Football instead.

I retired in 2006 and moved to Arizona where my wife had taken a job with the prestigious Mayo Medical Clinic. Retirement allows me to play golf as much as I can and take advantage of the beautiful weather that we have all year round. I also enjoy taking care of the wonderful flowers that we can grow all year. I miss the dales for its scenery, particularly the rivers where I loved to fly-fish, and wish it were closer than five thousand miles away.

JOHN BAYNES WHITTON May 2010 in Scottsdale, Arizona, USA jbwaz@cox.net.

Editor's note: John was asked to submit his story to ensure that we recorded a 'living' emigrant's experiences.

71. The FAWCETT family of Ivelet Heads, Swaledale who travelled to Green Valley Road, Ree Heights, South Dakota

John FAWCETT and family

John FAWCETT was born in May 1826 son of John and Ruth Patience (Peacock) FAWCETT of Gunnerside in Swaledale. He married Margaret METCALFE in 1852 and their family consisted of a son John FAWCETT born in 1853, his sister Ann born in 1855 and George Metcalfe FAWCETT born in 1858. Another baby was born in 1860. After Margaret's death in 1863 John and the three children decided to move to the United States. They travelled on the ship *Erin* and settled in south west Wisconsin where many of his friends and relatives already lived. John married Hannah THOMPSON and they had another daughter Ruth, born 1865. The family later moved to Iowa and it is believed he died in a mining accident in Iowa sometime between 1865 and 1870. After John's death Hannah and the four children again moved back to Wisconsin.

After their father's death John, his sister Ann and his brother George Metcalfe moved to what was then known as Dakota Territory and each set out a claim for land signed in 1885. Dakota Territory later became North and South Dakota and this land is in South Dakota. The family probably moved to Dakota Territory by train and later set up a home at Alexandria, South Dakota. It is here where John and his brother George married sisters. Martha RADFORD was born in Dubuque, Iowa in 1861. It is believed the Fawcett and Radford families were neighbours in Iowa and both had moved to South Dakota. John and Martha were married at Alexandria, South Dakota on March 31st 1886.

Martha often talked about helping in the field and hauling hay. She worked all day in the field with John and each of them would bring a big load of hay home at night.

Four children were born at Alexandria, South Dakota in the early years of their marriage. Myrtle was born in 1888; Margaret Alice in 1889; John Leonard in 1891; and Ruby Hazel in 1893. At that time John and Martha packed their belongings and four small children into two covered wagons and drove to Girrard,

Kansas, each driving a wagon. Martha was pregnant at the time and Matthew Clare was born there in 1895. The family then continued their journey to Arkansas where they lived on a farm for one year. Ruby was twelve years old at that time and told stories of their experiences while living there. They called the Negroes "*Darkies*" and told of the poor treatment given to them. Ruby came down with Malaria fever and was sick the whole year they lived in Arkansas. A side effect of medication and high fever was the loss of all her hair, but it grew back, a mass of curls, which she hated because long hair was the 'in thing' for young girls in those days. Ruby remained very sick and the doctor recommended that the family move back to South Dakota. John had an auction sale of their goods and they moved back to Alexandria, South Dakota, this time by train. During these years three more sons were born, Edwin in 1897, Koran in 1899 and George Robert in 1902. John was 49 and Martha was 41 when the youngest child was born.

For a short period of time the family lived on a dairy farm near Clear Lake, South Dakota before settling in Hyde County, South Dakota.

A Deed of Land shows in 1906 that John purchased 800 acres of farm ground in Hyde County for Ten Thousand dollars dated June 4th 1906. On this property in the 1920's a house was built with battery operated electricity and running water from a cistern. Today in 2010 a fifth generation lives on that ranch/farm in Green Valley. Our son visited Swaledale last year and George BUXTON showed him where our ancestors had lived. On returning to the United States he said he could understand why John settled in South Dakota and Green Valley as it would reminder him of the area he grew up in England.

As we think of the events in the lives of our pioneer grandparents, we also think more about them as people. We realise that they had lots of courage and faith and they worked hard. They had many sorrows and disappointments and also joys and good times, just as we all do. We need to remember what people are and not just what they do. Here's a closing thought "*Our descendant's eyes are on us* – *let us make them proud, as our pioneer ancestors have made us proud of them.*"

At one time most of the children of John and Martha lived in Green Valley and even today some of the descendents live there. John and Martha are buried at Ree Height, South Dakota.

Ann FAWCETT was born in 1855 and married William BEEZLEY in 1884 at Mitchell, South Dakota, and moved to Kansas. William BEEZLEY died in 1910 and Ann (Fawcett) BEEZLEY died in 1925. Their family consisted of Benjamin, born 1885, George Fawcett BEEZLEY in 1887, Elmer Carl in 1889, and Roy Clinton in 1893. Ann wrote the letter in the exhibition to her cousin Ann BUXTON who was my grandfather's sister.

George Metcalfe FAWCETT married Ellen RADFORD, a sister of Martha (Radford) FAWCETT, in 1888. They lived at Alexandria, South Dakota and had three children who all died at an early age. The family is buried at Alexandria, South Dakota.

PATTY FAWCETT 20361 Green Valley Road, Ree Heights, South Dakota, 57371
dpfawcett@venturecomm.net

GEORGE BUXTON 20 Smisby Road, Ashby de la Zouch, LE65 2JL, Leicestershire.
g_buxton@talktalk.net

72. JAMES WATSON and family from Richmond – horse racing supremos in France

James WATSON, was the eldest son of Francis and Ann WATSON (née Nic(h)olson). Francis was, from 1814, a *lighthouse keeper* on the Inner Farne Islands off the Northumbrian coast, and was a friend and neighbour of Grace DARLING whose family were on the Outer Farne Islands. Robert, their second child was born in North Sutherland, and by the birth of the third child in 1817, Frances and family appeared to be in Rothbury. Nearby was the stud of Nunnykirk, owned by William ORDE, so presumably this is how James moved into the world of horses. As a boy he was apprenticed to Mr Watson Alcock LONSDALE and during that time he trained horses for Mr Robert JOHNSON at Tupgill in the dales. In about 1830 he was put in charge of the stud Nunnykirk and it was here that he trained the famous mare *Beeswing*. She won an incredible 51 times out of 63 entries. Her most notable victory was the 1842 Ascot Gold Cup.

James started as a *public trainer* in 1850 training at Back Flags, Richmond, soon moving to more extensive stabling at Church Mills. According to the census records, in 1851 he was a *lodger* at Low Channell, Richmond in the Richard DUNN household and by 1861 he was at Newbiggin, Richmond. At this time Edward GILL retired from Belle Isle and James then took over in 1863. He turned out several well known winners. At 46 years of age, he married Jane COOPER in 1858, eldest daughter of the famous York *saddler*, Matthew COOPER and twenty six years his junior. (see chapter 68) James was a man respected by everyone, rich and poor. Following his death in 1891, the *Racing World* said his *'hospitality was proverbial; he could relieve a beggar, and entertain a prince'*. Other newspapers at the time of his death said he was *'honest, game and straight as a gun barrel'*. James and Jane had eleven children, all born at Belle Isle. His four sons all became *trainers* and two of his daughters married trainers who were already established in Chantilly. Elizabeth Ann WATSON (1860-1946 York) married James MAXWELL, a York *tailor* originally from Penzance, who lived in York.

James Cooper WATSON (1862-1929 Chantilly, France) also later known as Jim, lived and trained at Belle Isle and in 1888 he took over the management of his father's establishment. His patrons included the Earl of ZETLAND, Marquis TALON and Capt Wilson TODD amongst others. In July 1893, with the decline of racing in Richmond, he accepted an offer to train for the Baron Edouard de ROTHSCHILD in Chantilly. He came back in December to marry Elizabeth BLADES and then returned to Chantilly, staying as *private trainer* to Baron ROTHSCHILD for many years.

Francis (Frank) WATSON (1886-1946 Rugby) also went out to Chantilly with his wife Ada EYLES in 1894 to become assistant trainer to his brother James, for the ROTHSCHILDs. He later became a *horse dentist* in Chantilly. Their two sons, Donald and Dalton both became *trainers*. After the family came to England during the war, Dalton returned to Chantilly to train and Don stayed in England as a *stud groom*. Jane (Jinnie or Mutty) WATSON (1867-1942 died in the Northampton area) married Wallace ENOCH, a *butcher*, and moved to Cambridgeshire. They had four children.

Kate WATSON (1868-? USA) married William CLARKE from Pateley Bridge and they emigrated to America and settled in Massachusetts. He was a *farmer/grain dealer*.

John (Jack) WATSON (1870-1934 died in Newmarket, Cambridge) started off as the north-country lightweight jockey and was then, for forty years, the *private trainer* to Leopold de ROTHSCHILD, and a few of his friends. John WATSON made winning early season two-year-old races a speciality and took the Brocklesby Stakes at Lincoln six times in seven years. Another important success was the 1912 St. Leger with *Tracery,* who also won the St. James Palace Stakes, Champion Stakes and Eclipse Stakes. His son, Geoffrey, trained at Chantilly, for Baron Guy de ROTHSCHILD, Baron Elie de ROTHSCHILD and Baroness Guy de ROTHSCHILD and married his first cousin Elizabeth, daughter of his uncle James. His racing record was remarkable. In 1963 he had charge of *Exbury*, the best middle distance horse in Europe, winning the Prix de l'Arc de Triomphe. In 1973 WATSON had 44 victories, and was the top French trainer. On retirement he went to Cannes in the South of France, where he died in 1994.

Annie (Nancy) WATSON (1871-1990 Weybridge, Surrey) remained with her mother until her death and then went out to Chantilly to live with her sister and brother-in-law, May and Elijah CUNNINGTON.

William WATSON (1873-1946 Newmarket) at first became *assistant trainer* to his brother John in Newmarket and then moved into the banking world and worked for ROTHSCHILDs in London. He married Isabella HOPPER in Newmarket.

Frances (Fanny) WATSON (1875-1958 Chantilly, France) went to France in 1893 with her mother and three younger sisters, May, Nancy and Ethel, to keep house for James for a few months until his marriage in December. Whilst there, they met the CUNNINGTON brothers George and Elijah (both successful trainers) and both fell in love. They returned to England and Fanny married George in 1895 in York but they returned to France and stayed there.

Mary (May) WATSON (1878-1955 Roubaix, France) married Elijah CUNNINGTON in 1899 and also remained in Chantilly. In 1924 Elijah won the Ascot Gold Cup with *Massine* and also won all the French Classics during his successful racing career. They left France in 1940, narrowly escaping the Germans, and lived in York, where he died in 1943. May and her family returned to France after the war and she died there in 1955.

Ethel (Etty) WATSON (1880-1963 Brighton, Sussex) remained with her mother until her death and then went to live with her sister, Fanny in France until the war. She returned to England where she lived with her sister-in-law, John WATSON's widow.

The lives led in Chantilly by this generation were very different to the ones they had known in Richmond. The English Colony, despite being in France, maintained a very English way of life. A cup of tea in the afternoon was still an important part of their daily lives. English was always spoken at home and the English training families out there almost all inter-married. Even the stable lads were brought out from England so French was rarely spoken! The early English trainers built their own Church in Chantilly, St Peters, around which English village life existed. Even after a number of decades of the English families having settled there, an English grocer in Paris, BETJEMAN and BARTON, used to come out from Paris regularly to take the English orders and there was even a Newmarket tailor who came over twice a year to measure them all up for their English suits! The Butchers used to have to produce typical British cuts of meat and the trainers wives taught the wealthy French owners to enjoy such dishes as steak and kidney pudding and roast beef and boiled leg of mutton. My mother remembers her grandmother telling her these dishes were not normally cooked in France. In contrast to the village lifestyle they enjoyed, was the very sophisticated and lavish world of racing and all the fame and fortune that this brought. From about 1835, it was the English who led the way in horse racing in France and as a result were always held in very high esteem by all around them. Racing in Paris was a grand affair!

CAROLYN McCARTNEY carolyn.mccartney@btinternet.com

73. John James FENWICK from Swaledale to Newcastle

John James FENWICK

John FENWICK moved go Richmond from his parents' farm in Feldom, Swaledale, where he started a *grocer's business* at 83 Frenchgate. John's wife, Mary, was the daughter of James COOPER of Reeth and Margaret WARD from Healaugh. Mary was the sister of Matthew, who moved to York and became a well-known saddler. (See chapter 68). John James FENWICK the son of John and Mary was born on 31st July 1846 in Richmond.

With eleven children born to the family, and living in a small house, some were sent to live with their grandparents. John James stayed with his Feldom family, and for a number of years with James and Jane in the Toll House at Ellerton, where they spent the last years of their lives. John James walked to the Wesleyan School in Reeth each day. When he reached the age of eleven, after his grandmother had died, he returned to Richmond and attended the Corporation School in Tower Street. There the master had to be of *"indisputable moral character"* and be able to *"instruct the boys in reading English grammatically, in writing and arithmetic"*, all of which seemed to benefit John James in his future business career. He remained there till he was fifteen years old, although fourteen was the age at which the boys usually finished schooling; perhaps he was used as a monitor, helping to teach the younger boys. He left with a certificate which said that he read fluently and worked sums as far as square roots, that his knowledge of the Holy Scriptures, geography and grammar was *"good"* and of English history only *"fair"*. His conduct was *"very good and exemplary"*.

He then helped in his father's shop, where he was put to making the *"farthing dips"*, slender little candles, which were affordable by the poor.

His mother died some years after she had undergone treatment in London. She suffered poor health for many years but continued to have more babies until her death at forty-four in 1860. She had been a caring and loving mother who wrote poetry and kept a book of her poems and those of others, and in which she even penned a few farewell lines to her children.

John James then moved to Middlesbrough with his father, who set up business once more. He did not continue working with his father. After a short time in a draper's shop, he started an *apprenticeship* with a draper in Stockton on Tees. In 1869 he wrote in his diary *"considering the time that is past, I remember with sorrow what a valuable part of my life has been wasted. I am bordering on twenty-three years of age and I can find nothing of importance that I have done to benefit my fellow man"*. After seven years his employer suggested he would have more opportunities in Newcastle, so he packed up and found employment in the big city with a draper's firm called MOSES and BROWN in Mosely Street.

He then moved to BRAGG and Co. in Pilgrim Street, where he remained for twelve years as a *buyer* and then as *manager*. In 1872 he married Mary Hannah BURNARD, the daughter of a well-known *master tailor*. They had four children, and he was able to send his sons to the Leys school in Cambridge.

During his time with BRAGG and Co. he took on some work as an *agent* for the National Provident Institution for Mutual Life Insurance. His employers made his involvement with the insurance company a reason for dismissing him. He sued the company for wrongful dismissal and won the case, receiving £2,000. Although he was offered a full-time job with the insurance company, after considerable thought and uncertainty he decided he would set up his own business. No doubt the compensation received was a great help.

In 1882 he acquired property in the well-to-do residential Northumberland Street. Here he established with great success the first FENWICK fashion shop. He was creative and had a flare for producing fashionable garments of good quality. As the business prospered he visited London and Paris. He enlarged the premises by taking in other houses along the street. Finally, although his wife was against this expansion, he set up new premises in London in 1891. His descendents followed into the business until the present day, opening shops in a number of other cities.

James John died from heart failure aged only fifty-eight. He left an estate worth £40,971. He was sadly missed in Newcastle, where he was known as a man of principle, a Wesleyan, Sunday school superintendent, and a genial, smart man who embraced the innovations of the Victorian world.

The actress Ellen TERRY, who patronised his shops, is said to have knelt to pray before his portrait, hanging in the shop. When she rose she said, "Now, please show me something beautiful."

A measure of the fame of his enterprises is perhaps seen in another tale: when a stranger asked someone the whereabouts of Northumberland Street, the reply was, "It's outside FENWICKs."

JOCELYN CAMPBELL jocelyncampbell@btinternet.com

74. Henry CALVERT and Jane BRUNSKILL from Arkengarthdale to New Diggings, Wisconsin

Front row: Henry CALVERT b. 1811, Elizabeth Calvert CAYGILL, Jane Brunskill CALVERT b. 1815
Back Row: Margaret Calvert Hillary WILLIAMS, Isaiah CALVERT, John Thomas CALVERT,
Mary Jane Calvert TRELOAR. Not pictured were Henry CALVERT Jr. and Simon CALVERT

My 3rd great grandfather Henry CALVERT and four of his brothers and one sister left Arkletown, Arkengarthdale and moved to the area near New Diggings, Wisconsin between the years 1835 and 1842. Henry's parents were Henry CALVERT born 28th April 1784 in Muker (died 3rd November 1850 in Arkletown,) and Margaret RAW the daughter of Martin RAW and Jane HIRD. Margaret was born on 25th December 1778 at Healaugh (died 10th September 1837 at Arkletown). They were married on 13th February 1804 in Grinton Parish. Their children were:

Isaiah CALVERT, born 1805 in Arkengarthdale; died 22nd November 1850 and buried at the Shawnee Cemetery, New Diggings, WI. He married Ruth GILL on 29th June 1829 in Arkengarthdale; she was born 1807, died in 1858 and was buried Shawnee Cemetery, New Diggings, WI.

Margaret CALVERT born on the 22nd October 1805 in Arkengarthdale. She died after 1871. She married Joseph HILLERY on 7th August 1827 in Arkengarthdale who was born on 5th April 1800 in Standish, Lancashire.

Martin CALVERT, born 1807 in Arkengarthdale; he died 6th May 1859 at New Diggings, WI. He married (1) Elizabeth WAGGOTT 13th Dec 1834 in Grinton. She was born 1815 in Grinton and died before 1839. He married (2) Ann ALDERSON on 11th October 1849 in Jo Daviess Co., IL; Ann was born 12th March 1830 at Windy Hall, Reeth and died 9th January 1901 in New Diggings, WI.

Jane CALVERT, born 1810 in Arkengarthdale died after 1870 in Mifflin Township WI. She married Edward HUGILL on 29th June 1829 in Arkengarthdale. He was born 18th May 1806 in Smarber Hall, Low Row; he died on 10th September 1863 at Mifflin.

Henry CALVERT, born 17th August 1811 in Arkengarthdale died on 19th September 1895 at Calvert/Caygill Farm, Linden, WI.

Michael CALVERT, born 1813 in Arkengarthdale died 22nd March 1876 in Fairplay, WI. He married Elizabeth SPARKS 19th Mar 1841 in Jo Daviess Co., IL; she was born 1820 in England and died 16th May 1882 at Fairplay, WI.

John Nathan CALVERT, born 1816 in Arkengarthdale died on 20th August 1862 in Vernon Co, WI. He married Emily Rosetta HAMILTON on 13th May 1855 in Dodge Co, WI; she was born 7th January 1830 in Tioga Co., New York and died 18th Aug 1866 in Vernon Co, WI.

Thomas CALVERT, born 7th February 1819 in Arkletown and died on 6th October 1868 in Faggergill Mine, Arkengarthdale. He married Ann SLACK on 26th June 1841 in Arkengarthdale. She was born in 1818 in Langthwaite, and died on 13th February 1864 in Arkletown.

James CALVERT, born 6th January 1822 in Arkletown, died 12th April 1822 at Arkletown.

Ruth CALVERT, born 1823 in Arkengarthdale, died after 1854. She married James STUBBS on 27th September in 1845 Arkletown.

Simon CALVERT was born in 1824 in Arkletown.

Henry married Jane BRUNSKILL, daughter of Simon BRUNSKILL and Mary METCALFE on January 10th, 1835. Henry left Arkletown with his wife and three children, Margaret, Simon and Mary during May of 1840. They travelled on the ship *George Washington* and before reaching New York their youngest daughter Mary died and was buried at sea. They journeyed to Jo Davies County, WI and lived near East Fork. Henry bought a quarter section of land and twelve fine milk cows. A few years later Henry sold the land and cows for $1000 and moved to Iowa Co, WI and bought a farm three miles west of Linden, WI. Henry's sister Jane Calvert HUGILL arrived in Wisconsin in 1835 with her husband Edward HUGILL and owned land to the northeast of where Henry settled. Edward died on 19th September 1863. Jane is listed on the 1870 Wisconsin Census as a *widow* and caring for some of her grandchildren. She probably died before 1880.

Before his death Henry sold his land to his next door neighbour Thomas CAYGILL who was also his son-in-law. Thomas's wife had died soon after they moved onto the land next to Henry. Thomas was widowed with two daughters and married Henry's youngest child Elizabeth CALVERT on 30th June 1885. Their houses were within shouting distance of each other. Henry and Jane lived on their farm for the rest of their lives. Jane died on 30th May 1895 and Henry 18th September 1895.

Henry's brothers Martin, Michael, Isaiah and John also went to Wisconsin. Isaiah left Arkletown in 1842 and arrived in New York on 17th May 1842 on board the *Prentiss* with his wife Ruth and four daughters. He owned land south of New Diggings. Isaiah died on 22nd November 1850 and was buried in Shawnee Cemetery, New Diggings, WI.

Martin arrived on board the *Roscius* in 1839. He married Anne ALDERSON on 11th October 11 1849. Martin died on the morning of 5th June 1859 at New Diggings, WI.

Michael came to the New Diggings area before 1840 and married Elizabeth SPARKS. He died at Fairplay, WI on 22nd March 1876. At one time he owned the Wisconsin House Hotel in Fairplay.

John CALVERT is mention in our family bible as having lived in Bad Axe Co, WI. That county is now known as Vernon Co. There was a John CALVERT who died there on 20th August 1862. He was married to Emily HAMILTON in Dodge Co, WI and shown on the 1850 Wisconsin census living in Vernon Co. with two daughters, Helena and Mahala CALVERT. I have not been able to verify if this was Henry CALVERT's brother John.

Henry had three siblings who did not leave Arkengarthdale, Margaret, Ruth and Thomas CALVERT.

Thomas's son Henry CALVERT married Sarah Jane COATES on 10th October 1878. Henry and Sarah were not found in England after the 1881 census. There is a record of a Henry CALVERT on the 1885 Iowa census in Lucas Co, IA with wife Sarah. Their birthdates are similar and both are from England. Thomas's daughter Ruth CALVERT born in January 1859 was listed as a *cook* in Cheshire, England on the 1901 census.

SUSAN CALVERT COSGROVE 242 B Leslie Lane Ballwin, MO 63021 Sncsgrv@yahoo.com

75. Reginald and James ORTON, Military surgeons from Hipswell to India

Reginald ORTON and Anne THOMPSON became the parents of two sons who both became surgeons in India. Reginald became the *curate* to the Rector of Ormside in 1776 and transferred as the curate of the combined parish of Hipswell and Hudswell, eventually becoming *rector* of Hauxwell.

Their son Reginald ORTON (1790- 1835) was baptised in Hipswell, died in Blackburn and was buried in Catterick. He served in the Medical Service of the British Army between 1810 and 1821 in India, and four letters have survived which he wrote to his family in Hauxwell. There was a detailed death notice in the Leeds Mercury on 14th March 1835 which described him as *"eminently distinguished for his professional talents, and for his indefatigable and successful researches into the cause and remedy of Indian Cholera."* His Will dated 16th June 1830 was proved by his sisters Anne and Elizabeth ORTON, spinsters and mentions "my little freehold property in Murton."

In his letters he mentions his older brother James who was born on 20th April 1784 in Hipswell and died in 1857 in Gloucestershire. James was apprenticed to George HOBSON of Middleham, a surgeon and apothecary. He became a *surgeon* with the Bombay Medical Service and became President of the Bombay Medical Board (1838 – 1840), retiring in India in 1840. He returned to England in 1842 with his wife Barbara from Bedale, and settled in Cheltenham.

The following letter was extracted from the Oriental and India Office Collections, Mss Eur. D.1036 and was originally transcribed by Nancy McLAUGHLIN who descended from James.

"Bombay Septr. 10th 1810

My dear Mother

I am afraid the wonderful things which I am just going to tell you about will give you a great deal more pain than pleasure. My last, if it has reached you, will partly have prepared you to hear of them, what I then thought "unlikely" has now come to pass – (not to keep you longer in suspense) I have left the Armiston and am appointed Assistant Surgeon to H.M's 65th Regiment! – this is not all!! I have another equally great piece of news, which you shall hear as soon as you have digested this; let me now explain how this wonderful event has happened. James and I began as soon as I arrived here and left no stone unturned to bring it about. We applied to a member of Council that he has interest with, who recommended us to a member of the Medical Board – he could do nothing, so we went back to the other great man and got him to write a letter to the Capt of the ship desiring him to set me at liberty – this he positively refused, and I had lost all hopes of succeeding when a most extraordinary and unexpected event brought about all my schemes in a moment – the Compy's regular ship Earl Cambden was burnt, and the Surgn mate of her gladly accepted a situation which I as gladly gave up – an exchange was made – all the formalities got over – and I received the permission of Governt. to remain in India.

Half my plan was now executed – it only remained to get an appointment. An Assistant Surgeon was wanted for H. M's 34th Regt. lying at Jaulnah a place about 30 miles in the interior of the country and I fully expected to get that situation till a few days ago when we received a letter informing us that it was likely to be filled from Madras. That being the case I applied for and obtained this which I now fill in the 65th which regiment will in the course of a day or two sail for the Isle of France! -- I assure you my dear mother, it was not without the greatest reluctance I gave up hopes of seeing you again for so long a time as it is likely to be – but all-powerful interest carried everything before it.

If I had remained in the service it was most likely it would have been a number of years before I should have got to be surgeon of a large ship, till which happened it wd. have been scarce possible for me to save anything --- indeed the products of the voyage I had begun would hardly have paid my debts, much less have enabled me to prosecute my studies in London. --- On the other hand by accepting this appointment I am put in possession of a salary of upwards of Thirty Pounds a Month --- an unanswerable argument. That is the Pay at present and will be as long as they remain on active service, or are stationed at any distance from Bombay, and if the Isle of France is taken there is little chance of our returning for some time. But it is not so easy to save money here as you will imagine -- one is obliged to live like other people -- to mess with the officers which is very expensive; however I hope to be able to pay my debts soon, which are by the by much greater than you think.

I have had a great deal of money of James, for with fitting out and one thing and another (everything so dear at this place) I have been at a great expense. James has been proposing to me a plan which will contribute much to your comfort, and which I hope we shall be able to put in execution ere long -----It is now about five weeks since I was released from the Armiston, all which time I have been spending at Versovah ...... in expectation of the appt. in the 34th Regt...... have got a very good house......

This letter has to go to Versovah before it is sent off. Give my kind respects to Mr & Mrs GOODWIN and the GALES ---- I intend to write to Anne if I can possibly find time before we sail which will most likely be in two or at farthest three days; I am to go in the small Company's cruizer Thetis; perhaps you will see it mentioned in the account you will receive by & bye of the capture of the Isle of France.

Give my best love to Fanny who I hope is still (with Anne) doing very well in the way of business – not forgetting my dear little creditor Bessy---------Farewell my dear Mother, I hope no rascally cannon-ball or pistol-bullet will make this the last letter you have to receive from Yr ever affectionate Regd ORTON."

This is the final letter written to his sister Anne from Madras on 6th May 1821

"My dear Anne,

I have at last got this long talked of charge of the regiment. I am nominally in receipt of an immense income, there is not much of it falls to my share, as I was obliged to agree to give up the principal part of it to the Surgeon to induce him to go home. However I get about 900£ a year, and will save 700 of it; and if the regiment remains in India a year and a half or two years longer, I shall have realized quite enough to enable me to go on half pay and spend my time as I like. When I go home I will find out some pleasant place to set myself down in -- probably Richmond or some place in your neighbourhood, maybe Hauxwell itself. ....Rely on it however nothing shall hinder me to stay more than about a couple of years more. ......My constitution is a good deal weakened by the climate, but without proving the least danger to my life.

I wrote to you in August last, and sent you some copies of this book of mine by an officer of the regiment, who was going to Hull. The book has succeeded very well, and I must say (though it comes ill from me) has gained me credit. I have received the most flattering letters about it from all the Medical Boards of the three Presidencies. I have a good number of copies disposed of by private sale, and the Government have purchased from me 100 copies, for which alone I get about 140£. .... My life is a (blank) at present, and hangs rather heavily on my hands. In this country very few have quiet domestic female society; and that is certainly the greatest charm of a man's life. My almost sole amusements are books, and laying schemes of happiness to be put in practice some couple of years hence at home. .....you will find a vast change in my appearance since I saw you. I am always thin, and between the sun and the Seringapatam fever I have got a vile complexion. Besides this, I have within this year or two back made the unwelcome discovery of a number of curved lines in my cheeks, which had no business to be making (an appearance?) for many years to come. .....

God love you all, says Your ever affectionate

R. ORTON."

Oriental and India Office Collections, Mss Eur. D.1036.

The Manchester Times recorded on 21st October 1843 'in the garden of Miss ORTON of Hauxwell near Richmond, there is a splendid fuchsia, six feet in height, fourteen in circumference, and now richly covered in bloom."

Nancy McLAUGHLIN, New Zealand riversidenz@gmail.com

76. John, Joseph, Jonathan and James CLARKSON from Preston-under-Scar to London

Preston Mill, Preston-under-Scar

Joseph CLARKSON, *farmer and miller* of Preston was born about 1767 in Preston-under-Scar. In 1799 at Wensley, he married Mary ALDERSON daughter of William ALDERSON and Margaret LUNN born about 1773 also from the village.

Joseph and Mary had seven children, six sons and one daughter. Four of their sons moved away from Wensleydale to start new lives in London. The reason for them moving to London has not yet been discovered. This account attempts to chronicle briefly the careers and lives of these brothers, John, Joseph, Jonathan and James CLARKSON.

John CLARKSON was born about 1801 in Preston Mill. The earliest found record of him living in London was a notice in the *London Gazette* of 9th October 1832 which showed him as a grocer at 171 Strand, Westminster, London. He married Fanny (FOOT?) in Brompton, Middlesex, in 1830 and they had two children. Fanny died in 1839 when her second child John CLARKSON was born. By 1841, in addition to his grocery business at 171 Strand, he was also a *grocer* with an Italian warehouse at Somerset House, Somerset Place, and a *grocer and tea dealer* at Bouverie Street, in the City of London. He terminated his partnership as a *grocer* with his brother Joseph CLARKSON at 63 Fleet Street, London. In 1846, he relinquished his business as *grocer and tea dealer* at 171 Strand and, by 1861 was living in Herne, Canterbury, Kent (presumably retired), where he eventually died in 1864.

Joseph CLARKSON was born about 1810 in Preston-under-Scar. By 1841 he was a *grocer and tea dealer* at 63 Fleet Street, London, with his elder brother John. This partnership was dissolved by mutual consent in 1843. An entry in the 1841 *Post Office Directory of London* showed Joseph and his younger brother Jonathan as *grocers* in both Marylebone Lane, and 160 Oxford Street, London.

In 1846 Joseph married Elizabeth Mary ARCHBUTT in St George's, Hanover Square, London. Elizabeth was the daughter of Samuel ARCHBUTT and Elizabeth LEICESTER, born 1813 in Chelsea, Middlesex. Samuel was born in Cottingham, East Riding of Yorkshire in 1781. A *journeyman joiner*, he moved to London and married Elizabeth at St Martin-in-the-Fields in 1807. Elizabeth was born about 1786, and died in 1840 in Chelsea. Samuel died in 1852, also in Chelsea.

Samuel was a *builder* of some note. *British History Online* described him as a prosperous builder who operated extensively in Belgravia and Chelsea. He was also a prolific collector of paintings and bought a number of John Constable's paintings at Constable's post-mortem sale in 1838.

The 1851 census showed Joseph living at 24 Motcomb Street, Belgrave Square in London, where he was a *tea dealer and grocer*. In 1861 he was living at 15 Walton Street, Chelsea, working as a *wine merchant,* and by 1884 he was operating as ARCHBUTT and CLARKSON, *wine merchants*, still at 24 Motcomb Street, Belgravia. The 1884 trade directories include an entry for Joseph CLARKSON Son and Co., *wholesale tea dealers*, at 11 Miles Lane and 132 Upper Thames Street. In 1866 Joseph was living at 10 Hans Place, Sloane Street, Chelsea, when he appeared in court for having been adjudged bankrupt. He died in 1867 in Chelsea and Elizabeth his wife died in 1892 in Wandsworth.

Jonathan CLARKSON was born about 1812 in Preston-under-Scar. In June 1833, and at least until 1834, he was a *grocer* in Middleham. In March 1834 Jonathan and Anne BOWMAN were married in the Collegiate Church, Ripon when Anne was about 20 years old. By 1838 Jonathan and Anne had moved to London and were living at 160 Oxford Street where Anne died in June that year. On 10th November 1840 in the parish of St Luke, Chelsea, Jonathan married Mary Ann ARCHBUTT, sister of his brother Joseph's wife Elizabeth. Mary Ann was born in 1809 in Chelsea, Middlesex.

The 1841 census showed Jonathan and Anne living at 171 Strand, Westminster, and an entry in the *Post Office Directory* that year showed Jonathan and Joseph as *grocers*, also in Marylebone Lane. At some point he was also a grocer at 36 Wigmore Street. In April 1845 he was living in 1 Hereford Terrace, King's Road, Chelsea, where he was a *cheesemonger* for eight months before becoming insolvent the same year. He continued to fight his bankruptcy during the following nine years. However, on 24th Feb 1855 he was in danger of losing his total estate and effects due to bankruptcy. His case was postponed until January 1856, and in February of the same year he was released from bankruptcy. He appeared to have suffered substantially by fighting for his release from bankruptcy and subsequently he moved away from London. In 1861 he was living in Herne in Kent, where he continued to live until his death, carrying on various occupations, including *schoolmaster* at the local grammar school and employment as a *cashier*. His wife Mary died in 1879. He was *living off income* from house property in 1881 and died in 1903 aged 90.

Jonathan CLARKSON and Mary Ann ARCHBUTT had five children, including three sons and two daughters. Their second eldest son, Alexander Thomas carved out a very successful career as an *optical instrument manufacturer*. He was born in 1847 in Chelsea, Middlesex, and in 1876 married his cousin Elizabeth Mary CLARKSON, the daughter of his uncle Joseph CLARKSON and Elizabeth ARCHBUTT, at St George, Hanover Square. He was variously described over the years *as a scientific instrument maker, an optical merchant and manufacturer, and a telescope maker*. In 1873 he took over the optical instrument making business started by Benjamin MARTIN. The founders of the business set up as optical instrument makers in the middle of the 18th century, not long after astronomical telescopes first became available. Benjamin MARTIN established an instrument-making business in 1750. His son Joshua joined him in 1778 and in 1782 he patented a method for producing brass drawn tube. The firm prospered and Alexander CLARKSON took it over in 1873. Mr BROADHURST joined the firm as a partner in 1892, and moved it to 63 Farringdon Road, EC1 in 1908, naming the building *Telescope House* but trading as BROADHURST CLARKSON & Co. Alexander later retired and lived in Wandsworth where in 1918 he died aged 71. The BROADHURST & CLARKSON business enjoyed a worldwide reputation and was bought out by Fullerscopes in 1973. Telescope House was closed in 2005 and the company moved to Tunbridge Wells, Kent, where it is now trading as BROADHURST, CLARKSON and FULLER Ltd.

James CLARKSON was born about 1817 in Preston-under-Scar. The 1841 census recorded him as a *grocer* living at 51 Gloucester Street, Holborn, Middlesex. He died on 22nd Feb 1850 and was buried on 25th February 1850 in Wensley, his residence having been given as London.

Thanks are due to Dudley Fuller, Chairman of BROADHURST, CLARKSON and FULLER Ltd. who provided the photo of Telescope House and gave permission for its use in the exhibition.

PETER KENNEDY peter@pmkennedy.co.uk

77. Catherine BROWN also know as CALVERT, WALLER and ELSWORTH

Standing Alice CALVERT, Richard's sister. Front row left to right Philiatersia, Catherine seated, Albert on her knee and Elizabeth standing, taken outside Ivy Cottage, Low Row. 1905.

Catherine was born at 81 Whitefield Lane, Everton, Liverpool on 24th January 1881 and died on 25th March 1952. She was the daughter of Jane BROWN from Low Row, who worked as a *cow keeper* in Liverpool.

Jane had been sent to Liverpool sometime before 1881 to work in the cow keeping business of John MOOR where she met John HOLMES of Garsdale and became pregnant with Catherine.

It appears that the relationship did not last because Jane returned home to reside with her mother at Hatters Roof in Low Row, Swaledale and she appeared there on the 1881 census.

Catherine attended school in Low Row and knew Cherry KEARTON well as she was at school with him. Many years later she would tell Norma her daughter about special places of interest in Low Row, and her school days and often mentioned Cherry.

On January 7th 1889 Catherine's mother Jane married William CALVERT of Oxnop Gill Farm and Jane and Catherine are recorded on the 1891 census as living there. In 1892 Jane gave birth to James CALVERT who went on to farm at Lanehouse Farm, Whitaside and married Elsie HILLARY.

Catherine gave birth to a daughter on 9th April 1901 at Oxnop Gill and named her Philiatersia. She was always known as Elsie and she married a SUNTER. There was no named father on her birth certificate.

In July 1902 Catherine married Richard CALVERT of Feetham Holme Farm in Melbecks Church, Low Row. Richard and Catherine went on to have another two children Elizabeth and Albert CALVERT. In 1910 Richard took the great step of emigrating to Australia to make a better life for his family and his plan was to send for Catherine and the children when he was settled.

In the 1911 census they are recorded as resident at the first house in the row of houses up from the Punch Bowl in Low Row.

Between 1910 and 1911 Catherine began a relationship with John William WALLER, son of James Harker WALLER and Mary Jane COURT who resided in Low Row, not far from Catherine's home. John William WALLER was the grandson of the Rev. Boyd of Low Row. During this period Richard sent for Catherine to follow him to Australia but she refused to go. The suspicion is that she refused as she was pregnant with my mother Gwendoline Louella WALLER whose father was John William WALLER.

Sometime after May 1912 neighbours made it obvious that they were not pleased with what Catherine and John had done and they were forced out of the village, apparently leaving during the night. They left Catherine's three older children in the care of their grandparents Metcalfe and Elizabeth CALVERT.

There is no record of where they went after leaving the village but the presumption was that they may have gone to Hartlepool as John William had family residing there at the time.

The next record was of their marriage in 1917 at the Registry Office in Stockton on Tees where they were residing. Catherine called herself a 'widow'. This marriage was bigamous because Richard was still alive and did not die until 1935. It is possible they 'married' in 1917 because John William had enlisted in the army and if he died Catherine would receive a pension to support her and Gwendoline.

John WALLER was stationed at East Fortune airbase in Scotland. Descendants assume that he did not return to Catherine after the war because either John or Catherine had met someone else. Catherine gave birth to a daughter Norma in 1922. Norma was named on her birth certificate as Norma ELSWORTH, and again no father was named. She could have been named CALVERT which was her mother's married name. On Norma's marriage certificate to Herbert GREENWOOD her father was named as George Elsworth WALLER. It appears that Catherine had added WALLER to George's name because Norma had always been known by this surname, to match her sister Gwendoline. Catherine appeared to change things on certificates to suit herself.

In 1931 Catherine married George ELSWORTH in Stockton Registry office, once again describing herself as a 'widow'. This was yet another bigamous marriage.

Catherine went on to spend the rest of her life in Stockton on Tees married to George. She continued to visit Low Row and her family because there are records of her being in Low Row in 1917 and right through until she died in Stockton on Tees on 25th March 1952

SANDRA CAPES (née Campbell) sandra.capes80@ntlworld.com

THE METCALFE SOCIETY

Founded in 1980, The Metcalfe Society today stands in the forefront of the world of Genealogy as one of the largest and most respected one-name study groups, with almost 1,900 members past and present, home and overseas. It is dedicated to supporting anyone interested in their Metcalfe (and all spelling variants) family history and acts as the principal link between branches in the home country and those settled worldwide. Membership gives access to our online database of over 120,000 Metcalfes, as well as the services of our archivist. For further details please see our website at www.metcalfe.org.uk or write to The Metcalfe Society, c/o 22 Webser Crescent, Rotherham, S61 2BP.

78. Joseph Edwin CLARKSON, Royal Protection Detective to Edward VIII when Prince of Wales

Joseph Edwin CLARKSON (On Left)
With the Sydney Chief of Police during the visit of the Prince of Wales, Sydney 1920

Joseph Edwin CLARKSON was born in 1874 in Coverham Low Mill, Coverham in Coverdale, the third eldest son of William Thomas CLARKSON, miller of Coverham Low Mill, and his first wife Isabella YEOMAN. His father, William Thomas CLARKSON (son of Thomas CLARKSON and Elizabeth WINTER) was born 1846 in Griff Mill, Melmerby, and was married to Isabella YEOMAN (daughter of William YEOMAN and Mary SPENSLEY) in 1868 at Coverham in Coverdale. Isabella YEOMAN was born 1848 in Ashes, Caldberg. They had a total of five children.

In 1891 at the time of the census, Joseph Edwin was living at Marske Hall, Richmond, employed as a *footman and domestic servant*. It is not known when and why he moved to London, but in December 1895 he joined the Metropolitan Police in London as a *Police Constable*. In 1898 he married Lillie GOLDSMITH in Paddington, London. Lillie was the daughter of Henry G. GOLDSMITH and his wife Elizabeth and was born about 1873 in Southwold, Suffolk.

Joseph's police career progressed quickly, and within two years of joining the Metropolitan Police, he had been promoted to Scotland Yard's Commissioner's Office Executive Branch. By 1901 he had progressed to the C.I.D. whilst still a Constable. However by 1904 he had achieved the rank of *Police Sergeant C.I.D.* He was promoted again in 1912 to *Inspector (2nd Class) C.I.D. and Detective Inspector (1st Class) C.I.D.* in 1919.

Although the precise date is not certain when Joseph became a member of the 'CO.SB' Special Branch at New Scotland Yard, in 1920 he was engaged as a *royal protection officer* and *personal detective* to accompany the future Edward VIII on his visit to Australia, when he was still the Prince of Wales.

Joseph retired from the Metropolitan Police in 1929 as *Detective Inspector (1st Class) CO.SB. CID*, aged 55 after 33 years service, and died in 1954 in Coulsden, Surrey, aged 80.

PETER KENNEDY, Buckinghamshire peter@pmkennedy.co.uk

Free Homesteads of 160 Acres.

Reliable information, Pamphlets, Sailing Lists, &c., Free on application to

T. HISCOCK, Hawes,

Agent for the Allan, American, Canadian Pacific, Cunard, Dominion, Orient, and White Star Steamship Lines.

By booking at the Hawes Office intending emigrants have the choice of the best Steamship Lines, and can book on precisely the same terms as at the Head Offices.

EMIGRANTS SHOULD EXCHANGE THEIR MONEY INTO

DOMINION EXPRESS MONEY ORDERS,

Issued by T. HISCOCK,

and save time and trouble on arrival in Canada or the United States. No charge made for issue.

This advert from *"Hiscock's Wensleydale Almanack"* together with the photograph were in an article found by Christine AMSDEN in an old American genealogical magazine.

The picture was labelled as a group of emigrants waiting in Leyburn market place for transport to Liverpool and friends seeing them off.

79. Robert SUNTER born 1876 at Thwaite Bridge and died 1941 at Manchester

Old postcard of Thwaite Bridge circa 1925. It shows the 1768 turnpike road crossing the river Ure, on a handsome, arched, stone bridge. In 1932 the road was widened and straightened, and a new steel-girder bridge was built about 100 yards downstream, leaving the stone bridge to serve only the farm.

Members of the SUNTER family have lived in Swaledale since the Parish Records began, and probably much longer. Around 1783 Robert SUNTER (1732-1820) migrated "over the top" to Wensleydale, and took a lease on Carpley Green farm from Lord Grantham.

This farm lies about a mile south of Bainbridge. Much earlier, in 1757, Robert had married Elizabeth ALDERSON of Park House, near Low Row in Swaledale, and they had nine children, before moving to Wensleydale. Their eldest child was Elizabeth SUNTER (1758-1823) who married Alexander METCALFE (1759-1830) at Stalling Busk on 7th December 1789. They farmed at the remote Camhouses, which is set high on Dodd Fell, close to the boundary between the parish of Hawes and that of Horton-in-Ribblesdale. It is not to be confused with the similarly-named Camshouse, near Askrigg.

Alexander and Elizabeth had four daughters and a son. The son, John, was born in 1802 and in 1830 he married Elizabeth SLINGER at Hardrow parish church. They farmed at Thwaite Bridge farm, which lies about three miles west of Hawes, on the Garsdale road, and is now known as the A684. So began a 121 year connection of my family with Thwaite Bridge farm.

In 1874 Thwaite Bridge farm came into the possession of Robert SUNTER, a first cousin twice removed, of the above John METCALFE. Robert had just married Elizabeth TENNANT at Aysgarth. It was a very rare double-wedding as Robert's sister, Barbara, married Elizabeth's brother, Richard, at the same ceremony on 22nd August 1874.

Robert and Elizabeth had five sons and their second son, John (1878-1945), was my grandfather. This résumé however, concentrates on their eldest son, Robert (1876-1941). Robert and his brothers grew up on the farm, and amongst the many skills they learned was that of butchery. When he was just 24 Robert decided to seek his fortune by making his living as a *butcher* in Salford, Lancashire.

At that time Salford had the largest cattle market in the country. Robert may well have become familiar with it whilst working as a young cattle drover, taking cattle to Salford market. The railways had made this task much easier by that time. It was then only necessary to 'drove' the cattle to the nearest railway station, either Hawes or Garsdale, and they would soon be in Salford. It was then another short 'drove' from the railway marshalling yards to Salford cattle market.

In 1900 Robert opened his first shop on Cross Lane, Salford, about 100 yards from the cattle market. Once he was settled, he returned to Hawes to marry his childhood sweetheart, Esther IVESON, whose father Nehemiah IVESON was a Hawes *blacksmith*. His forge and cottage were located just opposite the school. They were married at St Margaret's, Hawes, on 17th January 1901, and after the celebrations, Robert took his bride to Salford for a working honeymoon.

Three children soon followed with Alexandra May being born in 1902, Robert in 1904 and Norman Kenneth in 1909. Alexandra and Norman were always known by their middle names. The boys eventually went into their father's business, and took it over after his death in 1941. Eventually, when Kenneth retired in 1970, he bought the *Old Dairy*, by the bridge over Gayle Beck, at Hawes, and enjoyed eleven years of retirement there.

For 40 years, until his death in 1941, Robert was a very successful retail butcher, at a time when there was no competition from modern supermarkets. He had over 15 butcher's shops in Salford and Manchester, and became quite wealthy. He owned a large modern house in Wilmslow, south Manchester, and had all the usual trappings of a successful businessman.

In 1932 Robert was elected president of the Manchester & Salford Meat Trader's Association.

Sunter Shop at 251 Stretford Road, c. 1935.

About 1930, Robert also went into the property business, buying fifty houses on a new private housing estate at Heaton Norris, near Stockport. This was at a time when his business was supporting not only himself and his wife, but also the families of his two sons. It seems unlikely that his business would be capable of raising sufficient capital for such a venture, and so it seems that he must have had another income stream. One suggestion, in the family, is that he operated as a 'bookie' or turf accountant, which although commonplace was illegal at that time.

Robert also persuaded two of his brothers to follow his example. James (born in 1883) followed his brother to Salford, in 1901, but about 1906 he left for Blackburn where he made a small fortune of his own. John (1878-1945), my grandfather, followed Robert to Salford, circa 1907, but he was content with just one butcher's shop, so his fortune was rather less grand, but still comfortable.

The two youngest brothers Bernard (born in 1881) and Richard (born 1886) were left at Thwaite Bridge and helped their mother to run the farm. Sadly Richard died in 1907, from injuries caused by an accident at the farm, and their mother, Elizabeth, died in 1921. Bernard continued to run the farm until he retired in 1951, when he sold it, thus severing its connection with the SUNTER family.

To-day there are still SUNTER families in the Dales, and they all share a common ancestry. If any would like a comprehensive family tree, I will be happy to oblige.

RICHARD MCGARRY rick_mcg@tiscali.co.uk

80.   A Family Trail – Anthony SPENSLEY from Swaledale to Dubuque

According to family lore, one Anthony SPENSLEY, his wife Ann (WHITEHEAD) and children, emigrated to America in 1839, first to Pottsville where Anthony worked in the coal mines, and then to Dubuque where they were to remain.

Anthony was one of the first emigrants from Swaledale to venture across the Atlantic and we may never know what prompted his choice. His passage overland would be by wagon. Later emigrants often went on the recommendation of earlier ones, or to join family there. I believe this was how he went, following his brother John.

We know that Anthony was one of the first white settlers and that he built a log cabin for his first home there. This home was the oldest in West Dubuque and was still occupied in the early 1900s. And just to show how facts can be altered by memory over time, online resources now reveal that Anthony actually left in 1834 not 1839.

The Ship's list of 1834 shows Anthony actually emigrated that year.

Ship North Star Liverpool to Philadelphia
(http://istg.rootsweb.com/1800/northstar18340603.html)

50	Anthony	SPENELLY	29	Male	Minor	England
51	Ann	SPENELLY	29	Female		England
52	Willim	SPENELLY	23	Male		England
53	Sarah	SPENELLY	2	Female		England

A few years earlier than Anthony's departure, a John SPENSLEY also left, going first to Pottsville, then to Dubuque in 1834. John's first wife was Betty PEDLEY and they had two sons, Ralph (1819) and John (1821). Following Betty's death in 1825, John remarried to Elizabeth SPENSLEY (daughter of George SPENSLEY AND Margaret HARKER) and the family emigrated. A son William was born in Wisconsin. John became a miner and smelter at Potosi in Wisconsin but suffered ill health and made what must have been a heart-wrenching decision to return home to England. He left a Will in America dated only a few days before his departure.

His Will was dated June 15th, 1838. It mentioned his property containing the blast furnace which was owned by him jointly with Joseph WOOLLEY and Matthias HAM. His address was Dubuque at that time. The Letter of Administration was dated 13 June 1844. It named Elizabeth as his widow, represented by Wm LIGHTFOOT, Anthony SIMPSON as the guardian for minor son William (age 9), and John SPENSLEY and Ralph SPENSLEY. Real Estate was described as 1/3 part of a certain tract of land on which was a blast furnace situate on W1/2 of NE 1/4 Sec #33 T 3 R N3 known as the Palliser's blast furnace in Rigsby Hollow. It looked like that would go to William and Elizabeth and that a sum of $92 each was to go to John and Ralph SPENSLEY. Final Settlement was dated July 6, 1844.

When John returned home he carried a notebook in which he recorded the amounts of money he carried on behalf of other emigrants for their families back home:

Joseph ATKINSON – 2 sovereigns to his mother Margret ATKINSON living at Eggleston; Jos BRUNSKILL 2 sovereigns to his mother Mary BRUNSKILL of Gunnerside; Anthony SPENSLEY, 5 sovereigns to his mother Jane of Low Row; Wm SPENSLEY, £4 to his mother Jane; Anthony SPENSLEY, £2 to his mother Mary WHITEHEAD and Obediah; Anthony SPENSLEY $1 to Wm WHITEHEAD, to drink; Simon HARKER, £1 to Ann HARKER of Barfend.

This document has helped to determine the relationship of Anthony, John and William SPENSLEY as brothers, and sons of Ralph SPENSLEY and Jane WATTERSs. John died of consumption in May 1839 and was buried on the 30th May at Low Row. His notebook was passed on to Robert BONSON who was leaving for Wisconsin, and contained instructions for goods to be bought for John's wife Elizabeth and children in America. Thereafter, Robert used the notebook as a diary and it is now in the archives at Loras College, Dubuque. Elizabeth's obituary contains the following:-

"Mrs. Elizabeth LIGHTFOOT, a lady much respected and beloved, died at the residence of her step-son, Mr. Ralph SPENSLEY, at Asbury, Dubuque County, April 26, aged 76 years. The remains were taken to her home in Potosi, and buried the following day in the cemetery at British Hollow. Mrs. Lightfoot was a native of Yorkshire, England, and came with her husband, John SPENSLEY, -- the father of Mesers. Ralph and John SPENSLEY, of Dubuque county, Iowa -- to America and settled first in Philadelphia, in the year 1832. The following year they removed to Dubuque, then a mere mining camp consisting only of one log tavern, a store and a few cabins. Indians were plentiful enough in those days, and the old lady was often heard to remark about them, and of having shaken hands with Blackhawk who was at that time a prisoner. Her husband's health failing, he left her and returned to his native land in the hope of that climate's benefiting him, but his hopes were vain. He never returned, and she was left a widow in a strange land with four little ones to guide and protect uncheered by a husband's loving aid and counsel."

CHRISTINE AMSDEN camsden@mymts.net

81. The COATES Family from c. 1800

My late mother told me that her grandfather had been an engine driver, working between London and Liverpool, so that was a good lead. For a long time I just could not find this gent and thought she'd been making him up.

I assumed that my grandfather, John COATES, had been the son of someone quite different and so it was a shock when I sent for his marriage certificate and found another John as his dad, and lo and behold! The entry said he was a *locomotive driver*. Got him! My mother would have said, "I told you so!" My aunt in law has told me that there were 13 John COATES, all blacksmiths.

The first John COATES that I found surfaced around 1800 and had married Nanny – Nanny who I have not been able to track down, as there were at least two, if not more, in 1799. Their son, John was born c. 1804 and he married Sarah HUGILL born 1808, daughter of John and Elizabeth (HARKER), in 1827 and had eight children, among which was another John.

Sarah died in Gunnerside in 1850 and John remarried to Isabella METCALFE born 1797, daughter of Thomas and Ann (HIRD?), John SMITHSON's widow, in 1851. Mining was beginning to fail and the population was on the move in the Dales. John and Isabella went off to the Rockdale area of Dubuque in Iowa, taking sons James, George and Thomas William (blacksmith) and his wife, Mary Hunt WALLER, and their two children, Sarah Jane and Thomas William, with them.

Blacksmith John had his shop in Table Mound township. He died on or about the 15th December 1871 and his Will lists "....*George and James COATES Executors, sons of deceased, and others: Ann MILLER (daughter) $25.00, John HARKER (grandson) $175.00, John COATES (son) $200.00; Jane (daughter) $200.00, Simon COATES (son) £200.00, Thomas COATES (son) $200.00, Elizabeth [Isabella] COATES (Widow) for her reasonable & comfortable support during her natural life., Elizabeth RADFORD (daughter) $200.00, to James and George COATES (sons) the rest and residue of the Estate real and personal....etc.*" John obviously had plenty of money to leave. *(Book 17, page 520 of Dubuque County Courthouse, and supplied by P Haase).*

Meanwhile, back in Swaledale, John Jr. had met and married Isabella ALDERSON, daughter of John and Elizabeth (Peacock) ALDERSON of Birk Park, Healaugh. Unfortunately for John and Isabella they had only 3 children and the last one had spina bifida and lived for two days. Isabella died on the same day as her son. John married again, to Mary COATES, born in Crackpot 1840, daughter of Ralph and Jane (CANTRELL), in May 1869 at Melbecks and they did not appear to have had any children. John died in Gunnerside in 1913 and I haven't been able to find Mary's death date.

John, son of John and born Melbecks June 1854, four months after his parents' marriage, was the above mentioned engine driver, although, like his forefathers, he was a blacksmith by trade. John married Sarah Ann PEACOCK, daughter of James and Elizabeth (Thompson) PEACOCK, in 1876 in Grinton and shortly after their first child's birth in 1877, moved to 127 Parkhill Road, West Derby, Toxteth Park, Liverpool then in the County of Lancaster. Grandmother Elizabeth PEACOCK lived round the corner in the 1881 census. In the same census John was listed as an *engine smith* from "Roth", so he was still following his trade. In the next decade the railway expansion in Liverpool and elsewhere became so intense that drivers were needed immediately. Instead of working their way up and graduating to full-blown driver status after a set number of years, men were drafted in at short notice and this must have been what happened to John the engine driver.

In 1880 along came another John, my grandfather. He was the first to break away from blacksmithing, wanting to become a Methodist minister and to study at the Methodist College. Apparently, he was a bit too keen and was turned away, so he went back to Swaledale and became a *farmer*. One can imagine his bitter disappointment but he soon found a similar mind in Isabella Guy HILLARY, who he married on 11th June 1911, at the Wesleyan Methodist Chapel, Reeth.

This wedding photograph appears in Sandra K WOOD's book *The Spirit Speaks Loud*.
1. John; 2. Isabella; 3. James Usher, 4. Mary Ann Usher, 5. Sarah HILLARY, 6. Jane Elizabeth HILLARY.

John and Isabella GUY had three children; the first were twins, born 19 June 1912: John HILLARY and Mary Isabel, my mother. The third child was James Ralph who was mad keen on aeroplanes, building models (whilst his father smashed them up – calling them nonsense), and going on to build one which he flew to Arkengarthdale. This was in the local papers and eventually he joined the RAF in World War II and earning a Distinguished Flying Cross for bringing home a Halifax on one engine when all the aircrew were wounded. The makers didn't know they could be flown on one engine. He was on the Queen's Flight and then became a designer for Hawker Siddeley in Bedfordshire. One of his aircraft – *Swalesong II* – is at Breighton Museum in North Humberside. He died in 1987 and his eldest son, the last John COATES of the line, died in 2007 aged 54. Neither were blacksmiths. It was his mother and my aunt-in-law who has prompted me to do the research.

However, to return to *engine driver* John: my aunt told me that he had married a second time to a PRITCHARD lady who had a son of her own and that John had left a HILLARY family farm to him when he died. So I looked for Sarah Ann's death which was in 1909, in Fazakerley, from cancer. John and she had had six children in total who married into various professions: Isabella married into paper making (LOVATT); John married into Lead mining (HILLARY – see Hillary Family); Elizabeth, a prison warder at Walton Prison in Liverpool married her father's *fireman-stoker* William Dent BELL and stayed in West Derby; James Peacock, also a *fireman*, married Alice Ann PICKSTOCK whose father was a *lighterman* on the Mersey; Ralph Arthur, another *fireman*, married Nellie Ada HUDSON whose father was a *baker*; and Ethel Mary married Frederick Reginald PRITCHARD, from Hawarden, Chester, who was a *cotton porter* in Liverpool. However, Frederick's mother was not "the PRITCHARD" who caused the Family Row! John COATES did marry again, to Rachel BELL, born 1855, mother of William Dent BELL. William was illegitimate, born in Feetham in 1885. His mother married Francis Sayer METCALFE in 1888 in Aysgarth and they had three girls. Francis died in 1896, leaving her with three very young children and somehow she met John COATES and married him in Walton, Liverpool in 1910. Rachel died in 1930 in West Derby, Liverpool. John died in 1942 in Southport.

MALISE MCGUIRE malisemcg@aol.com

82.   The HILLARY family from c 1790

John and Jane HILLARY and daughters

George HILLARY, *lead miner* and parents unknown, married Susannah GARTHWAITE, daughter of William and Mary, on 10th January 1814 in Marrick Parish Church. George and Susannah's first child was Mary, born in 1815, then John, 1816, George, 1819, William 1822 and Ann 1824.

Susannah died in 1826 at Levelhouses in Hurst. George with young children to care for, married Sarah HIRD, daughter of Robert and Elizabeth (STEVENSON), in May 1926 in Grinton and went on to have a further eight children – Robert born in 1828, Catherine 1829, Ann 1832, Thomas 1834, Eleanor 1836, David 1839, Elizabeth 1840, Hannah 1845. The similarity of some of the Hillary names to others makes me think that perhaps George's father was John who married Hannah GARTHWAITE in 1784, but this is only speculation on my part. George died in 1851 and Sarah died in 1880.

John HILLARY, senior, became the *mine agent* for the Hurst Mines. He had to learn to read, write and count and kept an exercise book in his office. When he married Isabella GUY, daughter of Henry and Isabella (SIDDLE), in 1842 he added the births and dates of his first four children to the book – John born in 1843, Susannah 1845, Sarah 1848, Isabella 1850, Mary 1852, George 1853, Isabella 1856, Henry 1858, Ann 1861 and Alis 1872.

John spent some time in the evenings designing and working on a four foot long geological time scale of part of the mine (now in my possession). They both died in Hurst, John in 1885 and Isabella in 1879.

John HILLARY Jr., was also a *lead miner* but along the way he was a *mason and farmer* living at Slack Hills. He married Jane METCALFE, one of three surviving daughters of William and Rosamund ALDERSON, in 1872. Jane was a *teacher of dressmaking and needlework* at the local Board School and had made her wedding dress which we still have. John died in December 1915 at West House, Arkengarthdale and Jane died in August 1930 at Hurst House, CB Terrace in Arkengarthdale. John and Jane had five daughters, one died aged three in 1881 and there was an Inquest. The eldest daughter born 1875, Sarah, never married as her fiancé died in the Great War and she died in Austwick in 1957 after living for a while with her niece Mary and family in Giggleswick.

Next there was Mary Ann, born in 1877 who met her future husband, we think, in the Haltwhistle area of Northumberland when accompanying her father on mining work. Her husband, James Williams USHER was one of nine children born in the Haltwhistle area

James Williams trained to be the *gamekeeper and estates manager* at Unthank Hall. He and Mary Ann were married in 1899 in Richmond and he subsequently worked for the Duke of Northumberland at Kielder. They also worked at Scar House, Arkengarthdale – Mary Ann as housekeeper to the WILSON family and James as *estate manager*. James eventually had work at Malham Tarn House, where Mary Isabel lived with her young family in 1944 at what is now called "Miss HILLARY's Cottage" because that was where Sarah HILLARY lived when the estate was sold to the National Trust in early 1950. Mary Ann died in 1950 and James W. in 1951 and both are buried in Kirby Malham churchyard.

Isabella Guy was born in 1880 and met John COATES in Reeth. John married Isabella in 1911 and had John Hillary and Mary Isabel on 19th June 1912 at the Kearton Farm in Low Row followed by James Ralph born in 1917 at Hurst, probably at the Hillary Farm.

Isabella died in 1960 and John died in Barnard Castle in 1967, possibly in a pub to which he had been taken when collapsing in the street (this is supposition – based on the fact that it IS a public house now). He had a severe kidney condition and as a strong Methodist he didn't believe in public houses. The shock of finding himself in one may have hastened his death.

The family story goes that Mary Isabel was born first and was classed as a "goner" so all attention was concentrated on John Hillary, the son and heir. Jane however decided that the "goner" was going to live and performed mouth to mouth resuscitation and when the "goner" set up a wail there was consternation. Isabella wasn't well enough to look after two babies, so which one was to stay?

They kept John Hillary and Mary Isabel was looked after by the aunties and her grandmother, eventually being officially adopted by Mary Ann and James W. I have since met my cousins who say that their father, John Hillary, had been the "goner" and was kept because he was so frail, so which story is true I do not know. John Hillary died in 1977 in Scunthorpe leaving a widow and two daughters and Mary Isabel in 1993 in Derby, Derbyshire, leaving three daughters and several grandchildren.

Jane Elizabeth, born 1882, and last daughter of John and Jane, married late in life to Ralph WHITE, son of Christopher and Elizabeth (CANTRILL), on 20th December 1920 and had one son, Christopher John Hillary in October 1921 in Arkengarthdale. Hillary married twice, first to Joan DIXON, and then to a widow from Colne in 1966. There were no children and Hillary died in 1992 in the Ilkley Hospice.

Mary Isabel met Kenneth Wainman WOOD in Saltburn on Sea where she was on a Workers' Educational Association course in Speech and Drama. Mary Isabel had definite ideas about her future, which included owning a hair salon and going to RADA. The first she was in the process of doing. Kenneth was on a motorcycling holiday and was a young *teacher* from the other side of Yorkshire. He saw where she took a film in to be processed and went in the following day and collected them himself!

Kenneth, son of Clarence Wainman and Bertha (Brearley) WOOD, was also born in 1912, the eldest of four children: two boys and two girls. His parents were from Cleckheaton in the West Riding textile area. He was a *teacher* at the Preparatory School at Catterall Hall, Giggleswick in 1940. When he moved from Malham Tarn to Giggleswick in 1945 he was made *head of history and librarian* at Giggleswick Grammar School. Their youngest daughter was born in 1947. The first two daughters were born in Settle Nursing Home in 1940 and 1942.

Kenneth Wainman WOOD died in New Plymouth in 1981 from chronic asthma and Mary Isabel came back to England in 1983 and lived for ten years in Derby, dying in 1993. Kenneth's ashes were scattered in the Tasman Sea and Mary's at Callanais in the Outer Hebrides, where she and he had been on a holiday.

Their grandchildren were born in Germany, Sierra Leone and Kenya. The great grandchildren were born in Newcastle upon Tyne and twins were born in Bedfordshire; there are also two great grandchildren in New Plymouth, New Zealand and who now living in Australia.

MALISE MCGUIRE malisemcg@aol.com

83. Matthew CALVERT

From the left back row: Matthew CALVERT (1866 – 1910), Elizabeth, Isabella, Mary Ann (OLDHAM); front row centre: Ellen, Thomas Richard c. 1900.

On Sunday, 18th May 1823, John CALVERT and Nancy (WARRINER) presented their new son, Matthew, for Baptism at Gunnerside Methodist Chapel. John and Nancy were married at Redmire on 24th April 1820. John was born in Middleton-in-Teesdale in 1794, the eighth child of Henry CALVERT, a mining agent, and Ruth HUNT. Henry was from Gunnerside and returned to Swann House in Redmire with his family of 11 children. Nancy was born in Redmire, the sixth child of Matthew WARRINER, a *miner*, and Eleanor ALDERSON. John and Nancy already had one child, Henry, and went on to have three more boys, John, Michael and William. John (senior) was a *carpenter and joiner*.

Matthew learned the trade of *carpenter and joiner* as did his brothers, the 1841 census recording all six males in the family as carpenters living in Gunnerside with the boy's mother Nancy. He married Elizabeth REYNOLDSON on Saturday, 3rd May 1845. Elizabeth was the fourth child of George REYNOLDSON, a miner, and Mary S. DAYKIN. Matthew and Elizabeth christened five children in Gunnerside, Nancy born in 1846, Mary Isabella born 1850, John in 1852, Elizabeth in 1856 and Dorothy born in 1859. Matthew and Elizabeth then left the dales with their five children.

Matthew's brother, William, and his family also decided to move. The local economy could not support six carpenters and their families in such a small community so the decision was made: Mathew and William would move and John senior, Henry, Michael and John Jr. would stay. Matthew and William and their families arrived in Burnley around 1860. They settled in an area of Burnley that already had a community of carpenters between the railway lines and Westgate. In the 1861 census, Matthew was described as a *joiner and Methodist Preacher* and was 37 years old. Nancy, the only child who was of working age being 15, was a *cotton weaver* in the mills that had sprung up in the area. His other children were aged ten, eight, five and two respectively. Matthew and Nancy also had two more children, Margaret born in 1864 and Matthew Jr. born on Wednesday 25th July 1866. Sadly, Matthew died on Thursday, 20th September 1866 aged 43 and just eight weeks after the birth of his youngest son, Matthew Jr. He had been diagnosed with cancer of the mouth some 18 months before and this was the cause of death given on the death certificate. There was a one line obituary in the Burnley newspaper of the time that only stated when he had died.

John was only 14 when his father died and Matthew Jr. just two months old. Dorothy (the baby who came to Burnley in 1860) died in 1861 at the age of two whilst Nancy died in 1869 aged 23. Mary Isabella, Elizabeth and Margaret were all *cotton weavers* and lived through to the new century. John became a cotton weaver and was described as a *cotton loom overlooker* in the 1881 census. By 1891 he was a *cotton manufacturer* and ten years later was a *loom overlooker*. He died in 1906 aged 54. Matthew Jr. was a cotton weaver all his short life.

Having had five children, Elizabeth, Isabella, Ellen, Thomas and Charlie (who died aged about 12 months), Matthew died on Friday, 9th June 1910 of a combination of influenza, perithyphlitis (appendicitis) and peritonitis, at the age of 44, just one year older than his father.

In summary, Matthew CALVERT (1823 – 1866) was an educated man who had a good trade that would take him anywhere. He was also a Methodist lay preacher who had strong family values. In order to escape impoverishment in the dales he moved himself and his family to a town that was up and coming in that mills and factories were being built or needed repair. That town would provide a steady income from his trade for the family. His skills were lost when he died and so his children went into those same mills as cotton operatives. They would not have considered themselves as being "better off" necessarily, but as keeping the family together and surviving. This branch of the family continues down through Matthew Jr. and his daughters Isabella and Ellen to the present day and it was only in the 20th century that the family could be considered better off and dispersed from Burnley.

It was in the six years that Matthew resided in Burnley that he constructed a large piece of furniture which the family still owns today. Known as a *chiffonier*, it comprised a glass fronted cupboard that sat upon a base, the top part of which was a drawer with a drop front that revealed a writing area and a series of little drawers. However, one would have to stand to write or to sit at a tall clerk's stool. The bottom part was another large enclosed cupboard. This was regarded to be the work of not just a carpenter/joiner, but of a true cabinet maker. At a time when having an education was a rarity, Matthew was himself a rarity. Given his occupation, he would have had basic numeracy and literary skills in order to carry out his work, and to collect payment for that work. However the family possess a book that has been hand written by Matthew. This book is titled *A Companion To The Wesleyan Hymn Book*. The frontispiece states: *"Being A Selection of Tunes, from The Works of the Most Celebrated Masters Coprising (sic) All The Metres in the Hymn Book and Supplement"* and concludes by *"Matthew CALVERT Keldside 1859"*.

It has many tunes within its covers all written on music rulings and the tunes were written in "chapters" by metre and type of verse. Usually, the voices are written in the order Soprano/Treble, Alto, Tenor and Bass. In this book Matthew has written them Tenor, Alto, Soprano and Bass as if he has written them so that he can follow the tenor line easily. He added harmonies and slightly transposed some of the music too, almost as if he were hearing the music in his head as he wrote. The precision was remarkable in that the notes were written clearly on or between the lines of the staves as musical notes are meant to be. Marion Moverley has concluded that Matthew was quite a remarkable man to have produced this book, and in all probability did it by candlelight, which in itself was an achievement. Matthew was a Methodist Local Preacher in Gunnerside and not just in Burnley. I now have confirmation that he was quite well known in the Methodist Community in Swaledale. *Please see Margaret Batty's book "Gunnerside Chapel and Gunnerside Folk" Chapter on "Emigrants" page 48.* It is not known from where Matthew got his education but with a grandfather and uncles who were mining and land agents and from a keen Methodist family, one may guess. As to his musical ability, who knows?

JANET BAILLIE 44 Clarence Street Lancaster LA1 3BB Telephone 01524847059
janet.baillie@talktalk.net

84. BROWNS from Crackpot

Elizabeth (Lilly) SMITH and Lambert Horner SMITH, my parents.

My submission about a family that left the dales is a simple one of a single family, my own. My story began with Richard BROWN and Mary SPENSLEY who lived on Crackpotside in Swaledale. In the 1861 they were recorded as having six children, one of whom, Jane, was to become my maternal great aunt. By 1871 they had moved to Bankheads at Whitaside and the family started to split up. The only boy, Thomas was a *farmer* at Trawden, near Burnley. Jane, one of the five daughters, went to Liverpool where she became pregnant and gave birth to a baby girl in February 1881. Immediately after the birth Jane and her baby Catherine returned to Low Row to live with Jane's now widowed mother, Mary BROWN. By 1901 Jane was married to William CALVERT and lived at High Oxnop Farm with Catherine recorded in the census as *step daughter*.

Catherine then married Richard CALVERT of Feetham Holme (Usher Top) in 1902 and lived in Low Row, where they had three children. These were Elsie, Albert and Elizabeth my mother. Richard subsequently went off to Australia to make a better life for them but the marriage broke up and the children were brought up by relatives in Swaledale. On my paternal side John Horner MUDD and Elizabeth PERCIVAL were married in Aysgarth in 1864. Their daughter Hannah Elizabeth, born in 1865 met and married John Pollard SMITH from Kildwick, near Skipton. It is possible that the movement of cattle from the dales to Liverpool via the railhead at Skipton may have been the factor in both Jane and Hannah meeting suitors. Hannah MUDD and John SMITH had a son, Lambert Horner SMITH, who married my mother at Stockton in 1930.

My earliest recollection of my family is living on a farm at Broaks near Richmond with my father working as a *lorry driver* for J. W. RAINS near Richmond railway station. I remember my mother taking me to school in Richmond every day, a round trip of about four miles each time. We then moved into Richmond living in Beachfield Avenue where my sister was born and my father continued to work for J. W. RAINS. Our next move was associated with work and was to Great Ayton about 1936 where we stayed until the outbreak of World War II. The War Office directed where dad worked as a *driver* doing Ministry work. This took us to South Bank, Middlesbrough, where we continued to live during the war years. When failing eyesight prevented dad from driving he worked in the local shipyard and steelworks until his death in 1952.

During all these changes, my mother Elizabeth, known as Lilly, was the loyal housewife and mother who fed, clothed and looked after us, not always an easy task during the war years of shortages and rationing, but her experience of dales living helped in this. Despite all her other roles she also found time to work in a munitions factory for a time, then as a *painter* in the shipyard and lastly in the shipyard canteen. She lived the rest of her life at South Bank close to her children until her death in 1984. My sister and I both married and continue to live in the Middlesbrough area.

RAYMOND SMITH raymond.smith12@ntlworld.com

The photograph of this sampler was provided for the exhibition by John WITTON
John METCALFE born September 14th 1822
Thomas Whitton METCALFE born 11th September
Jane METCALFE born 13th May 1827
The faded part in the centre is a quotation from Proverbs, Chapter 31, Verse 10:
"Who can find a virtuous woman? – for her price is far above Rubies"

These were the children of George METCALFE 1795-1863 and Mary WHITTON 1802-1834

John believes that Jane METCALFE 1827- after 1891 was born at Gilling and was living at Brough Hill, Near Bainbridge when she made this sampler, aged six.

John METCALFE born in 1822 at Brough Hill, was noted as *"imbecile"* in the 1871 census.

Thomas Whitton METCALFE 1824-1894 was also born at Gilling.

It is thought that there were two more children born at Brough Hill, George METCALFE in 1832 and William in 1834 who died 1838. Their mother died in 1834.

85. The WOODs of Askrigg

Ottiwell, son of John Rider WOOD and Ann CAUTLEY

Some of my ancestors were *clergymen* who started life in the Yorkshire Dales. The line began with Richard WOOD and his wife, Elizabeth RIDER, who married in 1754. They had three sons, one of whom was from my direct line. He was John Rider WOOD, a partner in the Richmond and Swaledale Bank. His brother, the Rev. Jeoffrey WOOD, married Elizabeth BURTON in 1792. One of their sons, Richard was at Cambridge University (Corpus Christi), from 1817, gaining his B.A. in 1822 and M.A. in 1825. He was ordained *deacon* (Chester) in 1822 and went on to serve in Askrigg from 1823-68. He was also a *Vicar* of Wollaston with Irchester, Northants between 1829 and 1868. He resided at Woodhall Park, Bedale, and died April 18th 1868, aged 68. He was the father of Charles C. WOOD (Cambridge Alumni 1856). Charles Claypon WOOD was born 7th August 1837 at Askrigg. He entered Marlborough School in August 1849 and was recorded there in the 1851 census along with his brother, Geoffrey Palmer WOOD. The 1861 census records the three clergymen – Charles and his father (Richard) and grandfather (Jeoffrey) at Woodhall Park, Askrigg.

The Leeds Mercury on Saturday, 23rd July 1864, records the marriage at Mansfield Woodhouse of Charles, youngest son of the Rev. R. WOOD, *incumbent* of Askrigg, to Ellen Mary, the youngest daughter of Capt. ROBINSON RN of The Priory, Mansfield Woodhouse, Nottinghamshire. The 1871 census showed Charles living with his wife and their two daughters, Katherine Sophie and Lillian Mary and an eight month old son, Charles George Bertram WOOD. Ellen died in 1874 and by the 1881 census Charles was living with his daughters and servants in Hastings. Two years later he married the children's governess Marianne WITHERBY. The 1891 census records the family in Pembrokeshire, Wales, moving then to Brecon where Charles was *Vicar* in St. David's Church in 1901. By the 1911 census Charles had moved to Ashbourne, Derbyshire, and with him were his unmarried daughters Lilian Mary WOOD (aged 44 years) and Katherine Sophie WOOD (aged 45). Charles' death was registered in 1912 at Calderwood, Torquay.

Geoffrey Palmer WOOD, brother of Charles Claypon WOOD was born about 1835 in Askrigg. He left Marlborough School at Christmas 1852. The next documented record I found was from New Zealand where he was admitted as a *barrister solicitor* aged 26 years in 1861. He was admitted to Canterbury Lunatic Asylum (in Gaol) on July 24th 1862. His admission was stated as *'Debauchery and Drunkenness – principally by action of mercury.'* He stayed there until his death in 1875, a total of 12 years and five months! At the Coroner's Court held on 21st March 1875 the verdict of the jury was that he died *"of disease of the membranes of the brain."* The nearest next of kin Marmaduke DIXON of Caistor, Lincolnshire, was informed of his death. He was the son of James Green DIXON who had married Rev. James Suttell WOOD's daughter Eliza Agnes in 1859. Marmaduke and Eliza then moved to New Zealand where they had six children. Two sons died young, while Marmaduke John (Duke), Richard, Rosa and Catherine lived to inherit the Eyrewell Estate near Christchurch, New Zealand.

Ottiwell WOOD, youngest brother of Charles and Geoffrey, born about 1839 lived a very short life. *The Morning Chronicle (London)* recorded his death on 21st June 1858. According to the *Gentleman's Magazine* he died of fever, in County Cork, Ireland.

Rev. James Suttell WOOD was my fourth great uncle. He was the son of John Rider WOOD and Ann CAUTLEY and the grandson of the Rev. Thomas CAUTLEY, *Vicar* of Ouseburn, York. James was educated at Clare College, Cambridge, gaining a BA in 1805 and M.A. in 1810. James was mentioned in BARKER's "*3 days of Wensleydale*", and Charles Fothergill's 1805 diary described him as "*.....an agreeable genteel young clergyman elect."* He was also a *Lieutenant* in the Loyal Dales Volunteers. His marriage "*At Whixley Church, Mr. James Suttell WOOD, of Bolton Castle, to Miss DARVALL, only daughter of Roger DARVALL esq. of Green Hammerton"* was recorded in *The Monthly Magazine* of 1805. On 27th December 1809 James was instituted as *Rector* at Cranfield, Bedford. He appears however to have had a troubled time there:

"*Recognizances: Jas. Suttell WOOD, clerk, Rector of Cranfield; to prosecute Wm. FORD, Cranfield for threatening to kill him."* and also *against Wm. FORD for threatening to shoot him.* George, Bishop of Lincoln agreed that he could be absent from the benefice until 31st December 1819 on account of the delicate state of his wife. They resided subsequently at Askrigg. James died in 1857 in Caen, Normandy. James was the father of George E. W. (1825 Trinity College) a *physician* in Winchester and James (1832 Magdalene) a *clergyman* in Bath. In 1851 Eliza Agnes WOOD was staying with her brother James in Walcot, Bath.

Anne WOOD was the daughter of Ottiwell WOOD (son of John Rider and Ann WOOD) and Jane HODGSON, and grand-daughter of Francelina BENN. Anne WOOD was my 3rd great aunt. Born about 1815 in Wensley, she married Robert Marsden CARTWRIGHT in 1837. He was a *surgeon* in Cartmel, Lancashire. They emigrated to Goulburn, New South Wales, Australia, at some time between 1837 and 1841. They had four children, all born in Australia.

The New South Wales Medical Board in Sydney on 3rd January, 1848 recorded that he had submitted to the Board the necessary testimonials, of qualification. In the *Maitland Mercury & Hunter River General Advertiser, Saturday 13 June 1846*, he was recorded as having £600 in debts. By the 19th April 1848 the newspaper recorded him being £425 in debt. He was also mentioned in 1848 as being insolvent in the *New South Wales Government Gazette*. His death was reported on 25th March 1853: "*At his residence, Elizabeth Street South, after a short illness, Dr Robert Marsden CARTWRIGHT, in his 37th year, leaving a beloved wife and four children to lament their loss. No burial details."*

Ann's brother, Thomas John Hutton WOOD was christened on 27th February 1814 at Wensley. Following his father, Ottiwell's death, in Annan, Scotland, he was mentioned in Ottiwell's Will of 26th December 1824, along with his mother, Jane, and his siblings: John, Ottiwell, Richard and Ann WOOD. A further document of 1839 records the names of Jane ALDERSON (2nd wife of Christopher ALDERSON) of Askrigg, formerly Jane WOOD, widow of Ottiwell; John Rider WOOD of Carmel, Lancashire, *gent;* Thomas John Hutton WOOD of 10 Felix Place, Liverpool Road, Islington; and Robert Marsden CARTWRIGHT of Cartmel, *surgeon* (in right of his wife Ann, d/o Ottiwell). In 1840, Thomas married Lydia Margaret DOBSON, daughter of John DOBSON, a *chemist and druggist.* The 1841 Census recorded Thomas and Lydia living at 10 Felix Place, St Mary Islington West, London. Jane POWELL, (listed as a *governess*) was living next door. Thomas died in 1871 at South Stoneham, Hampshire aged 57. Jane POWELL was in attendance at the death at Peartree Park Woolston. The 1871 census recorded her still there *living off interest* in the property.

The descendants of John Rider WOOD were also to be found in the Everton area of Liverpool, from 1861 until 1942, when my late father, Harold WOOD joined the Navy in World War II and finally settled in the Midlands after the war. I am now living a few miles away from where Thomas John Hutton WOOD lived in Woolston, Hampshire back in 1871.

JACQUELINE BROWN jakimbrown@googlemail.com www.woodfamilyhistorians.org.uk

86.   John WHITTON 1789 – 1850 Askrigg to Tasmania

During the 19th Century many people, from all parts of the British Isles, decided that a better life could be found in other parts of the world and emigrated to other countries either with or without their families. Others had no option but to do this, being sent by the judicial system for crimes which seen from a modern angle, seem minor transgressions. John WHITTON was such a person, being sent in 1846 to what is now Tasmania for the theft of two sheep valued at 40 shillings (£2.00) each.

John WHITTON was born at Brough Hill, Bainbridge on the 28th June 1789 the eldest of ten children, to Thomas WHITTON and Jane HEWGILL of Scarborough, his wife. Little is known of his early years, he appears to have worked in agriculture being described as an *'agricultural labourer'* in his court appearances. He married Margaret HOLMES at Aysgarth in 1819. For reasons that will become apparent later, either he had employment which took him away from Wensleydale, certainly to Lancashire, or else left the Askrigg area to seek employment. By 1833 his family consisted of his wife and six children and he may have been a butcher. At Christmas 1845 he was in Askrigg and this was the last Christmas that he spent with his wife and family. Depositions by George TERRY, one of the Constables for the township of Askrigg and Thomas CHAPMAN of Worton, Askrigg made by them to Justices of the Peace sitting at Leyburn on December 26th, told what happened.

Thomas CHAPMAN said that on Sunday December 21st he had four sheep in a field at Askrigg and he last saw them at four o'clock in the afternoon. He took one home with him and on the morning of the 22nd returned to the field where he found only two remaining. The gate was open and he searched for the lost sheep to no avail. He knew he had fastened the gate and that the fences were in good condition. For reasons not stated he suspected that John WHITTON had stolen the sheep and sought a search warrant. By Wednesday, Christmas Eve, he had obtained the warrant and sent it to the Constable.

George TERRY, the Constable stated that he was given a warrant allowing him to search the premises of John WHITTON and along with another Constable and Azariah CHAPMAN, the son of Thomas, he went to WHITTON's house on Christmas morning. On arrival he found only WHITTON's wife by the fire who told him that her husband was down the yard killing a sheep. He went down the yard and spoke to John WHITTON who told him he could search where he liked. A search of the butchering shop revealed nothing but the prisoner having left him, he went back to the house. He called out for him and John WHITTON's reply from upstairs was that he was changing his breeches. Upon going upstairs with Azariah he found a sheep's skin in a sack up the chimney. Azariah recognised it as that of the missing sheep. Thomas CHAPMAN said to the Constable before seeing it, that if it was his gimmer sheep's skin it would be *"shaggy with a long tail, fine long ears and some black marks on them"*. The Constable showed the skin to CHAPMAN and he confirmed it as being the skin of his gimmer sheep.

On December 26th John WHITTON appeared at Leyburn Magistrates' Court and was committed for trial at the Quarter Sessions at Northallerton on a charge of felony. On January 6th 1846 he pleaded guilty and was sentenced to be transported for a period of 10 years.

Studying the contemporary documentation revealed that this was not the first charge of that sort faced by John. It was not the first time he had been sentenced to transportation and it was not his first period in gaol.

The 1846 Northallerton documentation showed that a Deputy Governor of Liverpool Gaol attended the trial to confirm that John had been imprisoned in Liverpool for felony, again sheep stealing, and that the conviction was still in force. The register of indictable offences for the County of Lancaster for August 1840 showed that a John WHITTON, 54 years, received a sentence of 10 years transportation at Liverpool Assizes on August 17th.

Moreover, a search of the 1841 census record showed that John WHITTON, an agricultural labourer, born in Yorkshire was a prisoner in Millbank Prison in June of that year. Millbank was the depot for prisoners destined for transportation drawn from all over England. However, John escaped transportation and, for whatever reason, did not serve out his full sentence of ten years in prison because five years after the Liverpool sentence he was back in Askrigg. Presumably his reputation had led Thomas CHAPMAN, the sheep owner, to say he had cause *"to suspect that (John) was the person that had stolen it"*.

In any event this time the wheels turned and did not stop. No doubt after a further spell in Millbank and the hulks at Woolwich, John found himself aboard the *John Calvin* which sailed on May 9th 1846. It arrived not in Tasmania but Norfolk Island, a place renowned for the harshness of its regime. He remained there until June 1847 when he sailed on the *Tory* for Tasmania.

The records of his behaviour and locations survive in the Tasmanian Archives along with a most detailed description of his age, appearance, religion, family etc. Apart from an unauthorised possession of a towel on Norfolk Island which resulted in 14 days hard labour, his behaviour clearly improved, and in 1849 he gained a remission of 100 days through *'hard work'*. This improvement was all to no avail however, as on October 13th 1850 John's death was recorded, *"Died at the Hunting Grounds"* where he had been kicked by a horse.

Bearing in mind the meticulous nature of the Government records in Tasmania it must be presumed that some notification of his death reached his family back in England. It is unclear as to whether his family in England ever knew of his death. His descendants spread across England and eventually elsewhere in the world whilst some remained in Bainbridge in public office until the early 20th century and still remain in the local farming community.

BARRIE McKNIGHT daband@mckstoulton.go-plus.net

**A pair of gloves typical of the 1870s, provided for the exhibition
courtesy of Christine Amsden and Ian Spensley.**

Christine writes that more than a hundred years after they were knitted, and after years of her research for descendants, the appearance of these gloves, one set either side of the Atlantic, provided tangible proof that long lost lines were reunited. Neither family possessing the gloves know what to do with them in the future but each is pleased to have matched them!

87. William, Robert, and Elizabeth Pratt CARTER from Arkengarthdale to North America

The Evergreen Cemetery, Leadville, Lake County, Colorado

The story begins with a poignant Memorial Inscription in Arkengarthdale churchyard.

"In remembrance of JANE CARTER wife of WILLIAM CARTER of Booze Bank,
who died April 20th, 1879, aged 30 years.
Also PHILLIS MARGARET, their daughter who died in infancy.
Also PHILLIS MARGARET, their daughter who died at the age of 3 years.
Also of the above WILLIAM CARTER who died at Leadville, USA, on September 16th, 1884, aged 36 years and
was interred in the Evergreen Cemetery,
affectionate husband and dutiful son, a faithful brother."

The Evergreen Cemetery in Leadville, Lake County, Colorado, was created during the Silver Boom in the 1870's. Situated at 10,000 feet, the cemetery has surprisingly flat terrain. It is laid out in sections, including a Hebrew area, Masons, Elks and babies sections. There are many Civil War veteran markers, though many more Union than Confederate. There is a great variety of markers including Woodmen of the World variations, zinc, marble and wood.

It is estimated that there are over 2,500 graves in the cemetery. There are monuments to people killed in snow slides, mine disasters, child birth and illnesses such as influenza. Because of the high altitude, the weather is usually cool, even in the summer. The cemetery is covered in snow during the winter, which starts early in the high country.

ROBERT CARTER, the son of William CARTER and Hannah (née STONES) had also gone to the booming mining town of Leadville, Colorado, probably to join his cousin William, son of Joseph CARTER and Elizabeth (née HIRD).

Robert emigrated in 1883. In 1894 he married a German immigrant widow, Johanna, who already had a son called William Ricks. In the 1900 American census Robert was a *labourer* in a zinc mine.

In the 1910 census he was still in Colorado as a freight handler and in the 1920 census he had progressed to being a *farmer* growing fruit and hay. Neither he nor his wife appeared in the 1930 census.

His uncle George STONES in Arkengarthdale died in May 1886 leaving a will dated March 15th, 1886, bequeathing the then considerable sum of £30 to his nephew Robert in America.

The parish records and British census records from 1871 to 1891 revealed three more children of Jane and William Carter in Arkengarthdale.

John Joseph CARTER born 24th June, 1869 and baptised 27th June 1869 at St Mary, Arkengarthdale.
Elizabeth Pratt CARTER born 2nd December 1873 and baptised 24th October 1875 at St Mary, Arkengarthdale.
Sarah Jane CARTER born 23rd September 1876 and baptised 20th October 1876 at Arkengarthdale Methodist Chapel.

After the death of their mother and William's departure for Colorado they were cared for by uncles and aunts, but all three children had disappeared from the dales census by 1901. The following information came from the 1901 and 1911 British censuses and from family descendants in Canada.

John Joseph, aged 31, was recorded in the 1901 census as a *married policeman* with three children, living in Toxteth Park, Liverpool. He and his wife Alice eventually had eleven children, two of whom died in infancy.

There was no information about Elizabeth Pratt CARTER or Sarah Jane CARTER until Louise COATTA in Vancouver, British Columbia posted a message to the Upper Dales email group asking *"What happened to William Carter?"* This was seen by Sybil REED, granddaughter of Elizabeth Ann CARTER, the half sister of Robert and the cousin of William.

Elizabeth Ann, born, bred and buried in Arkengarthdale never left the dales but what a story emerged of the much travelled Elizabeth Pratt CARTER!

From her childhood in the remote dale she moved to Lancashire, Leeds, New York and Vancouver, Canada, where she died in 1952. She married twice and brought up her own four children and a number of step children. She was the great grand mother of Louise COATTA's husband.

On visiting a grandson of Elizabeth Pratt CARTER in May, 2010, Louise discovered that Sarah Jane CARTER had also left the dale, married George FAREY and in the 1901 census was living in Castleford, Yorkshire. With Sarah Jane and George was the now widowed Elizabeth Pratt's 4 year old son, William Evan Percy FLITCROFT. He, too, went to Canada with his mother and her new husband.

By 1911 Sarah Jane and her husband George had two children in Castleford and they then moved to Scorton, near Richmond where two further children were born. Sarah Jane had returned to within twenty miles of her birthplace.

There must be two lessons from this story. Never give up looking for your lost relatives and join the Upper Dales Family History e mail group.

LOUISE COATTA louise_coatta@shaw.ca

SYBIL REED sybilreed@aol.com

88. The Livelihood of the dales

We have to recognise that, for some four centuries, the livelihood of the dales people, particularly for those in Swaledale and Arkengarthdale was dependant on lead mining. Without it the sparse hillsides of the upper dales provided a living only for the hill sheep farmers and even the more lush areas of the lower dales provided little scope for arable farming.

It was these conditions that affected the comings and goings of the population. Until the middle of the 16th century, recovery from earlier depopulation had been slow but a new era of prospecting for lead both by individuals and by partnerships, brought visions of prosperity and lured incomers into the area. By the end of the 17th century, the population of Swaledale and Arkengarthdale had increased by some 4,000 people and lead mining was developing into a major industry which attracted many more incomers.

Not everyone welcomed the mining era. The large PEACOCK family, which had dominated Arkengarthdale for many generations, had no wish to become involved in mining. They were by nature an intellectual family and there was anger at the loss of their local leader Anthony PEACOCK in the Pilgrimage of Grace. They began to move out of the dales and probate and other records of that time show how widely they dispersed, and the various new occupations they undertook.

The mining industry prospered until the latter part of the 19th century when some of the smaller mines began to close and realization came that the whole industry would run down before long.

There was a gradual move away by 1850 and people went looking for work in the Durham pits or in the mills of Lancashire. It became known that lead mining was developing in the Mississippi area of America and that land there was readily available for farming. This prompted many young men and families to think of emigrating.

Those who went first sent back word that there was indeed a future to be had in Wisconsin and the Fever River area. Many more made the decision that they too would go despite the traumas of the journey and having to leave their relatives.

I have visited the areas to which they went and have told their stories in my book *"The Dalesmen of the Mississippi River."*

DAVID MORRIS M.B.E. morswale@richmond104.orangehome.co.uk

Editor's note: David is shortly to publish a new booklet called *"Are you a PEACOCK?"*

89.   The families of the three sons of William and Agnes PARKER

Francis and Ann PARKER

Of their four daughters, only the eldest married. Her husband was John FOTHERGILL and their descendants remain in North Yorkshire and Cumbria.

John and Sarah PARKER

The 1901 census records John PARKER aged 42, a *platelayer* on the railway, living with his 46 year old wife, Sarah PARKER née Dinsdale, and four of their children at the Weaving Shop, Cowgill, Dent. The family at home were Jeffrey Dinsdale PARKER aged 12, Alice PARKER aged 9, John Francis PARKER aged 4 and Edmund PARKER aged 1.

Their eldest child was William, who was born at Burtersett in 1881. At the time of the 1901 census William aged 20, had left home and was lodging in Walton on the Hill, Liverpool whilst working as a *locomotive* engine cleaner. A daughter, Jane aged 17, had also left home and was in service at Low Houses, Snaizholme, the farm of Edward and Ellen JOHNSON.

William had heard of the exploits of his uncle, Jeffrey DINSDALE, who had emigrated to the United States of America in 1888 and when he was 21, made the decision that he would also emigrate. In fact, he persuaded his parents and siblings to join him and in May 1903 the whole family arrived in Red Lodge, Montana. John and Sarah were able to stake their claim to some land and commenced farming. Their children found work in and around Red Lodge. All their descendants remain in the United States and two of them, Fred PARKER and Ruth Parker SILVESON have provided much of the information relating to the family trees.

William could turn his hand to anything because the list of jobs which he undertook included stonemason, farmer, miner, lumberjack, and oil field roust-about. He also cooked for the Forest Service and at one time was contracted to carry ashes, trash and garbage for the town of Red Lodge, Montana, and during the Second World War was contracted to dig holes for the electricity supply. This latter job enabled him to earn enough to buy his home.

Simon and Martha PARKER

At some time between February 1902 and April 1905, William PARKER born in 1880, Margaret PARKER born in 1883 and Agnes PARKER born in 1887, the eldest children of Simon and Martha PARKER, emigrated to Montreal, Canada. Simon and Martha PARKER emigrated to Montreal in 1906 with their four other children – Alice PARKER born 1890, Martha Jane PARKER born 1893, John Ralph PARKER born 1895 and Ethel PARKER born 1899.

The 1911 Canadian census lists Simon's occupation as *Night Watchman* at Fairbank's, the same company where his son in law worked as a *journalist*.

Whilst Simon and Martha remained in Montreal, their family did not stay in Canada for long. They were attracted by the lure of the many jobs available over the border in Detroit, a move which was to prove tragic for their youngest son, John Ralph PARKER, who was killed at the young age of 33 whilst at work. Many of their descendants remain in this area of the world.

MALCOLM McCALLUM, Hunters Lodge, Bowling Green Lane, Manfield, Darlington DL2 2RL
malcolm.mccallum2@btopenworld.com

90. Richard YEOMAN from Coverdale to Huron County, Ohio

YEOMAN house in Coverdale (Photograph courtesy of Pat RYDER)

Richard YEOMAN the son of John and Margaret of Horsehouse in Coverdale, baptised at St Botolph's, Horsehouse, on 25th June 1815 emigrated to America from Horsehouse near Coverham, around 1842 where his father, John YEOMAN, was an *innkeeper and farmer*. Margaret died just before the 1841 census, and was buried at Horsehouse on 9th April 1841 aged 53 yrs. John YEOMAN died on 25th April 1867 aged 83 years and was buried at Horsehouse on 29th April. John and Margaret had twelve children between 1808 and 1832. After his father's death Richard was contacted about returning to England to take control of the estate, but he decided not to return.

Richard's brother Nicholas YEOMAN wanted to go to America but spent the rest of his life in England and died 12th October 1871. He was buried at Horsehouse on 15th October aged 49 years. Richard met and married Fanny AXTELL in Ohio in 1846. There they worked with the underground railroad during the Civil War, providing safe passage for the slaves heading North. Fanny's father Daniel AXTELL and mother, Jane Wellman AXTELL made their home in Pittsfield, Lorain County, Ohio. They moved two years later to the "Home Place" in Russia Township near South Amherst, Lorain County. It is said that his home was the first frame dwelling erected in Lorain County. Jane WELLMAN was the daughter of a Revolutionary War soldier Abraham WELLMAN, of Belgrade Maine.

Richard and Fanny moved to Cedar Township in Mahaska County in 1865 along with their seven children, Margaret, Franklin, Orsemus, Elinor, Ida May, John Darius and Burt. Three more children, William, Edna and Mary Jane were born on the homestead. William "Billy" YEOMAN fought in four wars served with the South Dakota Militia at the battle of Wounded Knee in South Dakota.

Richard YEOMAN died in 1886 at the age of 71. He and Fanny and many members of the YEOMAN family were buried in Cedar Township Cemetery, located across from the original family farm. Orsemus YEOMAN continued farming the family homestead amassing some 600 acres of land that were eventually divided into smaller farms and passed on to his children. In 1860, he married Marybelle KING of Cedar Township. Orsemus and Marybelle raised seven children on the homestead, Harry, Denver, Leonard, Marchie, Stella, Thressie and Cecile.

The following letter was sent by Nicholas YEOMAN to his older brother Richard and was addressed to Mr. Richard YEOMAN, Monroville Huron County Ohio North America. It was postmarked in Middleham and again postmarked *"Boston Ship MS Aug"* Horsehouse -June 24th 1846.

"Dear Brother and Fanny:

I take the present opportunity of writing a few lines to you in answer to yours which we received on the first of this month. My Father is quite well and all my brother's and sisters accept my self and I am recovering from a long illness I have had twelve weeks bed and I have been not much better then in bed since the Martinmiss but I hope I am getting better. I have four runnings on me two on my back and two on my thigh and they are drying we think.

John BARKER & Jane is very well and Doing well and the little boy is well and a very fine Boy his name is John after both his grandfather's and his father. Christopher and Mary and all their Children is well and they have four and nearly five and Jane BARKER is on the way again Francis has gone apprentice to A Butcher at Gelling near Richmond for one year he has been there about three months Elizabeth has married one George HONDALE of Dallagill his mother was one of Betty Stanley Daughter's She has done very well they and they are gone to a Farm in Dallagill not far from his Father's his Mother is dead her Name was Bella I think Francis will not Mary yet he says you are to look out first hear has been a good many deaths since you would hear from us last time old Betty TENNANT is dead & old Pollie WILKINSON of Woodlelate of Bradley and old Margret WILKINSON Abie COATES oldest Boy and Bob COMB is dead he married Ann THOMAS about fifteen months since and he was scarce ever well after he has gone of in a consumption or a decline and a child of John TENNANT of Arkelsit is Dead Fanny LOFTHOUSE has been confined of a girl and Thomas HAWMAN wife has been confined of a girl Margret SPENCE of A Sone Margret COATES She married William SPENCE and Hannah SIMPSON of A Sone She Married Mathew LAMBERT John TENNANT Wife of a boy and Nell CALAP of a daughter it is the fourth Child Mary RAYNER Rodger RAYNER Wife of a Daughter you must give Margret RYDERTS Respects to her son John and tell him he has a father & a mother alive yet and some brothers and they never was such bad parents to him they think as well as others that he ought to write to them he ought to forgive or else how can he expect to be forgiven.

The Railway is not decided whether it will come up Coverdale or up Bishopdale if it comes up Coverdale it Will cross our highside land East and our Head west and it will come from Bedale and from Northallerton if it come up Coverdale they have got Mannby Ralph LOFTHOUSE will get his fathers share & Robert will get his Uncle Ralph's Share Rodger LOFTHOUSE will get Ned BALL's First wife's share and his own and Robert of Bradley gets his Father's. We have got two fields of hay without rain east paddock and the field on the high side of the road east we have had a long drought oats appears to be bad and wheat good. Potatoes are missing and they have Been very bad this last winter they have been in the same way as they were in America. The wages at the railway are good now on account of haytime they are about a guinea per week. Our Margaret is living at Richmond and John is in Lepton near Huddersfield and he has not been hear for five years he came to see Me at Leeds Infirmary and we have not heard from him since I have yet some thoughts of America if ever I get better and am able Elizabeth HANLEY of Middleham has got Married Mary CLARK is getting better she has been bad above a year. I am very sorry I cannot send you the receipt to kill Rats with from your friend Tinker BOBLEY for he has not been hear of a long time he Stoll a pair of Shoes of My Fathers nearly new and he has only been hear once since and Martha Blew him up about them and he said Stew as God Stew as God is in Heaven I never meld with them if God may Strike me Dead I never Meld on them,

Joseph SPENCE Wife was confined last September of a Son and it has only one Hand & two Ann BELL of Pickle Daughter of Robert BELL late of fathered a child on James Rawman HAMMOND yesterday and he has 18 pence per week to pay until it be 13 years old 10/- for Doctor & 4/- for Summons R. POTTY is writing to his Brother My Father has got $100 out of Pickle CALOPT's Arkelside Moor Shippherd we have to pay Tythe for Fetterholme all through utbley now I must conclude ever well wishing you hoping to meet you in Eternity and I don't doubt seeing you in America yet yours in heart

Nicholas YEOMAN"

Richard YEOMAN's cause of death was recorded as *"dropsey, rhenomatism and inflammation of stomach Duration: 3 Months."*

JAMES L. YEOMAN siksika2004@yahoo.com

91. The family of James SPENSLEY (1773-1848/49) from Swaledale to America

My paternal great-great grandfather James SPENSLEY emigrated at age 69, with his two youngest children. His sons John and James remained in Swaledale; two sons were already in Dubuque, Iowa. In June of 1842, James, William (age 19) and Margaret (age 22) reached New York on the ship Roscius. Their journey continued by water and land until they reached the lead mining region near Dubuque, where sons Richard and Mason SPENSLEY were settled. These three sons of James---Richard, Mason, and William---prospered and enjoyed long and productive lives in America. They were life-long Methodists. Little is known of Margaret. She supposedly became Mrs. RICHARDS and was, in 1901, living in California. James was the son of James (1737-1817) and Elizabeth Alderson SPENSLEY of Whitaside and the grandson of James (born 1712) and Ann Bullock SPENCLEY (sic) of Whiteyside (sic). The emigrant James (1773-1848/9) married Rosamond MASON in 1798; she died in 1824 in North Yorkshire. James' life in Iowa is not well documented and it is only through written narratives of his two grandsons in 1889 and 1901, that we know James died in about 1848/8, No evidence of his death has been found nor has his grave been located.

Richard SPENSLEY (1805 Feetham Holme, Swaledale – 1892 Galena, Jo Daviess County, Illinois)

Richard was the first of James' children to leave England. His father-in-law was Robert BONSON who, with Richard and Robert WALLER, erected what local history claims was the first furnace built in the United States for the smelting of lead ore. This was situated on the Little Platte River in Wisconsin, about halfway between Dubuque and Mineral Point, Iowa. The company sought financing from back home and recruited dalesmen to help construct and operate three more furnaces by 1836. One of those recruited was Richard SPENSLEY who held the position of *banksman* in the famous Barnsley coal mines in Yorkshire. Richard, his wife Alice BONSON, and their six children reached New York after an ocean voyage of six weeks, then took the canal to Buffalo, then sailed across the lakes to Chicago, and from there went by team to Dubuque. It is said Richard walked the entire distance (175 miles). Richard erected a log cabin near Dubuque in which he and his family lived for many years. This is recorded in the *Historical Encyclopedia of Illinois*, Newton Bateman and Paul Selby eds., and the *History of Jo Daviess County*, Hon. William SPENSLEY, ed. An online transcript of the sketch of Richard SPENSLEY at a Jo Daviess County website is in error and readers should consult the original work at <www.archive.org>.

Many of Richard's children married descendants of Yorkshire families who had migrated to the Galena area. Eleven children survived to maturity:

1. Rosamond (1825-1903) married Ralph SPENSLEY in 1841. They had at least ten children, including: Richard W., Isabel, Ralph Jr., Robert V., and John F.
2. Mary (1828) married Benjamin MATHER in 1845.
3. Elizabeth (1831-1875) m. John FERN.
4. James (1833-1916) had three marriages producing thirteen children.
5. Bonson (1835-1884) married Ann HARKER.
6. Margaret (1837) married Thomas ALLISON and had five children.
7. John Robert (1839-1872) married Mattie E. DAVIS.
8. William (1841-1910) married Mary Jane LOW.
9. Alice Ann (1844) never married.
10. Ellen (1846-1923) married John GRAY.
11. Richard Mason (1849-1922) married (1) Agnes A. GRAY; (2) Jessie A. VIRDEN.

The above comes from *Portraits and Biographical Album of Jo Daviess County Illinois,* (Chicago: Chapman Bros, 1889) included a sketch of Judge William SPENSLEY.

Mason SPENSLEY (1814 Feetham Holme, Swaledale – 1884 Smelser, Grant County, Wisconsin)

My great-grandfather Mason emigrated in 1841 at the age of 27. In 1853 he married Frances Ann TAYLOR (1835-1921). Mason's work always centred around mining. In 1850 with partners, Mason rented a smelting furnace, one of only two in the Platteville area with double hearths. The partnership later dissolved but Mason continued to be active as a smelter with Richard STRAW for the next 30 years. In 1883 Mason sold his interest in the furnace and more than 100 acres of property to STRAW. After Mason's death in 1884, the widow and her children moved to the city of Dubuque, Iowa. Mason and Frances had twelve children, all born in Platteville, Wisconsin. The nine who survived to adulthood were:

1. James (1854-1924) became a *silver miner* in Lone Pine, Inyo County, California where, at the time of his death, he owned some valuable mining claims. He never married.
2. Rosamond (1857-1939) married William DASHMAN in 1882 and lived in Dubuque City, then Maywood, Illinois, then Grand Junction, Michigan. There were no children.
3. Frances Ann (1860-1926) married Frank M. LITTRELL in 1889. They lived in Dubuque, Chicago, and Maywood, Illinois where they died. They had six children: Blanche, Richard Elmer, Gladys May, Frances G., Cora "Dollie", and Alice.
4. John Thomas (1861-1916) died in Dubuque at age 55. He never married.
5. Margaret Ellen (1867-1945) married Charles LITTRELL in 1895. They had two daughters and a son. The son died in infancy. Margaret died in Dubuque, Iowa.
6. Richard Mason (1869-1910) died in Chicago of nephritis associated with *dropsy*. He never married.
7. Mary Maria (1871-1895?) married William RUTH in 1890. Mary died 21st May 1889 in Chicago. She is buried as "Mary" (no surname) with her parents in Platteville, Wisconsin.
8. Alice 1873-1950) married Charles WATTE in 1897. They had a daughter (1898-1900) and two sons born in Chicago. Alice died in Chicago.
9. My grandmother: Cora (1877-1964) married Amos HARGREAVES in 1897 in Chicago. They had five children (1) Mary Ruth (1900-1956) two children; (2) Wilson (1905-1970) two children; (3) Mason (1908-1979) five children; (4) my father Milton (1910-1994) married Lois C. MERTES in 1937, three children; and (4) Vivian (1914-1971) who never married. Cora's children lived mostly in Elmhurst, DuPage County, Illinois.

William SPENSLEY (1823 Feetham Holme – 1902 Vermillion, Clay County, South Dakota)

The youngest of James' children, William, immigrated 1842. In 1851 he married Elizabeth CHALDER in Rockdale, near Dubuque. William was a *farmer,* first in Table Mound, Dubuque County, Iowa, then in Vermillion Township, Clay County, South Dakota. William died in Clay County in 1902. They had seven children:

1. James Mason (1852-1931) married Virginia (Jenny) J. BUCKINGHAM in 1877. They had five children: Lottie P., James Elmer, Ella, Dora, and Muriel.
2. Rosamond Anne (1854) married Charles R. GRANGE. Children were Charles Herbert and Mildred.
3. Alice (1856) married William H. WHITAKER in 1881 and they had one child Alice.
4. Margaret (1859) married John CARSON and had a son Irvin W. (1887 SD).
5. Thomas or Joseph (1862) married Ida WASHBORN 1885/6. They had four children Arleighet B., Flossie Mayone, Lloyd Bernett and William James.
6. Robert Ellsworth (1863) married Alice BAKER 1884/85. They had five children: Lillian May, Laura, Robin (or Lena), Alice, and Howard Ellsworth.
7. Mary E. (1868) married William Morgan BARNETT in 1894 and had two children: William and Margaret Elizabeth.

The descendants of the children of James SPENSLEY are now spread throughout the United States

SANDRA HARGREAVES LUEBKING, 12202 Sumner, Lemont, Illinois 60439
12202wl@sbcglobal.net

92. Descendents of Henry YEOMAN (born February 1798 in Carlton Highdale)

Richard the author and Joseph Yeoman born 1878

My knowledge of Henry and his life is sketchy but I believe him to be a son of Joseph YEOMAN (born 1741 Arkleside) and Ann LOFTHOUSE (married 13th November 1781 Horsehouse).

Henry moved to Upper Nidderdale probably in his late teens where he married Miriam HORNER in 1821 at Middlesmoor. They had 10 daughters and Miriam died in 1850. Henry remarried to Elizabeth LOFTHOUSE in 1863 and at some point after then moved to Leeds where he died in 1877 and was buried in Beckett Street Cemetery. Elizabeth died in 1880.

I believe Henry had an earlier marriage which produced four children including Ellen born in 1818. In 1847 she married James WALKER (born 1805 at Grewelthorpe) at Pateley Bridge. They had a son Henry Walker YEOMAN (born 1849 at Fountains Earth) who is my great grandfather.

Henry Walker YEOMAN was an Agricultural Labourer and married Mary WRAY (born 1845 in York) at Ripon Cathedral on 15th November 1872. On the 1911 census he was listed as a *cowman* and as a widower and lived at Littlethorpe with a John NICHOLSON *(farmer)*, Louise Emily NICHOLSON, their son Frank and a *servant* Maud SMITH. Henry and Mary had three daughters and two sons:

Lillie born 1873
Harry born 1875
Rose born 1877 – interestingly she was born in Northallerton
Joseph born 1878
Maud born 1879

Henry Walker YEOMAN lived in Littlethope for a number of years then moved to Bondgate, Ripon. His wife Mary worked as a servant at Littlethope Hall.

On 19th April 1897 Lillie married Ernest FRANK (born 1871 in Harrogate) at Ripon Cathedral.

Harry married Elizabeth SUFFELL (born in 1882 at Stillington, York) on 31st October 1903 at Ripon Cathedral. In 1901 on the census he was listed as a *general farm carter* and on the 1911 census as a *carter small holder* but on his death certificate (16th June 1962) he was noted as a *chauffeur (retired)*. They had no children and variously lived in Wormald Green and Ripon.

Rose married Charles James MARRITT (born 1880) on 16th August 1902 and, as far as I have been able to trace, they had three daughters – Constance, Clarice and Renee.

Maud married Henry Edward CAPEIL (born 1879) on 1st June 1901 at Ripon Cathedral.

Joseph married Sarah SUFFELL (born December 1877 at Stillington, York) at Woodhouse, Leeds on 28th November 1906. Sarah was Elizabeth's sister. They had two children Frank Leslie (born 3 December 1906) and Kathleen (born 13th March 1909). Joseph was listed in 1901 as a *general labourer*, on the 1911 census as an *agricultural labourer* and in 1945 as a *groundsman*.

Joseph served in the First World War. On 2nd December 1915 he was listed as a Private (38464) in the Yorkshire & Lancashire Regiment and was discharged on 7th February 1919 as Private 79251 from Northumberland Fusiliers. He died at Rose Cottage, Copt Hewick near Ripon on 5th February 1959. Sarah died on 24th March 1968 at Cookridge Hospital Leeds.

Kathleen married Harold DALE (born 11th July 1897) and they lived at Copt Hewick and had one daughter Eileen born 26th July 1939.

Frank Leslie (my father) married Ethel PINCHBECK (born 27th November 1914 in Hull) on 4th September 1945 at Ripon Cathedral. He went to Ripon Cathedral School and became a *cordwainer (or cobbler)* and held a contract to repair footwear for the RAF bases in the Vale of York during the Second World War. He suffered from polio as a youngster and had a "withered" leg which meant he was unable to serve in the war. They lived at Ure Bank Terrace in Ripon and had one son, Richard Anthony (me – born in 1949).

Frank died on 28th July 1989 at Ripon Hospital. Ethel died at the Pines Nursing Home in Harrogate on 23rd June 2002.

I married Marilyn CHANDLER, who is related to the Chandler families which originated in West Tanfield and Dallowgill (born 1947 in Pudsey) in 1975 at St James the Great, Pudsey and we have three children:

Martyn Richard born 1979
Louise Helen born 1981
Julie Michelle born 1986

In summary, it would appear that this particular branch of the Yeoman family have, so far, not moved very far from Carlton Highdale where they originated.

RICHARD YEOMAN richardyeoman@talktalk.net

93. WALKERS of Askrigg – Thomas Lewis WALKER (1825-1907) and Peter John WALKER (1832-1910)

Thomas Lewis and Mary Ann (Thomas) WALKER Family (1904)
Taken at Thomas and Mary Ann's 50th wedding anniversary

Thomas Lewis WALKER and Peter John WALKER were the two youngest sons of James and Dorothy (Pratt) WALKER and were both born in Askrigg.

James WALKER was born in 1792 in Askrigg, son of Francis WALKER and Anne COATES. He died in 1843 in Askrigg. He was a *stonemason*. Dorothy PRATT was born in Woodhall in 1790, the daughter of Thomas PRATT and Elizabeth METCALFE. She died in Askrigg in 1835.

Thomas and Peter were recorded on the 1841 census in Askrigg living with their father James, and sister Ann.

Losing their parents whilst they were still so young was probably influential in the boys' decisions to try a new life in America.

Thomas sailed on *The Saxony* from Liverpool in February 1849 with younger brother Peter who was only 16, arriving in New Orleans on 30th April 1849. From there they took a Mississippi steamer to Galena, Illinois. Within a short time of leaving the port many passengers were dead from cholera. In a biography in 1901 it was noted that the steamer captain had suggested they add alum to their drinking water and take brandy and red pepper as a preventative. Thomas and Peter were among the few who survived the journey.

They then went to Benton, Wisconsin where Thomas worked in lead mining. As he was a *mason* he returned to Illinois to continue his trade during the summer and worked as a *miner* in the winter. He later worked at Big Patch Furnace purchasing minerals.

This well paid job, plus further periods of mining and a year at a smelt works in Hazel Green, enabled Thomas to purchase a 240 acre farm near Muscoda which he exchanged a year later for another in Clifton, Grant County, Wisconsin.

Thomas married Mary Ann THOMAS in 1855 and the couple had ten children, four of whom predeceased him. In 1864 Thomas enlisted in Company H, 7th Wisconsin Volunteer Infantry Regiment and served to the end of the Civil War. At the battle of Petersburg four bullets struck the buckle of his cartridge belt but he was not injured. This souvenir buckle was one of his prized possessions. The war took its toll on his general health but he continued farming and survived to celebrate his 50th wedding anniversary. He sold his farm to his son Ulysses and moved to Preston, Grant County, Wisconsin where he died aged 82 in October 1907. He was such a respected member of the local community that the Preston M.E. church could not accommodate all the friends and veterans who came to pay their respects.

Peter WALKER settled in New Diggings, Wisconsin and married an English girl Tamer Jane CLAYTON in 1855. They had four children, two dying in infancy. Tamer died only six years later on 20th Mar 1861 at Big Patch, Grant Co. Wisconsin.

Peter may have followed his brother into lead mining and in 1857 had enough money to purchase 80 acres of land in Castle Rock Twp, Grant Co.

Peter married a widow with one son Sarah Ann ROBINSON in 1863 and had nine children by her. A letter from Peter in July 1864 to cousins in Askrigg showed that he was puzzled as to why Thomas had gone to war when he was not compelled. However he was given $500 on enrolment for three years whereas for new volunteers the bounty was less.

Peter was unsure if he would volunteer or even be drafted. At the time Peter was living about two and a half miles from Thomas and had been there seven years. He considered himself unfortunate, firstly, as his first wife was *"a very sickly woman"*, which made life difficult on a farm, and secondly losing two children. His wife then died leaving him with a three year old to look after and a baby who was brought up by another member of the family.

He seemed to have lost touch with his sisters back home in the dales and a drought and bug infested crops made life hard. In one of his letters he wrote of selling some of his land to move about fifteen miles from his brother. In 1869 the family moved by covered wagon to Algona, Iowa. Another letter in 1895 fills in details about Peter's family life.

Peter died on 13th January 1910 in Algona, Iowa.

JILL THISTLETHWAITE jillythistle@hotmail.com

94.   Peter LEYLAND from Bainbridge to China

Friends Ambulance Unit (FAU) near Kweilin, China

This account was published originally in the Darlington & Stockton Times June 6, 2008 and is included with the kind permission of Pip LAND the author and Peter LEYLAND.

The earthquake in China has brought back memories for Peter LEYLAND of Bainbridge in Wensleydale of transporting medical aid to Sichuan Province during the Second World War. One month remains particularly unforgettable and that was June 1942. First he lost a very close friend and then he heard that his father, John, had died. As he was a *volunteer* with the Friends Ambulance Unit in China, with the Japanese having cut off the road link to Burma, there was no way he could get to his father's funeral in Bainbridge.

Coming from a Quaker family his father had inspired him to follow the Society of Friend's pacifist doctrine. But to many in Bainbridge John LEYLAND had been just another "skiving" conscientious objector. It therefore came as a big surprise to them to hear, at the funeral, that he had been awarded the Croix de Guerre for his bravery with the Friends Ambulance Unit (FAU) during the First World War. He had earned that by continuing to drive ambulances to the front line to collect the injured even when the road was being shelled.

Peter was articled as an *accountant* in London when the Second World War broke out. He served with the FAU in London during the Blitz and then joined the "China Convoy" as it became known. After lessons in Chinese, mechanics and first aid he and about 40 others headed for Burma late in 1941. Ten months later, on June 10th, when in West China, he wrote in his diary that the unit was at its lowest ebb in morale – and that was before he heard of the death of his friend, Douglas HARDY. Doug, from Darlington, had attended the Society of Friends school at Ackworth with Peter. They had shared a cabin on the *City of Baroda* when it sailed from Glasgow in September 1941 during the height of the U-boat war in the Atlantic. On Saturday June 13th 1942 he wrote: "*Doug died on Thursday. It seems he developed typhus and with the dysentery just hadn't the resistance. Poor Doug – I suppose he is the last of us I should have wished to go, having known him since school and being such great friends during our time together in this convoy. He has been buried at Anshun. I am gathering Doug's things together.*" For the China Convoy this was the second death from typhus for John BRIGGS had died on June 9th. John was from Horsforth near Leeds and his parents built almshouses there in his memory.

While Peter was confined mainly to an office as the unit's *accountant* John and Doug were *convoy drivers* and *mechanics*. Doug and Peter had been at sea between Calcutta and Rangoon when news of the Japanese attack of Pearl Harbour broke. Most of the coolies left Rangoon after the Japanese bombed the city and Peter and other FAU team members themselves loaded valuable hospital equipment straight from the docks onto their trucks ready for the drive over the Burma Road to China. Peter helped with the drive north to Lashio and on into China. On January 2nd 1942, the scenery was so awe inspiring that he almost forgot it was his 22nd birthday. The day before they had driven up Maymyo Hill, a rise of 3,000 feet in six miles in a series of 22 hairpin bends. *"Rather like a long stretch of Kidstones Pass, Wharfedale side, at the top. The view from the top across the plain with the Irrawaddy meandering in the distance was striking"* he wrote.

The following day they headed towards the Goktech Gorge. *"We came over a hill and saw this steep narrow gorge down below, with mist hanging in its depths. In the distance we could see the railway viaduct, which crosses 1,000 ft above the river. We drove down into the gorge, having to reverse on some of the bends in order to get round them. My hand brake behaved very badly. Crossing the bridge at the bottom we climbed very steeply by means of another series of hairpins. This time I had to reverse on just one, but having to back towards the edge is not pleasant. I believe that some chaps had to reverse on three or four of these bends."*

It was not long before the Burma Road was closed by the Japanese and the FAU made its headquarters near Kunming in China. There was a desperate shortage of petrol and so most of their lorries were converted to run on charcoal. Doug had been one of the pioneers of using such adapted lorries. Peter explained:

"Our job was mainly to transport these medical supplies with our charcoal burners throughout west China to the various hospitals. The Government of China was established in Chongqing and we were transporting these medical supplies brought in over the Hump throughout this west China region mainly Yunnan, Guizhou and farther north Sichuan. Chongqing was in the middle of Sichuan on the Yangtze."

The Hump was the name given to the air supply route over the Himalayas from India to Kunming over the Himalayas.

Peter's main problem was the level of inflation which was often at 20 per cent per month. Foreign currency for the China Convoy was sent to the British Embassy in Chungking and was only converted into Chinese dollars as and when needed. When drawing Chinese dollars from the bank Peter had to take a rucksack because he received the money in huge wads of notes.

In November 1945 as he came to the end of his time with the FAU he was asked to travel home via North America to talk to some of the donors about inflation accounting. But then he got a telegram informing him that his only brother, Derrik, had died. He headed home to support his mother but was held up in India for three months waiting for a berth on a ship. Within days of his reaching Bainbridge she introduced him to her fiancé, Anthony PIM, who was a master at Bootham School in York where Derrik had also been teaching.

Peter returned to London to complete his accountancy training. He went on to become the *finance director* of Scott Bader Commonwealth Ltd.

It wasn't until 1992 that he and a fellow China Convoy man, Theo WILLIS, who grew up in Carperby, went back to China with their wives. The tourist group they were with was taken to see the house in Chongqing where Chou En-lai, had lived during the war. Chou En-lai was later the Chinese premier.

Peter commented *"When inside Theo looked to the right and said – 'that's where Duncan WOOD and I sat with Mao Tse-tung and Chou En-lai who had organised a meeting to thank the FAU for the help we had given by getting medical supplies to them in Yenan.' All of our group was quite overcome with surprise at this – a bit of living history and several afterwards said it was the best bit of their whole trip."*

PETER LEYLAND as told to PIP LAND jleyland@freeuk.com and pip.land@virgin.net

Editor's note: Peter died in the Friary Hospital, Richmond, on 13th June 2010, aged 90, just prior to the publication of this book. I feel honoured to have known him and to have had the chance to listen to this shy and modest man, who was only reluctantly convinced that his story was worth telling. He and Janet both contributed to our first exhibition, and we are grateful to Janet for allowing us to publish this account.

95. William ATKINSON 1830-1905 a dairy farmer in New Zealand

William ATKINSON Jr., his son and wife buried in Hamilton Cemetery New Zealand

William ATKINSON, son of George ATKINSON *blacksmith* and Rosamund CHERRY, was born in the hamlet that he and his family called Gownleyfoot and he was baptised at Healey Parish Church on 30th December 1830. In 1841 William lived at Pasture End Cottage in Healey cum Sutton with his parents, six brothers and one sister. Pasture End Cottage is semi detached and I visited the cottage next door when I visited Masham in 2009. It was difficult to imagine where they all slept as the cottage had only two bedrooms, one of which was very small. In 1851 I believe William was living at Spring Hall, Grewelthorpe and working as a *servant/ and farm labourer* for the owner John HARRISON.

Subsequently, I received copies of letters written by William ATKINSON senior and his son William ATKINSON Jr., from Esther POGUE in Texas. They had both written letters to a Joseph ATKINSON living in Burnet, Texas, the brother of William ATKINSON senior. The letter written by William Jr. gave the names and ages of his siblings and with this information I sought help from people in New Zealand. They helped me locate William ATKINSON senior and his family on electoral rolls and supplied me with sources of information.

My research indicated that William ATKINSON (1830-1905) went originally to Bendigo, Australia in 1857 and worked as a *gold miner* for four years. He then moved to Otaga, New Zealand and worked as a *gold miner* at the Shotover Diggings on the South Island for several years. The Shotover Diggings were on the banks of the Shotover River and were part of a rich gold mining area. He returned to England in 1869 or 1870 and married Elizabeth BURTON on 14th May 1870 at Ripon Cathedral before returning to New Zealand in 1870 on a ship called the *Aboukir*.

The *Aboukir* landed in Auckland on Sept 6th 1870 and records show that there was a couple named William and Elizabeth ATKINS on board which I believe to be William and Elizabeth ATKINSON. According to a letter written by William ATKINSON Jr. on 23rd November 1898 to the family in Texas, their life was not initially easy: *"I have heard them say they had with the settlers to all stop together at one place at night for fear the natives who were very savage would attack them if they scattered about all over the district. Anyhow those times are all passed now and instead of a wilderness it is now close by settled."*

William ATKINSON purchased two plots of land in the Waikato region of the North Island of New Zealand, one in Pukerimu and the other in Pukekura. In the letter written by William ATKINSON Jr. on 23rd November 1898 he stated *"Father has 100 acres where we live & 70 a 1/4 of a mile away all first class land worth on an average from 8 to 10 pounds an acre or as you would say over there from 40 to 50 dollars"* and *"The Waikato is a great dairying district, there being about 29 or 30 butter & cheese factories in it all together. We are milking nearly 30 cows and supplying between 70 & 80 gallons of milk each to one of the butter factories on an average about three-pence a gallon for it all the year round."*

William ATKINSON senior and Elizabeth BURTON had four children who were all born in Pukerimu:-
George Henry born 1872, died 1944 in Pukerimu.
Elizabeth born 1875, died 1931 in Pukerimu.
William Jr. born 30th September 1876, died 29th May 1953 in Hamilton.
Robert born 1877, died 1931 in Pukerimu.

Elaine MULLINS in New Zealand forwarded to me the Waikato electoral rolls for the years between 1882 and 1919. These showed the family managed a minimum of two farms between them. We know from family letters that these farms were dairy farms with a good return. William ATKINSON senior, *dairy farmer*, was found permanently at Pukerimu with his wife Elizabeth and in the early years his children were with him. Between 1897 and 1900 his son George Henry ATKINSON managed a farm in Cambridge West with his sister Elizabeth ATKINSON acting as his *housekeeper*. Cambridge West included the districts of Pukerimu and Pukekura. At this time there was no record of the brothers William ATKINSON Jr. or Robert ATKINSON. After their father died in 1905 all the children returned to the home farm in Pukerimu except for Robert who managed the farm in Pukekura. It appeared from the 1908 electoral rolls that William Jr. had a son also called William but I have been unable to find any evidence of a marriage or of the birth of this son. After 1908 William disappeared from the Waikato electoral rolls whilst George Henry and Elizabeth remained with their mother at Pukerimu and Robert was on the farm at Pukekura.

The Pukerimu cemetery records show that William ATKINSON senior died on 24th Nov 1905. The death printout confirmed that William was the son of George ATKINSON and Rose CHERRY and his wife was Elizabeth BURTON. Elizabeth, wife of William ATKINSON senior, died on 15th Jan 1924 according to cemetery records. Probate for a will does exist for William ATKINSON senior.

I have traced the children of William and Elizabeth ATKINSON and three of them died childless, George Henry ATKINSON, Elizabeth ATKINSON and Robert ATKINSON; all are buried at Pukerimu cemetery.

Recently I have acquired a death printout of a William ATKINSON who died in Hamilton, New Zealand in 1953. The printout confirmed I had found the second son of William ATKINSON senior from Gownley Foot and that this son had married and had children. When William ATKINSON Jr. died on 29th May 1953 in the Waikato Public Hospital, his occupation was given as *officer in the Salvation Army*. William ATKINSON Jr. married Marie THOMAS on 1st December 1909 in Hamilton, and they had four children all born in Hamilton.

George Henry born 28th Sept 1910 died 22nd June 1929.

Hazel Elizabeth born 23rd November 1912, married William Allen RAE in 1940 and died 6th September 1973 in Hamilton, New Zealand.

Irene May born 6th May 1916 and may have married a Graham BRITTEN in 1939, however there were other women of that name in Hamilton at that time.

Lloyd George born 29th May 1918 and died 5th January 1991, place unknown.

LIZ HOLDSWORTH 18 Argyll Street, Castlefields, Shrewsbury SY1 2SF.
yzzil.yrruc@btinternet.com

96. John ATKINSON (1835-1904) from Masham – a London Hotelier

St Paul, Black Notley, Essex.

My interest in genealogy began after my mother died in 2002; as I was sorting through her belongings I came across photographs of her mother and father. Her mother Bertha CURRY née LICKLEY died in 1921 when my mother was only 21 months old and her father William Henry CURRY in 1951 when I was only 11 months old, so they were people I had never known. However my mother had told me tales about her father and I knew the paternal side of the family came from Masham in the North Yorkshire Dales.

I had memories of a tale my mother used to tell about an ancestor called George ATKINSON who lived in Masham and was a *blacksmith*. She was told this tale when she spent holidays with her great aunt Margaret Jane HARRISON née ATKINSON who lived in Silver Street, Masham. According to this anecdote if George ATKINSON heard that any local child had ended up in the workhouse in Bedale he would get out his pony and trap and set off to Bedale to pick up that child. He took some children into his own household and others he found places with other local families. This tale always intrigued me.

Over the following two years I traced my family back to a George ATKINSON (1803-1877) *blacksmith* of Gownleyfoot and his wife Rose née CHERRY (1808-1886). Utilising *The Parish Register of Masham, 1800 – 1837* and *Pallot's Baptism Index for England, 1780-1837*, I established that George and Rose had six children baptised in the Masham District between 1829 and 1836. Census records and the purchase of four birth certificates established a further six children were registered with George and Rose ATKINSON as their parents between 1837 and 1851. I have not yet discovered any evidence that any of these children were adoptees although two further birth certificates are required.

During the two years of researching the ATKINSON family I made contact with two other descendents of George ATKINSON, *blacksmith*, Margaret HAWKINS and Sue WISHART. Working together we began to look at the offspring of George ATKINSON in detail, each of us concentrating on different children. Unfortunately Sue died before she had completed her research into the eldest son George ATKINSON (1832-1881) and all we know about him at present is that he was a *whitesmith* in Bradford and had five children, so was another resident who left the Dales.

John ATKINSON was baptised on 17th Jan 1835 the fourth child and third son of George and Rosamund ATKINSON of Gollinglith Foot. In 1841 he was found living with his parents and siblings at Pasture

End, Healey. It is now known as Gollinglith Foot. After 1841 I found it difficult to trace John until I communicated with a maternal uncle by letter and telephone. My uncle informed me that his father William Henry CURRY (1893-1951) attended a charity school in London after his father's death in 1898. While he was at school in London during the week he would spend weekends with his great uncle John ATKINSON who owned a hotel in London. According to my uncle, John ATKINSON had also been a *butler* to a titled family at some point in his life.

I located a John ATKINSON on the 1871 census said to have been born in *Marham, Yorkshire* and working as a *butler* to a Lady Bisshopp in Paddington, London. Looking at the original census record I believed his place of birth was incorrectly transcribed and it said Masham. He was married to a lady called Hannah and had a daughter Mary H. ATKINSON aged two months.

I obtained the birth certificate of his daughter and established the maiden name of her mother – Hannah PARKER. I then began the search for the marriage certificate of a John ATKINSON to a Hannah PARKER Unfortunately this couple were given different page numbers on the references for their marriage so it took me over a year to work this out, nowadays I know better! Having eventually acquired the marriage certificate I established that the father of John ATKINSON was a George ATKINSON, *blacksmith*.

During my time searching for Margaret HAWKINS I had established contact with Mrs Esther POGUE in Burnet County, Texas. Esther was in possession of letters written to Joseph ATKINSON that firmly established this Joseph ATKINSON as a son of George ATKINSON, *blacksmith* of Gownleyfoot. These letters stated that Joseph had a brother called John who lived with his children in London; this helped validate my findings.

John moved from being a *butler* and in the 1881 and 1891 census records he was recorded as a *hotel proprietor* at numbers 16 and 19 Thavies Inn, London. The clientele of the hotel indicate that this was a hotel for people in working class or lower middle class occupations. John ATKINSON had two sons living with him as well as his daughter, and through acquiring their birth certificates I established their mother was Hannah PARKER. According to the 1881 census he had a wife called Eliza and a letter written by his mother in 1876 indicated his first wife Hannah had died in 1875 which enabled me to find her death certificate. John ATKINSON married his second wife Elizabeth HERITAGE in 1879 but I have been unable to find any children born to this couple.

For some time I was unable to find John ATKINSON in the 1901 census although I was able to find his daughter and eldest son living at 197 Camden Road Islington. I located John and his younger son William P. ATKINSON (1875-1904) lodging at The Vines, Black Notley, Essex. This is still a public house which I have visited. John was recorded as a *widower and retired hotel proprietor*. Initially I thought they were visiting friends or taking a break from London life but the death of his son William Parker ATKINSON has raised other possibilities. John ATKINSON died on 13th Aug 1904 at Rectory Cottage, Black Notley, Essex, with bronchitis and cardiac failure. On the death certificate it gave his occupation as *labourer*. On my visit to Black Notley I found the Rectory to be boarded up and so was unable to establish which of the buildings in the grounds might be the Rectory Cottage. I searched the graveyard at Black Notley but was unable to locate a grave for John ATKINSON and many of the gravestones are eroded and difficult to read. I have discovered recently that he was buried on 17th Aug 1904 at the Church of St Peter and St Paul, Black Notley, Essex.

The son of John ATKINSON, William Parker ATKINSON, died on 15th December 1904 at Essex County Asylum, South Weald, Essex. His death was due to colitis of some weeks. His death record states he was admitted to the asylum from Braintree Workhouse but did not state the reason for his admission.

I have not yet searched the Essex County Asylum records held at Brentwood to establish why William Parker needed care in an Asylum, which in turn may give me a reason for his father moving to Essex.

LIZ HOLDSWORTH 18, Argyll Street, Castlefields, Shrewsbury SY1 2SF
yzzil.yrruc@btinternet.com

97. Thomas Atkinson (1836-1907) – Black sheep of the family?

Pasture End Cottage

Thomas ATKINSON was born one of twin sons to George ATKINSON, *blacksmith* and Rose CHERRY at Pasture End, Healey cum Sutton. He was baptised with his twin brother Henry (Harry) ATKINSON at Healey church on 12th September 1836. Henry was my maternal great great grandfather.

In 1841 Healey Pasture was a piece of common ground that lay between Healey and the hamlet known as Gownley Foot. Pasture End signified the area that lay at the edge of Gownley Foot and the cottage address reflected this but appeared to change to Gownley Foot from 1851 onwards. On a visit to Masham in 2008 I was informed that the hamlet is now known as Gollinglith Foot; however for historical accuracy I have used the name Gownley Foot in this summary.

Thomas lived with his parents in 1841 and 1851 and by 1851 was no longer classified as a *scholar* but as a *blacksmith's son*. The forge was to the rear of the cottage and from the records it appeared that the twin boys were working with their father. After 1851 Thomas left home and for at least 30 years moved from place to place with different occupations. There was no evidence in records that he ever married and family letters confirmed this.

By 1861 Thomas had left home and moved out of the dales to Rowley in the parish of Worsthorne With Hurstwood, Burnley. He lodged with a family called BAINES and worked as a *carter* and delivered goods with a horse and cart. Working at his father's forge probably gave him valuable experience with horses for such an occupation. In 1871 he was a boarder in Killing Hall, Middleton St George, Darlington, Co Durham and working as an *excavator*, he gives his place of birth as Masham. Most people in the local vicinity appeared to work as *stone masons* or *bricklayers* and it is possible he excavated stone for the *stone masons*. Then by 1881 he lodged at 14, Severn Street, Hunslet, Yorkshire, and worked as a *cab driver*, which I took to mean he drove a Hansom cab and again worked with horses.

During the years Thomas was away from his family home it appeared he rarely went back. He is mentioned little in the family letters discovered by Mrs Esther POGUE in Burnet, Texas and when he was the words used were often negative. His mother Rose (Rosamund) ATKINSON née CHERRY (1808-1886) complained about him in a letter she wrote to her son Joseph ATKINSON in Texas on 23rd February 1876: *"Tom is in Leeds and has a cab he has not been here for five years and has never written in that time".* This is the only time she mentioned him in the content of her three letters.

Thomas returned to Gownley Foot circa 1882 and moved into the family home with his mother. In 1884 his mother left to live with her son Robert ATKINSON in Harrogate and Thomas remained at Gownley Foot, which seemed to cause some bad feeling. Robert wrote to Joseph in November 1884 and said *"it is a year since the 3rd of this month we had a sale at Gownley Foot, mother got over lame and infirm to look after anything brother Tom had been with mother over 2 years previous to the sale and he durst not take a wife nor keep a woman to look after them"* he went on to say *"Anyhow mother cleared out from Gownley and Tom took it and I think it will not be much good to him for he as no one but his self."* On 13th July 1891 Robert wrote *"Brother Tom is a real old bachelor lives at the old House at Gownley foot by himself and you may bet ods I do not envy him of position."*

Thomas remained at Gownley Foot in 1891 and 1901 working as a *stone cutter* or *road repairer* and is not mentioned again in family letters until 8th March 1908 when his sister in law Mary ATKINSON, second wife of his twin brother Henry, writes to inform Joseph about Henry's death. In her letter she said *"it was a great trouble to him his twin brother haven such a death but no one was to blame but himself he might to have had a woman in the house and not to have lived by himself he had no one to help but himself and where he died he had nothing at all but we so (saw?) he was but (put?) away in a nice maner but it was a great trouble to harry."*

I became intrigued by the death of Thomas after reading Mary's letter and sent for the death certificate which stated he died from accidental burns and was registered by John Stamford WALTON, Coroner. With the help of North Yorkshire Archives I was able to obtain a copy of the Coroner's and Police report written by Thomas WALKER *acting sergeant* stationed at Masham. The following is a précis of the report.

Thomas had been unwell for a couple of days but refused to let his neighbours send for a doctor. His neighbours were a Horatio Nelson CRAIG and Laverna Beatrice MALLABY his married sister who was visiting her brother. At 6.15 a.m. one morning they heard moaning from the house and broke in to find Thomas lying on the kitchen floor with the lower half of his body severely burnt and almost suffocated. There was a large fire in the grate and they thought he had fallen in. A doctor was called but Thomas died at 12 noon. I have been unable to locate the grave of Thomas ATKINSON at either Healey Church where his parents and sister are buried or at Masham Church.

LIZ HOLDSWORTH 18, Argyll Street, Castefields, Shrewsbury. SY1 2SF.
yzzil.yrruc@btinternet.com

98. Thomas PARK of Grinton and Mary ROBINSON of Downholme to Pateley Bridge

The Half Moon Inn, Fellbeck

Thomas PARK and Mary ROBINSON were married at Downholme Church in the Parish of Grinton in November 1770. It is understood that Thomas was a *lead miner*. They had five children all born and baptised in Grinton:

1. Betty 20th October 1771
2. Mally 27th March 1774
3. Catherine 28th July 1776
4. John 5th November 1780
5. Thomas 3rd October 1784.

The family then moved to Pateley Bridge where they lived at Moorhouse, two miles southwest of the town. Lead mining was a major industry in the area.

They had two more children, George born in 1787 and Maria in 1789.

Betty married Thomas UMPLEBY in Pateley Bridge.

George married and moved away to Woodhouse, Bingley, and died in 1868 aged 81. His mother Mary went to live with him when her husband died. In his Will he left his goods to his siblings or their issues. Betty was not mentioned in the will, and may have died by this time.

Mally, later known as Mary, married George GILL in Hampsthwaite in 1793.

Catherine married William RAW in Pateley Bridge in 1798.

John married Mary FRIER at Bolton Abbey on 15th April 1805, and was believed to be an *innkeeper* in Bolton.

Thomas married Mary HULLAH in Pateley Bridge in 1806.

Maria married William COWLING in Pateley Bridge, a large family in the area.

When Thomas (1784 – 1842) married Mary HULLAH in 1806 he was recorded as a *lead miner*.

He was industrious and thrifty and by 1818 he had enough money to rent a farm. He prospered and became a property owner. He became one of a limited number of people in the area able to vote in Parliamentary elections. He was recorded on the list of voters for 1835-1837 and 1841. One of his properties was Laverack Hall.

In 1841 he was recorded with his wife Mary and daughter Elizabeth at Fell Beck; Thomas was a *publican*. The only pub in Fell Beck was the Half Moon.

Thomas as Mary had seven children:

1. Thomas born in 1807 who married Sarah BLEASFIELD. He was a *blacksmith* in Pateley Bridge. They had two children, Thomas Jr. christened in1834 who emigrated to Australia and worked as a *draper*, and Hannah born in 1835. She married Samuel SMITH from Keighley and they emigrated to Iowa (America) where her son Richard was born in 1874.

2. John born in 1809 was a *farmer* in Pateley Bridge. He was still alive in 1893 living at Ivy Cottage, in the village.

3. George born in 1812 took over the Half Moon Inn when his father died and was the *licensee* in both the 1851 and 1861 census. He also *farmed* 40 acres. My grandfather remembered visiting him there as a small child in the 1870s.

4. Mary born in 1815 married Aaron PARKER but died when she was 28 years old. Her son George of Hartwith inherited her share of the property in the Will.

5. Hannah was born in 1818 and married Henry KIRKBY, a *blacksmith*. She was widowed in 1893 and living in Bingley.

6. Elizabeth was born in 1821 and married Edward THACKRAY, a *farmer*, and lived at Carr Lodge, Dacre. Their eldest son Thomas of Manchester inherited his mother's share of the property. He was a *gardener*. Their daughter Mary married Whitwham HUTCHINSON, the parents of William born in 1870, my grandfather.

7. Ann married Robert THACKRAY, a *farmer*, and cousin of Edward. Ann and Robert lived at Lexmoor, Grewelthorpe. Robert inherited Ann's share of the property.

When Elizabeth and Ann married at Ripon Cathedral on 4th November 1847 it was a double wedding. Although their father had died in 1842 the family was wealthy enough to afford a lavish wedding.

Laverack Hall had wonderful views over the Nidd Valley and was sold by Thomas's descendants in 1893 to George METCALFE, the proprietor of an important local brewery. He owned flax mills and quarries. His son John Hawkridge METCALFE Member of Parliament was the signatory on the indenture.

Not bad for a lead miner!

CELIA POLLINGTON celia@mrspolly.wanadoo.co.uk

With acknowledgements to Ian CAMERON, Christopher CHAPMAN and Richard SMITH of Florida.

99. James WHITTON and Elizabeth HESELTINE from Askrigg to Ontario

Elizabeth HESELTINE and James WHITTON

This information was compiled originally for a reunion of the WEYMARK family in 2001.

I am descended from James WHITTON, born in Askrigg on 16th April 1819. I can now trace his family back further, to James WHITTON, born about 1721, in East Brompton. There is virtually no information included regarding any descendants prior to James. I did not include data on James' siblings, although two of them did come to Ontario. The rest remained in England.

James married Elizabeth HAZELTYNE on the 27th of January 1840, at St Andrew's Parish Church, Aysgarth. Her last name has various spellings, but HESELTINE is the preferred spelling in Ontario. Elizabeth was 17 years old when they married, and James was 20.

Elizabeth became pregnant soon after the marriage, and in October 1840 gave birth to their first child, Jane. James and Elizabeth decided to emigrate to Canada early in the 1840s. One can only imagine what the trip across the ocean was like with an infant. They arranged to purchase property, near Sorel Quebec, prior to their departure. When they arrived, they had a terrible shock. The land they bought was not owned by the person who sold it to them. This left them extremely short of funds. Somehow they made their way to Upper Canada.

They were fortunate to obtain a contract to run an inn at Glenburie, near Kingston Ontario. The inn was located on a farm owned by John MURRAY. They settled there for a few years, until they could replenish their funds. The inn became known as WHITTON's Inn.

Around 1849 they moved to Burnbrae, Seymour Northumberland County. They rented a farm to live on. By the 1851 census James' occupation was listed as *shoemaker*. Together, with his wife, they were listed as *tavern keepers*.

Although the exact year is not known, they had soon saved enough to buy their own farm. They built a very large three storey home. They thought of the farm houses they had known in Yorkshire and made a very heavy underground basement into which they constructed a vat to make cheese. James' wife, Elizabeth was familiar with the making of Wensleydale cheese and she had a friend, Miss BADGLEY, who came from Yorkshire to help her make cheese. They used the Wensleydale method of making the cheeses in the basement vat. This cheese was the first to be made in Northumberland County. It became so popular that even people in the next county, Hastings, were aware of this great tasting cheese. Elizabeth decided that an opportunity was there for money to be made. She suggested to her husband that a small joint stock company should be formed with James, William HUME, and James CLEUGH.

The name Brae Cheese Factory was given to the business. Their main aim was to serve the farmers in the area by organizing a co-operative effort, where the milk was obtained from these farmers. The company men decided to bring in an expert cheese maker from the United States. He was knowledgeable about the production of high grade cheese but unfortunately, he chose to leave after just six weeks. This left the factory in a precarious position. It was a great relief that Elizabeth had previously given her son, James, lessons in making the cheese. He and a young friend were taught by Elizabeth the process of manufacturing large batches and they were able to keep the company going without the assistance of the expert cheese maker.

Elizabeth stepped away from working at the factory. She was more the creative genius behind the scenes. In 1868 there was a situation that could have caused the demise of the cheese factory. Her son and his partner were having trouble with a large batch of cheese, and everything seemed to be going wrong. Elizabeth was sent for. She had to make her way through a storm during the night to get to the factory. She was able to help save the batch and disaster was averted.

By 1874, with the prosperity of the cheese factory, they decided to expand. A new factory was built in Wellman's Corners, Hastings County. More investors were gathered to form a wider joint stock company and it was renamed the Wellman's Cheese Factory. A wagon was used to collect the milk as before but the company had not considered that they would have to travel some ten miles by wagon in order to ensure enough milk for their batches of cheese. This greatly cut into their profits.

The factory was closed for a few years. In 1879, James and Elizabeth's son, decided to re-open the cheese factory. By this time his mother, Elizabeth, had died at the age of forty-five. His father had remarried to Elizabeth SIMPSON. James Jr. changed the name to the Plum Grove Factory and continued operating for the next 31 years. Cheese from this factory won many provincial and national awards.

James WHITTON Senior sold the family farm about 1883. He and his second wife, moved to Campbellford, a larger village near the settlement of Burnbrae. Elizabeth died at the age of 54 the following year. James then married his second wife's sister, Jessie TURNER, in 1885. Her first husband had died just four months after they had married. She had been on her own for 44 years. James died three years later.

He and his family were very well known in the area. James and his first wife had made a success of their life in a new country.

Many of their children's descendants are still living in Ontario. From the information I have gathered about James and Elizabeth's children, they were a close-knit and happy family.

KATHY BUZUNIS kbuzunis@mymts.net

100. The Poor Law Records (1834 – 1871)

The Poor Law Amendment Act of 1834 saw a radical reorganization of support for the poor in England and Wales. Parishes and townships were required to join together to form Poor Law Unions. Local parish poorhouses were replaced by larger Union Workhouses. The regime was intended to be harsh to discourage the poor from entering the workhouse and thereby becoming a burden on the rate-payers. Out-relief, or benefit as we would call it, was to be abolished for all but the aged, infirm or children – the impotent poor. This national system was overseen by the Poor Law Commission (PLC) and later the Poor Law Board (PLB), both based in Somerset House, London. It remained in place until 1929.

The PLC was very bureaucratic, developing a large number of complex rules for the workhouse system. This resulted in much correspondence with the Unions, most of which survives and is held in the National Archives (TNA), at Kew in London. In 2008 over 20 groups of local volunteers began work with TNA to digitise and catalogue some of this correspondence and make it freely available on the web. (See The National Archives Website at http://www.nationalarchives.gov.uk/catalogue/) What follows is from the work of the Reeth group.

Individuals feature mainly in returns from the Union to the PLC or where their circumstances raise an issue. Thus in 1835 there was a large return from William RAYNARD, the Muker Vestry Clerk, listing *'outdoor pensioners'*; i.e. those who were not in the workhouse but were in receipt of benefit. Whilst most lived in the dales there were a small number who had moved elsewhere and fallen on hard times. For example, Alice WAGGETT, aged 64, born Ivelet, was living in Bradford and in receipt of benefit since 1812, and received 1 shilling and 6 pence per week. Christopher HARKER, born Muker, a *collier* in Rochdale, received support *'because of a misfortune'*, perhaps a mining accident whilst Leonard METCALFE, also born in Muker, *a collier* living *'near Bradford'* had received £1 7 shillings and 10 pence in order to clothe and *'remove his family'* i.e. return him to Muker. METCALFE seemed to like Bradford since he was there again with his family in 1851, a *banksman* in a colliery.

In the 19th century every person had a legal settlement; i.e. the parish or township to which they belonged and which was responsible for supporting them in times of need. The law of settlement was complex and often Poor Law Unions sought guidance from the PLC/PLB. Thus in 1847 the Reeth Union sought permission to provide out-relief to Edward BIRD, aged 31, an *unemployed railway worker*, living in Austwick, near Settle, with his wife Betty, 31, and children George, seven, Thomas, three and William eighteen months. This was to avoid removing the family and putting them in the Reeth Workhouse. The PLB refused, commenting that to give relief to avoid incurring the expense of the workhouse would increase able-bodied pauperism by *'encouraging labourers to throw themselves out of employment'*. However, by 1851 Edward was back working on the railway near Settle. Whilst regular out-relief was frowned upon, it was allowable to provide temporary support as was the case in 1848 for Isaac ROBINSON, his wife and six children, residing at Colne. He was a *spinner*, destitute through want of employment.

Out-relief and the cost of the workhouse were not recoverable from paupers so to keep poor law rates down the Union tried to offer loans to help people through hard times. Thus in 1842 approval was sought for a loan to enable Samuel SMITHSON, Joseph SMITHSON, John CHERRY and their families, to leave the workhouse and move to Halifax where they had obtained work. The PLC ruled that this would be an illegal use of the rates but a sum sufficient to maintain the families for a week on leaving the workhouse could be granted.

Whilst many who left the dales remained in the north of England, some ventured overseas. The 1834 Act allowed Unions to meet the expenses of *'emigrating poor persons'*, but only to a British Colony. In 1845 the Reeth Union sought permission to enable Jane KENDALL, 8 years, *'belonging to Grinton'* to move to America with a relative. She received 2 shillings per week from the Union. The relative was willing to take her there if he was paid £10 8shillings, which was the amount she would receive from the union as a pauper, in the following two years. Thereafter he would indemnify the parish of Grinton of future claim for her relief. However, the PLC was unable to sanction this and suggested funds could be raised by private subscribers. It is not known if Jane went although there was a Jane KENDALL, born England, age not given, in the lead mining community of New Diggings, Wisconsin in 1850. Perhaps she made it there?

There are two references in the correspondence to women deserted when their husbands absconded to America. One refers simply to a man named HARKER of Bradford; the other, in 1849, refers to Ann BIRKBECK, 26 years, of Marrick, a single woman with two bastard children whose husband (sic) had absconded to America. She applied for out-relief but the PLB refused, saying that to make an exception *'would encourage immorality'*. In 1851 she was in the Reeth Workhouse with her two children Jane, aged five and Robert aged one.

Sadly, some who left the dales did so because they could not look after themselves; thus in 1861 the Reeth Union paid the maintenance of the following people in the North and East Ridings of Yorkshire Pauper Lunatic Asylum at York: Ann CLOSE of Melbecks, Deborah BALL, William BLENKIRON, Reeth, Dorothy RAINE, Arkengarthdale and Thomas STONES, Marrick.

There are many other people referred to in the correspondence and many more in the minutes of the Guardians of the Richmond and Reeth Poor Law Unions at the North Yorkshire County Records Office.

ALAN MILLS alanfmills@lineone.net

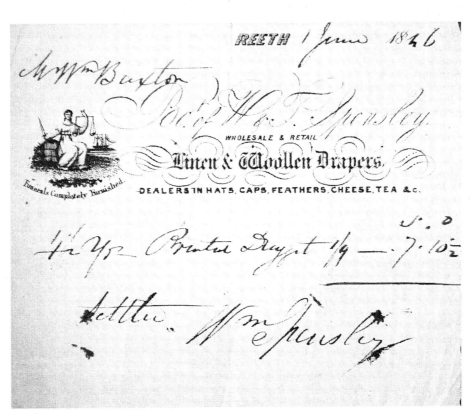

Bill of sale to William BUXTON from William SPENSLEY
Courtesy of George BUXTON

101. Rev. Benjamin PRATT (1853 – 1931) from Swaledale to India

Edith née BELL and Rev. Benjamin PRATT

Benjamin PRATT was the second son of Gunnerside-born Christopher PRATT who left Swaledale in 1830 when he was eleven years old. (See chapter 59). Christopher was taken to Bradford by his widowed mother where he served his time as a *cabinet maker*. Later, he founded the well known furnishing firm in North Parade.

Eventually, Benjamin joined his brothers in the business which became Christopher PRATT and Sons. In 1877 he decided to leave his job as a *designer – draughtsman* and went to college.

He trained as a *missionary* and was *ordained* as a Minister of the Wesleyan Methodist Church. Three years later he travelled to India to help the Rev. William BURGESS open up a new mission field in the Hyderabad district of Deccan. BURGESS began his work at Secunderabad and was appointed *Chaplain* to the British Troops. Benjamin became an *itinerant missionary* in the outlying villages.

He had to learn to speak Telegu, a native Indian language. With the help of a good teacher or "moonshi" he is said to have mastered the language in only six weeks!

He was joined by his fiancée Mary NEWSHOLME of Keighley in 1884 and they were married in India. Tragically, Mary died a week after the birth of their son Henry.

Edith Amelia BELL, the daughter of a Methodist Minister, trained as a *medical missionary* in Edinburgh, and was sent to the Hyderabad district where she met, and in 1887, married Benjamin. She became the mother of five more children as well as being an active participant in missionary work. Her *"vagrant dispensary"* as Ben called it, was an early attempt to alleviate bodily pains and sickness. Her medical practice included the removal of cataracts, and the vaccination for smallpox requiring the use of live vaccine. The cause of malaria, with which she had later to fight a running battle, was unknown at that time.

Edith started a lace-making workshop to provide young women with a marketable skill and source of livelihood. Widows without any skills were otherwise condemned to a life of near starvation. There was an impassable gulf of social and traditionally differences between the castes and outcastes (or *"untouchables"* as the Hindus called them), and whole communities were reduced to depths of degradation. Benjamin and his Indian colleague the Rev. Benjamin WESLEY, felt called to minister to these sick, illiterate and poverty – stricken people, giving them hope for a better life and encouragement in the growth of self respect.

Village life was basic, there were no schools or health care, but locals who had never seen a white man were friendly. The usual mode of transport on rough cart tracks was by bullock bandy. In his letters home Ben mentioned ponies and a *"springless country cart."* In his late thirties he acquired and learnt to ride a bicycle!

In 1907 Benjamin suffered a debilitating stroke and returned to England. Three years later he returned to India but was unequal to the work and returned to Bath. Later Edith and Benjamin joined their family in British Columbia, Canada where they both died.

When Benjamin left India he was able to look back on 30 years of progress in Hyderabad. The number of schools increased from five to 166, the five teachers to 133 and the 90 scholars to 3,091.

He left 282 villages under Christian influence in the state of Hyderabad, all developed from his own endeavour and leadership.

The solitary memorial plaque on a wall of the Wesley Methodist Church, Secunderabad says it all:

"Rev. Benjamin PRATT 1853-1931.

He was the first itinerant Wesleyan Missionary in the villages of Hyderabad,
and laid the foundation of widespread evangelism amongst the outcastes of the land.

For many years he was the Chairman of the district and spent his last years in retirement,
broken in health by his incessant toil.

By his friendliness and faith, his preaching and personal piety,
he won the love of all who knew him."

DAVID PRATT Hunterland, Turner Lane, Addingham, Ilkley, LS29 OLF

102. Sir Christopher WRAY

Sir Christopher WRAY, Speaker of the House of Commons and Lord Chief Justice.

Christopher WRAY was not only one of the earlier migrants from the dales, but he also made more of a splash than most by attaining important positions in public life.

Writing in *The Genealogist* in 1880, the Rev. George Octavius WRAY stated that the surname came from Raydale, south of Bainbridge, and described the 16th century WRAY family as a *"numerous clan, living in the parishes of Aysgarth, West Witton and Coverham,"* with the main concentration in Thoresby, Thoralby, Swinithwaite and Carlton. (I descend from WRAY's grandfather).

These settlements were all in the Royal Manor of Middleham, of which most of the WRAYs were *Crown tenants*. Christopher's father Thomas was probably born in the late 1400s, and in 1535 he was recorded as *seneschal* (steward) of Coverham Abbey, later owned by the WRAY family. Christopher's mother Joan was daughter and co-heir of Robert JACKSON of Gatenby, which no doubt accounts for Christopher's birth at nearby Bedale c. 1522.

Almost nothing is known of his early life. Later in life he became a *benefactor* of Magdalene College, Cambridge, though there is no evidence that he studied there. Well-educated he must have been, because in 1545 he was admitted to Lincoln's Inn in London, and called to the bar five years later. According to the *Oxford Dictionary of National Biography*, *"by 1553 he was MP for Boroughbridge...... In 1558 he became a bencher of his inn, and from January 1559 until 1563 was steward of Wetherby. But his future lay in Lincolnshire: by January 1559 he was "of Glentworth", having married Anne, widow of Robert BROCKLESBY of Glentworth."*

In those days there was no sensitivity about perks for holders of public office. When WRAY built a mansion at Glentworth, Queen Elizabeth helped him out with profits from the mint. He was a Justice of the Peace for Lincolnshire, and in due course for Middlesex, Norfolk and the North Riding of Yorkshire.

The *Oxford Dictionary of National Biography* (ODNB) notes his formidable reputation as an advocate: *"By 1562 WRAY was of counsel to (the) Earl of Westmorland, and sufficiently prominent a lawyer that the chancery plaintiff in Brend v. Hyldrache (1562) had to be assigned counsel by the court as none would act voluntarily, for 'the matter in question toucheth Mr WRAY of Lincoln's Inn."* He soon became *Member of Parliament* for Great Grimsby, *commissioner of sewers* in Lincolnshire and, from 1565, *treasurer of Lincoln's Inn.*

WRAY's promotion continued apace. Having been made *Queen's Sergeant* in 1570 he took the assizes in his native county and rode the Northern Circuit, dealing with the insurgents of 1569 at the York, Carlisle, and Durham Assizes. Conflict of interest did not trouble officialdom in those days and the flagrant use of influence was taken for granted. According to the *ODNB*, among the rebels' submissions which WRAY received were those *"of his brother Thomas, and John Gower, son of his sister Anne, for whose pardon (the) Earl of Sussex wrote to Sir William Cecil....... pointing to his relationship to WRAY, 'whom, I think, Her Majesty favours.' "*

In 1571 WRAY was elected *Member of Parliament* for Ludgershall, Wiltshire, whence began his short period as *Speaker of the House of Commons*. *"His oration on religion, authority, and laws expounded Her Majesty's absolute power in matters spiritual or ecclesiastical, touched on the necessity of treasure in maintaining authority, and commended Her Majesty for giving free course to her laws."* (*ODNB*). Though his time in office was short, Parliament being dissolved soon afterwards, WRAY's legal career continued to prosper. In 1572 he was appointed a *Justice of the Court of Queen's Bench*, and after being knighted in 1574 he became *Chief Justice*. Promotion brought a move to the sought-after Norfolk Circuit, from 1575 until his death.

Of the many cases over which he presided one of the most notable was that of the Jesuit martyr Edmund CAMPION in 1581. Although tortured whilst in custody CAMPION denied the charge of treason and many expected the jury to acquit him. When a guilty verdict was returned WRAY asked him why he should not be executed. He declared that, while he was prepared to die, adherence to his faith was not treason and he remained the Queen's loyal subject. The implacable WRAY condemned him to be hanged, drawn, and quartered. It was a brutal age and *"though the judicial murder of Campion shows that in crown cases WRAY was by no means too scrupulous, it is perhaps unfair to apply the moral standard of modern times to a judge of the Elizabethan age."* (http://wapedia.mobi/en/Christopher_Wray).

Five years later WRAY was among the commissioners at the trial of Mary, Queen of Scots, who once had been imprisoned in a stronghold well-known to his relations back in the dales, Bolton Castle. More mundanely in 1590 WRAY got the Judges together to reform the wording of the Commission of the Peace, a less than startling move, but of some importance in local administration. He had a reputation for decency and judicial impartiality, and was *"a most reverend Judge, of profound and judicial knowledge, accompanied with a ready and singular capacity, grave and sensible elocution, and continual and admirable patience"* according to Sir Edward COKE, Lord Chief Justice a few years later. Like many a senior Judge, however, he was an autocrat in the courtroom and was known to be intolerant of counsel who departed from the style of dress he favoured, or were under-prepared.

"Choice, it was said, in his friend, his wife, his book, his secret, and his expression and garb, WRAY was a self-made man, an able and ambitious lawyer whose rise was celebrated in his generous Lincolnshire benefactions, and was not to be hampered by obscure birth," (*ODNB*).

His son William was created a Baronet in 1611 and his two surviving daughters linked him with notable families: Frances married first Sir George St Paul, and second Robert Rich, Earl of Warwick; Isabel married first Godfrey Foljambe, second Sir William Bowes, and third John, Lord Darcy of Aston.

In religion WRAY played his cards close to his chest (as wise men did in Tudor England), but his wife came from a Catholic family and he probably inclined towards that religion.

He died at Glentworth on 7th May 1592 and was buried in the chancel of Glentworth church, where there is a splendid monument in alabaster, with effigies of Christopher, his wife and four children.

In addition to his legacy to Magdalene, WRAY provided in his Will for the school of Kirton in Lincolnshire, and for the inmates of his almshouse at Glentworth. The WRAY baronetcy bestowed on his son became extinct in 1809 on the death of the last male descendant. This ended a Lincolnshire dynasty of 250 years, with its ancient roots in the WRAY family of Wensleydale, Bishopdale and Coverdale.

JAMES HOGG JmsHogg@aol.com

103. West Burton School

West Burton School 1896

Since 1874 West Burton Church of England school has had a commanding presence in the centre of the small dales village near Leyburn. Today it is like a tardis with its Victorian grey stone exterior and an interior which, last year, was transformed into a 21st century educational facility.

In February a team of volunteers used the copying equipment loaned by the Records Office at Northallerton to make a digital record of the school's history. For Wendy Bennett copying the school's log books was especially exciting as her family has been in the village for about 100 years. *"To me it's that feeling of connection because you all know each other."*

The log books reveal both the continuities and changes that have taken place for what was once an isolated farming community. The Robinson Memorial School was founded with an endowment and relied heavily on subscriptions from well-to-do local families the pupils' lives revolved around the farming year.

Until the 1940s this dominated the school calendar particularly at hay time. The head teachers and managers often had to start the midsummer holiday early in July if the hay was ready to harvest, or to postpone the autumn term until late August if the season was "backward". On August 27th, 1920, a head teacher wrote:

"The majority of the absentees are in the hay field. There is still a large amount of hay to be gathered in and the farmers require the children to carry the 'drinkings' to the field and to do the light work."

For the first head teachers it was a tough, underpaid and often very lonely job. Until 1895 they had to cope with up to 70 pupils with no assistant teacher and just a sewing mistress. In 1893 the head teacher noted:

"Besides the difficulty of working this school single handed there is a still greater difficulty and that is, not having the children regularly enough at school to make satisfactory progress with work. Just now several of the older boys are kept from school to help their fathers to clip sheep."

One mother told him that she could not spare her daughter on washing and baking days. The reasons given for other absences included mangling clothes, collecting ling for bedding or sticks for making fires, nursing a baby, fishing and sheep dipping. Some older boys were employed by the school managers (as governors were then known) to act as *beaters* during shoots on the moor.

It was not easy to continue paying school fees for a child until he or she was 14-years-old when they could be helping on the farm or even earning a wage. For the girls that could mean becoming *domestic servants* and for the boys working as a *lead miner*, as a *butcher's apprentice* or even driving the horse and trap for the local doctor.

A head teacher remarked that many parents felt that the village feasts and fairs which were then held on weekdays were far more important than school. So many were absent for those in West Burton and Leyburn that the school was forced to close.

Merit holidays for full attendance were sometimes used for these special occasions but as the head teacher in 1902 noted he had been at the school for three years before he could record such a memorable event. Truancy wasn't the only problem. Year after year until the advent of antibiotics epidemics of scarlet fever, diphtheria, measles, chicken pox and influenza, as well as siblings sharing ringworm, meant exclusion and even the closure of the school.

And then there was the snow and the heavy storms in winter. Parents not surprisingly refused to send their children to an "ice-house" school in very wet weather.

For the first 50 years of its existence there were many occasions when the temperature in the school was almost at freezing point at 9 a.m. as the cleaner had not lit the fire early enough. One day in 1908 the head teacher commented: *"No fire, the children can't do good work because their hands and feet are cold."*

Now the temperature during winter is usually around 19 degrees centigrade, the fairs are held on Bank Holidays and the school cane is just an interesting artefact.

A case of truancy led to the head master using the cane for the first time in April 1874. He explained: *"His mother said I was to do with him as I pleased. I thrashed him before the whole school...."* But not all parents even then accepted that the head teachers had a right to cane their children.

The canings were recorded in the log books until 1904 and then in the Punishment Book until 1933. In the latter the offences which merited many canings by the second head mistress included silly behaviour and wasting time. The managers recorded in 1931, however, that she could not keep any discipline and asked for her to be replaced with a Master. They added *"the lads over twelve detest being under a mistress."*

They did get another headmistress but of her it was recorded: *"She has, by the exercise of firm but kindly discipline, improved the tone (of the school) and won the respect of the children."*

There have been many female head teachers since then, the latest being Carol Brotherton. Today truancy among its 43 pupils aged four to eleven is zero. North Yorkshire County Council has assessed it as being a highly effective school, and OfSTED judged it to be good with many outstanding features. Its creative curriculum has won it such awards as Fairtrade, International School, ICT mark, Healthy School, Activemark and bronze-level EcoSchool.

There is a whole team of teachers, teaching assistants, midday supervisors, dining room assistant, secretary, clerical assistants and a caretaker who work together to ensure that it runs smoothly to provide quality education in a school complex which now comprises four classrooms, school hall, and three offices plus an adventure playground and vegetable garden.

A far cry from the days of two-seater privies and one big icebox for a classroom!

PIP LAND pip.land@virgin.net

Editor's note: This article was first published in the Dalesman magazine and we are grateful to Pip for allowing us to use it.

104. The North and the East: The East India Company at Home, 1757-1857

The Swaledale Museum

Dr. Helen Bainbridge from the Swaledale Museum in Reeth is delighted to be working with Professor Margot Finn from the University of Warwick on an exciting new project that combines the skills and approaches of university based academics and family historians. The project aims to produce a group of detailed case studies of selected British interiors (in England, India, Scotland and Wales) that show the incorporation of Asian material goods—such as artwork, ceramics, furniture and textiles—into gentry and aristocratic homes in the later Georgian and early Victorian periods. The project also aims to survey and assess patterns of material 'Orientalisation' in British culture by collating, on a publicly – accessible online database, detailed information garnered by a network of family historians on a broad range of Asian luxury goods acquired by British families in the heyday of the East India Company.

Framed chronologically by Clive's victory at Plassey in 1757 and the outbreak of the Mutiny and Rebellion of 1857, the project focuses on a period that saw the East India Company expand its fiscal, territorial and military grip on the subcontinent, even as the British government imposed increasing regulation on Company servants' freebooting habits of rule. At the beginning of this period, the Company's servants (that is, its civil and military officers) enjoyed unprecedented access to the world of Asian goods, through bribes, ceremonial gifting, commerce and the spoils of war. These goods, together with the Company's official cargoes of Indian and Chinese commodities, entered British markets and transformed propertied families' domestic sensibilities.

Margot and Helen will be posing a series of interlocking research questions about the incorporation of 'the East' into the British domestic interior. These will include:

1) How and why did the acquisition, content, display and interpretation of Asiatic goods in British country houses change over time between 1757 and 1857?

2) In what ways did gender differences, such as the disproportionately male composition of the British population in India, influence the incorporation of Eastern wares into Anglo-Indian and British propertied households?

3) Do regional distinctions – for example, between southern English, northern English, Scottish and Welsh homes – mark the acquisition and display of luxury goods from India and China in Britain?

4) Were the narratives constructed around Asian goods by the gentry and aristocracy orientated primarily toward the articulation of familial genealogies or of national identities?

Helen is inviting family historians who have ancestors with links to the East India Company to contact her and become involved with this exciting project. Find out more about Margot Finn at www2.warwick.ac.uk/fac/arts/history/people/staff_index/professor_margot_finn/

DR. HELEN BAINBRIDGE museum.swaledale@btinternet.com

YORK PUBLISHING SERVICES LTD

Tel: 01904 431213

email: enquiries@yps-publishing.co.uk

www.yps-publishing.co.uk

YPS are recommended by the Writers' and Artists' Yearbook

INDEX

This index contains the names of everyone (including wives by their maiden names, where given, and nicknames), plus all the placenames, house names and significant buildings, mentioned in the book. To provide a wider context, the index also contains the names of employers, businesses and a few significant outside events and people, all mentioned in the stories but nor originally from the Dales, and a bit of old-fashioned terminology.

The index does not (in this edition) include an index of occupations, or migrant ship names, or states of health, or school names, or military units or specific wars, which I realise would be useful.

Please note the following conventions:

- MOST IMPORTANTLY - the numbers shown against each name in this index indicate the chapter number(s) in which they appear, *not* the page number.

- Places outside Yorkshire are identified by county or country (American State abbreviations - IL, MO - are used to save space).

- Places within Yorkshire are identified by old Riding or dale and, where sensible, grouped under the village or town although isolated farms are indexed under their own names. The chapter numbers indexed against individual dales indicate that no other place-name was mentioned in that particular story.

- SURNAMES are displayed in capital letters and have been grouped under one variation, since experience has shown that you can find unexpected links better this way. All the variants cross-refer to the main entry.

- Where children are only named by their forenames in the story, I have done my best to identify their surnames and index them accordingly. Sometimes the author has been able to give me other surnames even when not mentioned in the story and these are indexed too. Please let the editor know if there are anomalies.

- Where the same name belongs to different people in the same chapter, the index shows the number of mentions like this[3].

- If somebody has a formal forename and a nickname or informal abbreviation (Elizabeth and Betty, for instance), both are indexed separately and if I have been unable to decide that, for example, Peter Henry is actually the same person as Peter, I have indexed them both separately.

- Only family members named in the stories are indexed here; be aware that there may be more.

In the end, only two letters home contain names that have not been identified:

- In Chapter **13**, Mary HARLAND's 1834 letter to Quebec mentions: Fanny, Nanny, 'that wretch Bess', Old Nancy and Betty, little Jos who died of 'the meesels', Mary Elle, aunt Jane and aunt Betty, and finally little Bessy who sounds as if she was left behind with 'the old people'. If you recognise these people please notify the editor.

- In Chapter **90**, Nicholas YEOMAN's 1846 letter mentions: Betty Stanley, Christopher and Mary, Elizabeth, Francis, Robert[2] and Uncle Ralph.

MARION HEARFIELD